EASTERN EUROPE
IN THE SIXTIES

EASTERN EUROPE
IN THE SIXTIES

Edited by STEPHEN FISCHER-GALATI

FREDERICK A. PRAEGER, *Publisher*
New York · London

FREDERICK A. PRAEGER, PUBLISHER
64 UNIVERSITY PLACE, NEW YORK 3, N.Y., U.S.A.
77-79 CHARLOTTE STREET, LONDON W.1, ENGLAND

Published in the United States of America in 1963
by Frederick A. Praeger, Inc., Publisher

This book is Number 137 in the series of
Praeger Publications in Russian History and World Communism

Manufactured in the United States of America

EDITOR'S PREFACE

Eastern Europe in the Sixties is a pioneer effort. It is the first collaborative attempt to present and interpret the principal problems and developments in contemporary Eastern Europe on an "area" basis. This comprehensive approach is deemed preferable to the conventional "country-by-country" method, even at the risk of possible minor distortions creeping into the broader generalizations. It has the advantage of presenting an integrated picture of East European affairs in the proper perspective essential for understanding the workings of the Soviet bloc, Yugoslavia, and Albania.

The editor is most grateful to the authors of the several chapters for the high competence they brought to their tasks, for their cooperation and suggestions, and for confining themselves to the specific topics envisaged in our necessarily tightly drawn outline. He is also indebted to Dr. Joseph S. Roucek and Mr. Joseph Babicki for information on topics related to social and intellectual change and to Mr. Frederick A. Praeger and his associates for making our book possible. Indeed, without the publisher's willingness to underwrite projects on this area, the general knowledge of Eastern Europe would be even more meager than it is at this time.

CONTENTS

INTRODUCTION

In the 1960's, as throughout their existence, the Communist regimes in Eastern Europe have been confronted with problems inherent in ruling without popular support and, except for Yugoslavia and recently Albania, with circumscribed powers of decision and action in domestic and foreign affairs. Since the survival of all Communist states in Europe depends essentially on the power of the Soviet Union, most of them continue in their status as satellites. Whatever degree of independence the satellites enjoy is ultimately derived from the Soviet Union, which may—for broad strategic reasons—tolerate the insolent defection of Albania, the maintenance of a friendly Communist Yugoslavia or, more immediately, Gomulka's and other polycentric variations on a theme by Marx. However, as a consequence of the increased military and economic strength of the U.S.S.R. since the end of World War II and the subsequent changes in Soviet foreign relations, the issues subordinate to the elemental one of survival are assuming a character markedly changed from that of 1948. Although the Communist countries of Eastern Europe, with the notable exception of Albania, have developed new bases of stability, they must meet ever more complex challenges to the realization of "socialist" aims.

The strength of the East European nations rests not only in the police and the Red Army, but also on new or expanded industrial foundations. The industrialization of society and the ensuing transformation of the social order in the totalitarian states has permitted the establishment of a *modus vivendi*, however precarious, between populations aware since 1956 of the futility of revolution and governments anxious to avoid creating situations that could jeopardize the *status quo*. Thus, in the early 1960's, the East European regimes seek to consolidate their gains and eliminate, or at least reduce, weaknesses that tend to impede the process of "socialist construction" leading to the eventual victory of Communism, either under the necessary "leadership of the Soviet Union," or—in the case of Albania—under that of Communist China.

The Achilles' heel of each of the regimes is popular apathy toward Communist creed and practice. Even elements with vested interest in the continuation of the existing order (with the exception of the top Party and government bureaucracies) make demands incompatible with the socialist objectives, demands resulting in compromises that inevitably retard the realization of ambitious goals. This conflict is most apparent in the economic field, particularly in agriculture. In all parts of Communist Eastern Europe, whether agriculture is fully or partly collectivized—as in East Germany, Czechoslovakia, Bulgaria, and Rumania—or essentially private—as in Yugoslavia and Poland—the peasantry remains uncooperative. Lack of incentive, policies restricting private-property rights, insufficient and inequitable allocation of capital for agricultural development, adverse price structures for farm commodities, and the general relegation of the peasant and agriculture to low priority levels in socialist planning are responsible for continuing failures to supply farm produce adequate to the requirements of an industrial society. The only apparent remedy would be a modification of existing policies that, based on Marxian antirural theory, more immediately proceed from doctrinary and Soviet-imposed priorities on the development of heavy industry. The consequences of this fundamental weakness are manifold, affecting not only the peasant but the new industrial and bureaucratic society as well. For the continuing food shortages, the high prices of agricultural products, and resultant high cost of living erode the material gains realized by those engaged in industrial occupations. This situation and the exorbitant prices of consumer goods (in short supply because of capital-goods production priorities) are partially responsible for the lack of genuine support for government policies even among those who stand to profit most by industrial progress: the industrial worker, the technicians, and the various bureaucratic staffs. Moreover, the rapid industrial progress achieved by the nations of Eastern Europe since World War II, impressive though it is, has compounded the problems of the satellite governments and Yugoslavia. Efforts to build a rapidly industrialized economy are further impeded by serious shortages of raw materials and skilled labor as well as by unfavorable trade balances. These deficiencies, resulting from overambitious plans, inadequate natural resources, the absence of an industrial tradition, and, finally, economic dependence on the U.S.S.R., are obviously difficult to overcome. The economic and political needs of the Soviet Union impose such solutions as greater economic integration of the bloc nations through the Council for Mutual Economic Assistance (COMECON) and development of trade relations with the West and the rest of the non-Communist world. But these plans have been generally unsuccessful, primarily because of the economic nationalism of individual satellites and their exploitation by the principal supplier of materials and directives, the Soviet Union. Such modifications in planning as deceleration of economic programs on extended schedules, while demonstrating increased awareness of the difficulties in maintaining the pace of industrial development in the previous decade, do not represent any real departure from dogmatism, nor do they alter the priority of capital goods production over that of consumer goods. They cannot resolve the crucial tension between the people actually required to carry out industrial production, planning, or administration and the regimes unsympathetic to the economic aspirations of these people. It is noteworthy that the East European regimes, including Yugoslavia, have not satisfied the basic consumption requirements of the new technical cadres, the managerial class, the governmental bureaucracy, and the industrial workers, despite occasional palliative measures such as higher wages and lower prices. Understandably, therefore, other attempts of the regimes to secure mass support for their aims and policies and to inculcate loyalty to Communism have met with minimal success. Pragmatism and cynicism are the motive force of large segments of the population (including the young), and the attainment of a modicum of material well-being is the highest goal of all but a few idealists or the Party stalwarts whose economic position is secure, but whose political survival demands strict adherence to the ideology.

Yet given the effectiveness of Communist methods of political control, these same industrial factors, despite all their imperfections, confer stability on the regimes and provide the basis for future consolidation and progress.

Because Soviet power—often expressed in the delegated power of national police forces—dominates all East European affairs, it must be emphasized that neither existing nor potential deviation from Soviet norms, whether it assumes the form of polycentrism or even independent action, in any way threatens the Communist security of Eastern Europe. That the Russians would resolutely refuse to allow the establishment of non-Communist states in the bloc and that the West would not support direct attempts to suborn the Communist order was vividly demonstrated to the satellite peoples in 1956 and again during the Berlin crisis. Whatever changes occur in Eastern Europe are ultimately initiated or approved by Moscow; since the possibility of direct or indirect Western intervention by force in East European affairs is excluded, internal shortcomings, although recognized, need not be hastily rectified in fear of a repetition of 1956. Time, the essential element in the principle of "peaceful coexistence," has become an asset rather than a liability to Communist Eastern Europe because of the balance of military and political power attained in recent years. The East European governments may now slow down, as they have recently done, the timetable of industrialization; they may, if indicated, revise their agricultural policies; they may impose more or less rigid norms. In short, they may take any measures expedient or necessary in terms of domestic stability or attainment of Soviet-imposed goals. The progress of economic integration under COMECON and the generally greater degree of autonomy in the formulation and execution of domestic policies reflect the lessened concern over internal problems, which permits a broadened approach to interbloc, long-range planning. It is also significant that in the indoctrination of the youth, the emphasis is on training for social usefulness in industrial societies operating on a long-range basis rather than on hatred of the domestic and foreign class enemy bent on destroying the new order. The new order, having been firmly established through rapid progress under Stalinism and having withstood the pressures of 1956, is assumed to be on sufficiently solid foundations eventually to bring about the Marxian utopia. This will not be attained in the 1960's

—or 1970's or 1980's for that matter—but as long as Soviet military power balances that of the West, the Communist pragmatists and theoreticians have greater reason to believe that ultimately it will be achieved. Lack of popular support, shortages of raw materials, and possible challenges to East European economic development through the establishment of the Common Market and further integration of Western Europe and the United States are disturbing only in terms of immediate and short-range goals. Now that the masses are benefiting, however slightly, from the economic progress inherent in new industrial societies, now that they are released from the pressures produced by the crude police methods of Stalin's day and participating more and more in work directed toward the victory of Communism, their leaders are generally more relaxed and optimistic. Though they will not suffer any challenge to their power from domestic sources, whether social, intellectual, or (least likely of all) political, they seem more certain than ever of their conviction that the Marxian millennium is coming. The 1960's, in Communist Europe as in the West, appear to be transitional years, during which the two great opposing camps will strive to consolidate their positions in the mighty struggle for industrial supremacy.

STEPHEN FISCHER-GALATI

PART ONE

The New Social Order

1. THE NEW SOCIETY*

WAYNE S. VUCINICH

East European societies embody a blending of Marxist imperatives with deeply rooted and localized cultural traditions. Understanding the dynamics of these societies will be promoted by a closer look at (a) the applicability and sociological limitations of the Marxist-Leninist theories of social classes and of the nature of the state; and (b) the new values resulting from directed social change under Communist auspices.

The "Classless Society"

The Communist leaders of Eastern Europe claim that the postwar transformation of their countries has followed the sociological blueprints of Marxism-Leninism, according to which the liquidation of capitalism by proletarian revolution is expected to produce a society of nonantagonistic classes that will eventually evolve into a classless society. For we are told that the liberation of the proletariat invariably leads to a dissolution of social classes and the ultimate freedom of man.

A close scrutiny of the experiences of Communist states reveals many fallacies in Marxist-Leninist social theory. First, Marx and his followers exaggerate the historical role of classes. Secondly, in elaborating their class theory, the Marxists make the serious error of assuming that private property and authority are essentially and uniquely interdependent, so that by abolishing the former, the latter becomes redundant.[1] However, history has convincingly demonstrated that the abolition of private property does not lead to the extinction of authority. In the experiences of the Soviet Union and other East European countries, the state,

* The research for this article was undertaken as a part of the Studies in International Conflict and Integration, Stanford University.

instead of withering away, has grown stronger, and the old classes have been replaced by new ones. Third, the Marxists did not anticipate what Adolph Berle has called "the twentieth-century capitalist revolution," or the so-called managerial revolution, which modified the traditional relationship of property to power. Because they were ideologically committed to the premise of capitalism's inner anarchy, they did not foresee large-scale economic planning in capitalist countries. Dedicated to the idea of a growing abyss between the bourgeoisie and the proletariat, they failed to anticipate the rise of the "middle class" as the backbone of a democratic society.

The Soviet leaders have declared that their country has achieved socialism, that it has entered the stage of Communism, and that by 1980, it will become fully Communist. Among the other East European countries, only Czechoslovakia has advanced the claim that it has completed "socialist construction."

Communist theorists distinguish between two forms of proletarian dictatorship: (a) the Soviet form, and (b) the people's democracy. These are identical in their class character, because both are avowedly ruled by the proletariat, but they differ in specific institutional expressions of special historical circumstances and national peculiarities. At first, the Marxist interpreters told us that "the retention of some of the old bourgeois forms constituted one of the unique features of the People's Democracy."[2] This position has now been abandoned, although it is pointed out that "the smashing of the old forms had not been performed in one violent sweep, as during the Russian revolution."[3]

The essence of the Yugoslav Marxist interpretations of the classless society and the withering away of the state appears in the Program of the League of the Communists of Yugoslavia, adopted in 1958. Here it is explained how the socialist state "in its first phase" becomes "a powerful instrument of conscious action" that secures "the necessary material, social, and economic prerequisites for further development of socialist relations" by planning and so "creates conditions for its own gradual withering away."[4] "The uneven development of socialism and the diversity of its ways and forms" produce "inner contradictions in the socialist movement."[5] This is caused in part by initial compromises with "small-owner elements, even with the bourgeoisie," as well as by temporary reliance "on various forms of state-capitalist relations and methods." These accommodations breed "a number of contradictions and antagonisms," and yet societies "advance most swiftly precisely because of these contradictions."[6]

The Yugoslav theorists acknowledge the influence of "the economic and political remnants" of "the old society," which engender tendencies "toward a restoration of capitalism" and which "can become a real danger if . . . relations between the leading political forces of the socialist state and the working class itself should be seriously upset."[7]

Of great concern to Yugoslav leaders is the "retarded social consciousness of the working masses," which defies any process of accelerated remolding. The Yugoslav theorists believe that "in certain social strata, especially among the intelligentsia, the middle classes, and the petty-bourgeois elements, and equally among certain sections of the working class, anarchism often appears as a reaction to the difficulties of the transition period in general, as a retreat from the battlefront of socialism, cloaked in abstract liberalism, actually pseudo libertarianism."[8]

There is a difference in the way the Yugoslavs and the Soviets interpret the role of the state in the transition period, the idea of the "withering away of the state," the party's role in and relations to the state, the "lower phase of Communism" (i.e., socialism), and the state and socialist property.[9] Like other Marxists, the Yugoslavs expect the state to die out gradually as its functions pass into the hands of the workers. In the opinion of Edward Kardelj, Vice Premier of Yugoslavia, a state is not "really socialist until it begins to wither away," and the Yugoslav state is in this process.[10]

With the decentralization of governmental power and the transfer of industrial management to workers' councils, the Yugoslavs claim that the state in their country has begun to wither away.[11] They officially proclaimed this at the Sixth Congress of the Communist League of Yugoslavia.[12] State functions are said to be weakening as workers take over. The state in Yugoslavia no longer has "direct control by means of a bureaucratic apparatus."[13] Decentralization of the Party is interpreted as part of the withering-away process. The army's failure to wither away is ascribed to external threats that make a strong armed force necessary for national security.[14] How long it will take for the state to wither away will, according to Yugoslav theorists, depend on a variety of circumstances.[15] They expect it to be a long, difficult process.[16] In the meantime, as the state continues to wither away, the central state administration will remain only as a coordinating and planning body.[17] The Yugoslavs define the withering-away process as one "in the course of which the role of the state decreases perceptibly, its organs undergo transformation, direct democracy is ensured of continuous development, and the functions of the various organs of social self-management keep multiplying."[18] They concede that "the forms of this development have already been seen to differ and will also do so in the future."[19] It is essential to point out, however, that so far the Yugoslav notions about the state and its withering away remain in the realm of theorizing. There is no indication whatsoever that the Yugoslav state is withering away.

East European constitutions, like the Soviet document of 1936 (Article I), describe their countries as states of workers and peasants. Stalin painstakingly pointed out that the Constitution "proceeds from the fact that there are no longer any 'antagonistic classes' in society," that society consists of "two friendly classes, of workers and peasants."[20] This was an admission that two classes, allegedly "nonantagonistic," still existed in the Soviet Union. Beside the two officially acknowledged classes, however, the evidence from many sources indicates the existence of additional groups, which, by virtue of occupation, income, and authority, manifest varying degrees of group consciousness.

One sociologist thinks that social stratification in the Soviet Union is so firmly rooted that nothing short of a social and political revolution could produce anything like "a classless society as defined in classic Marxist terms."[21] Another confirms this observation and adds that vertical mobility is becoming increasingly restricted in the Soviet Union.[22] What has been said about Soviet social stratification applies to a great extent to other Communist states of Eastern Europe as well.

Although Lenin realized that social equality could not be

achieved immediately after the revolution, he did not anticipate the gross inequalities that developed under Stalin's aegis. The kind of society Stalin tried to impose upon East European countries was neither truly revolutionary nor truly socialist. What he primarily sought was the establishment of undisputed Soviet control over Eastern Europe. Under Soviet guidance and inspiration, the new Communist governments dispossessed and destroyed the propertied classes by legal and police action. The "class enemy" was either stripped of political and economic power or forcibly integrated into the new order.

The destruction of traditional classes in postwar East European countries and the building of societies on the principle of totalitarian conformity have not led to social homogeneity or a classless society. Many forces have been working against this Communist ideal. No one has so authoritatively portrayed the failures of Communist societies to eradicate the class barriers as has Milovan Djilas. Here is a disillusioned Communist who discovered that the fruits of the proletarian victory do not go to the people for whom they were intended but to a bureaucracy that "is nothing else but the party which carried out the revolution."[23] The bureaucracy, taking over the administration, the means of production, and the sources of power, establishes a monopoly of rule. The bureaucrats come to constitute a new ruling class with special privileges. The illusion of a classless society soon fades away.

The Communist social leveling has produced new social groups —the bureaucrats, the managers, and the Party leaders. In some regards, the "new class" resembles its historical predecessors; in others, it differs sharply. A member of the "private-ownership classes," for example, leaves his property to his heirs, but a member of the new class only bequeathes "the aspiration to raise himself to a higher rung on the ladder."[24] Djilas says that in the new class, "just as in other classes, some individuals fall by the wayside while others go up the ladder."[25] He contends that: "The new class is actually being created from the lowest and broadest strata of the people, and is in constant motion."[26]

A well-informed student of Soviet affairs remarks that "Communism had provided Communists with status, careers, and comforts, and latterly even reasonable security against arbitrary ar-

rest," and that "partly to meet its requirements of economic progress, and partly as a result of that progress, Communism has
created a new bourgeoisie, statist rather than individualist, but
otherwise much akin socially and psychologically to the salaried
middle class in the West."[27] The same author observes that this
"new class" is not made up of people who are "personally fanatic"
and that their belief is a "matter of conformity and comfortable
self-righteousness," unless they happen to be one of the "numerous
secret dissenters." For it would seem that while "the Communist
movement demands unquestioning loyalty to its authority . . .
belief plays no guiding role."[28]

The new class has two outstanding characteristics: collective
and monopolistic ownership, and totalitarian authority. Djilas,
still a Marxist, links ownership with authority. He declares that
the new class "possesses the nation's goods" and that "the use, en-
joyment, and distribution of property is the privilege of the party
and the party's top men."[29] For these reasons, in the opinion of
Djilas, the Communists "have transformed themselves into owners." Although it is doubtful that the term "ownership" is fully
meaningful in the context in which it is used by Djilas, such an
objection amounts to semantic captiousness. Much of what he
says is valid, especially in so far as the Stalinist period is concerned.

Others who have traveled a road similar to that followed by
Djilas share his basic views. Professor Alfred Kantorowicz, who
fled to West Berlin in 1957, had this to say: "The People's Chamber had become the chamber of the functionary. The welfare of
the people had become the welfare of the functionary. The people's factories had become factories belonging to the functionaries."[30] And so the new class was born out of a congeries of
bureaucrat-functionaries. It even has its status symbols: cars, special schools, shops, undisclosed salaries, servants, and vacations.
The Yugoslavs have coined a new term, "Dinar-ic society," for those
whose primary aim in life is the accumulation of personal wealth.*

Lichtheim thinks that since Soviet society "is asserted to be
classless by definition, social differentiation cannot become overt

---

* Dejan Djurković, "Razgovor o domaćem filmu," *Delo,* VIII, No. 3 (March,
1961), 340–60.

beyond a certain point without threatening the moral foundation of the regime." The doctrine of classlessness, however, "can be transformed into one of social harmony—especially if the inconvenient concept of 'class' is dropped and replaced by a politically neutral term." And, in taking this course, "the party would anyhow merely pursue its traditional role of re-interpreting the doctrine to fit the circumstances."* After all, Communism is the *ideology* of Soviet society; it is not Soviet society itself. In fact, it is primarily the ideology of the ruling elite "organized in the Communist party." Lichtheim suggests that "the official ideology rather than the state" would in the end wither away, but notes that the Party can "adapt itself to a situation where its function is simply to preserve the *status quo.*"†

Several authors have discussed the changes in Communist social relations since Stalin's death. In the opinion of one of them: "The fanatic Stalinists have gradually given way to hierarchically trained, pseudo-intellectual party *apparatchiki,* primarily interested in their own power; these leaders in turn are coming under pressure from the younger generation of technically trained intelligentsia, concerned with the domestic development of their countries."[31] Dumitriu, a Rumanian writer who defected to the West in 1960, shares this view.[32] According to him, the dogmatic, irrational, and militant orthodoxy of the ruling class is being increasingly challenged by a growing middle class of technocrats whose philosophy is dominated by rationalism and pragmatism.

This new middle class does not disregard national interests, and it presses toward further material progress. Its members favor the

* George Lichtheim, *Marxism: An Historical and Critical Study* (New York: Frederick A. Praeger, 1961), p. 399. Though Lichtheim is primarily concerned with the Soviet leaders' approach, his observation seems to apply also to Eastern Europe. Of course, it cannot be said that Communist leaders like Poland's Gomulka have openly given up doctrinaire Marxist attitudes toward class and the classless society. Yet it is clear that Gomulka has little understanding or sympathy for the Hegelian language of Marxism. As his writings show, he is primarily concerned with practical problems.

† *Ibid.* In Gomulka's opinion, "the fullest definition of the social content contained in the concept of socialism lies in the formula that socialism is a social system that abolishes exploitation and oppression of man by man." (Speech at the Eighth Plenum, 1956, in *Przemówienia 1956–1957* [Warsaw, 1957], p. 38.) See also the collected speeches in *Przemówienia* (Warsaw, 1959–61).

development of consumer-goods production at the expense of the
development of heavy industry, an obsession of the ruling elite.
This new middle class is large, and its influence cannot be dis-
counted. The somewhat static picture presented by Djilas, therefore, needs revision, although his statements on the authority
of the ruling class in Communist countries remain incontestable.
Brzezinski and Dumitriu suggest a willingness on the part of the
ruling class to make concessions but not to renounce power. The
new middle class is, on the whole, as much the child of the new
order as the ruling class itself, and its demands cannot be denied
without endangering the further success of industrialization.

Since 1945, two major trends have worked in opposite directions
in the East European countries. One is the gradual elimination of
old classes and old class barriers, the other is the creation of new
ones.[33] The outcome is a society roughly divided into four classes:
the ruling bureaucracy, the new middle class, the workers, and
the peasants. The remnants of the old classes are being assimilated
either by the working class or by the new middle class. The tensions
between these classes are considerable, and any talk of social harmony therefore is illusory.

The concept of the "transition to Communism" as a fulfillment of
this "social harmony" is merely an effort to ensure the "emotional
benefit of old socialist ideals." " 'Naturally, in a Communist society,'
says Khrushchev, 'there will be planned and organized distribution
of work according to various branches of production and social reg-
ulation of working time,' while 'certain public functions will remain, analogues to present state functions.' The idea of 'withering
away of the state' is thus redefined to mean nothing but the transfer of functions from central to local agencies or from the government to the organs of the Communist Party. . . . The 'dictatorship
of the proletariat' is officially terminated by the 1961 program, but
it yields only to 'the state as an organization embracing the entire
people,' while the role of the party as the leading and guiding force
of Soviet society, 'with all its unity, discipline, and ideological
rigor, is reaffirmed in all force with no terminal date whatsoever.' "[34]

What does all this mean? It simply means that "Soviet socialism
is merely a dictatorial alternative to capitalism as a system for

creating material wealth." Communism is only "another instance of modern and bureaucratized industrialism."[35]

"Socialist" education and extensive social legislation have been expected to instill "socialist consciousness" and to further the idea of social classlessness. These expectations have not materialized. Instead of engendering a trend toward social equality, the socialist order has produced new classes and groupings. Education has become an important determinant of social stratification.[36] DeWitt observes: "Contrary to the Marxist vision of growing egalitarianism on the road to communism, Soviet policy over the last forty years has, in effect, elevated the principle of differential rewards to the status of an immutable law of socialism: 'from each according to his ability, to each according to his work.' "[37] Educational achievement has become a criterion for determining the social value of "work," it has become, primarily, a means of advancement.

In East European Communist countries,[38] discrimination exists in both educational and welfare policies. "Social origin" is important in determining opportunities of university enrollment, although this discrimination is becoming less and less prevalent as time passes. While access to a resort or a sanatorium does not depend on one's political standing, members of the Party elite and their families have at their disposal special government clinics and resorts that are much superior to those available to the common man. Education, even though not a path to classless society, is undeniably an instrument of social mobility.

There is, however, a constant supply of young, able, and trusted "cadres" from the working and peasant classes who, after thorough training, can join the ruling bureaucracy. But this social mobility neither promotes nor blocks the trend towards a classless society. In other words: "Social mobility constitutes a type of recruitment of the personnel of given positions. Social classes, however, are phenomena which exist independent of the mode of recruitment and rate of fluctuations of their members."[39]

Sporadic campaigns to decentralize the government and planing do not affect social mobility; they do no more than broaden the base of the bureaucracy. They give "greater rights to the lower strata of the new class."[40] According to the decision of the Twenty-second Congress of the Soviet Communist Party, one-quarter of the membership of the Central Committee is to change every four years. This appears to be a new means of infusion instead of the out-of-date purges, but it does not alter the essence, the pre-eminence of the Party apparatus. The frequent antibureaucratic campaigns do not lead to radical changes, for no ruling class will relinquish its power and privileges voluntarily. The Hungarian writer Gyula Háy wrote, shortly before the uprising of 1956, that: "In the pruning of the bureaucracy the most bureaucratic bureaucrat will survive. The bureaucracy will be smaller, but as bureaucracy per se it will be more intense and virulent, ready to spread at any moment."[41]

In spite of the fact that the gap between the masses and the ruling class is diminishing, partly because of the rising living standard and partly because of the broadening base of the ruling class, the societies in Eastern Europe continue to be class societies, dominated by new bureaucracies.

The interwar history of the East European intelligentsia is tragic. Products of the age of crisis that saw a devastating war, economic depression, and failures of democracy, the intellectuals grew bitter and disappointed. Many of them clung to outdated concepts, rode on the waves of nationalism, and seemed satisfied with the existing order. Some were dragged into swirling eddies of racism and religious bigotry and came to speak for fascism. The young intellectuals were embittered by a lack of recognition and economic security and disillusioned by the evident inability of the existing political institutions to cope with national and international problems. They were drawn to volatile extremists who offered a wide variety of panaceas. Hounded by fascists and wooed by Communists, they supplied recruits for both, but particularly for the latter. World War II further catalyzed the participation of many members of the intelligentsia in Communist organizations. The Nazi extermination policies, which virtually decimated the Polish intelligentsia, and similar fascist actions elsewhere sharpened the desperation of Polish survivors as well as

that of intellectuals everywhere and catapulted them leftward—
often into Communist organizations.[42]

After the war, the Communists adopted plans to develop "a
body of scientific, artistic, and professional manpower" from "the
strata of the society" that would accept the Party's program and
identify "personal aims with the aims of the socialist system."[43]
Although the old Communists occupied the most responsible positions, many careers were open to members of the intelligentsia
who joined the Party after the war. In certain fields (science, arts,
literature), official honors were being bestowed on those who,
without joining the Party, were ready to display "a positive approach to new reality." Awards and decorations given to the most
prominent individuals symbolized the regime's desire to admit
to its favors all "old specialists" who were ready "to serve the people." (Among these favors were educational opportunities for
their children.) All this, however, did not apply to former civil
servants, politicians, judges, or the military, who were either removed from or not restored to their posts.

In Yugoslavia, Tito at first spoke of three classes: workers, peasants, and "respectable" (*poštena*) intelligentsia.[44] After the Communists consolidated their power, Tito explained that while the
"people's intelligentsia" had crystallized in Yugoslavia, the "representatives of the old intelligentsia" were still needed to help edu-
cate the youth.[45] He drew a clear distinction between the former,
which serves "only the interests of people," and the latter, which
had once constituted "a privileged caste."[46]

Developing a "people's intelligentsia," the Communist governments undertook to "re-educate" the prewar intelligentsia and to
elevate "the intelligent and politically active workers and peasants
into the managerial ranks in industry and administration." To
achieve this objective, special educational institutions were established for workers and peasants, and the school system was re-
formed. Children from peasants' and workers' families were given
educational priority, and all students were subjected to "ideological training, with stress on vocational preparation."[47]

The "spontaneous process" and the "planning" have produced
a powerful intelligentsia in all East European states. The number
of "working intelligentsia" (which in Poland is understood to in-

clude all the "mental workers," particularly everybody with full or partial secondary education) in the Polish United Workers' Party, for example, rose from 20.3 per cent, in 1949, to 39.5 per cent, in 1956.[48]

The people's intelligentsia is "highly differentiated and stratified."[49] One observer divides it into three "sociological categories," each of which is further subdivided into several "vocational categories." The first sociological category is the "creative intelligentsia"—the people who create the nation's representative culture (i.e., scientists, writers, artists, architects, actors, musicians, journalists). The second category consists of leaders and organizers of social, civic, and technical activities—i.e., engineers, technicians, judges, directors of nationalized enterprises, managers, workers in the Party apparatus, officials in planning, military officers, police, and workers employed in planning and organizing the cultural life of the population.[50] The third sociological category includes professionals, teachers, and all those who apply scientific knowledge to the solution of practical, vocational problems—i.e., physicians, teachers, priests (when fulfilling social functions), and white-collar workers in agriculture.[51]

The structure and function of the intelligentsia in East European countries has changed in the course of years. The term "intelligentsia" no longer refers to an intellectual elite but to those who have the legal status of "mental workers" and who constitute "a third toiling stratum of socialist society."[52] The Communist Party (and not the intelligentsia, as it was understood in the pre-Communist days) has the task of creating "philosophical and political ideas, shaping public opinion, and establishing value criteria." It is admitted, however, that some categories of the "creative intelligentsia" still have "an effect on intellectual and artistic values that serve as symbols and factors contributing to national coherence and continuity and to a sense of national identification." But the present-day intelligentsia has no "common institutions, no common economic interests, and no common ideology or social consciousness." Szczepański observes that "the process of institutionalization advances along occupational lines." He adds: "Some occupational groups of creative intelligentsia that traditionally exercised political leadership and public influence still maintain a feeling of responsibility and national mission, but their real influence is not at all commensurate with their ambitions. These groups are an organized social force rather than a political force."[53]

The "core of the people's intelligentsia" is represented by the new group of political leaders, who are to some degree interpenetrated by traditional intellectuals. The prestige of the "creative intelligentsia" is still very high in the popular mind. The fact that the arts increase the country's international prestige permits the creative intelligentsia to have "some independent action,"[54] while the mass of white-collar workers "can advance only through loyal service," as in any other state.[55]

The Marxist leaders frankly concede that not all objectives for the creation of a new people's intelligentsia have been achieved.[56] What has been accomplished is the "professionalization of the intelligentsia" and the reduction of "traditional barriers between the intelligentsia and the lower classes." Szczepański says that "the increase in numbers of intelligentsia, the specialization and institutionalization of its occupations, and its shifting status in division of labor, all pose new problems and create new situations in which the traditional pattern is losing its validity."[57]

Even a cursory examination of the Communist societies of East Europe reveals categories of the intelligentsia that are deeper than formalistic labeling. A special segment of the intelligentsia is made up of Party members, who speak for the Party, carry out its directives, and serve as models of Communist dedication in government offices, military barracks, classrooms, centers of research, publishing houses, newspaper and journal offices, and propaganda bureaus. They are the first to interpret new developments in science and the arts, in domestic and foreign policy, and in Marxism-Leninism, and the first to criticize those who do not conform. They are the eyes and ears of the Party and constitute the source from which top bureaucrats and managers are drawn.

The same group, however, gave rise to a number of prominent revisionists. Their position and character varied from one state to another, although in essence they were similar. This was the group that became disillusioned to various degrees with Communism, especially with its Stalinist form. Many were alienated from their governments and divorced from power. This was the group that spoke on behalf of those who carried through the revolution in Hungary and the Poznan demonstration. The latter event signaled "a merger between the restless proletariat and the disenchanted intellectuals."[58] Although "a large part of the Hungarian intelligentsia" was not ideologically transformed, "those who had been elevated into the ranks of the intelligentsia by the Communist system had gradually become repelled by it."[59] "The growing contacts between the alienated intellectuals and the workers" provided the "momentum" for the Hungarian revolution.[60]

On the Yugoslav scene, the picture is somewhat different. After 1948, Tito appealed for support of "the Communist intellectuals" in the name of "independent socialism."[61] But this split the ranks of his own intelligentsia. Most intellectuals took his path, but a few adhered to the Soviet Union. As time passed, Tito's tactics disappointed many Communist intellectuals, who saw little difference between Yugoslavia's system and the Stalinist model. Some, like Djilas, abandoned him later for not having carried the decentralization of power and democratization of the country to fuller and more meaningful ends. Many foreign Communists who had previously "attached great hopes to Yugoslavia's separate path" became disillusioned with Titoism.[62]

Another section of the intelligentsia consists of those who, although not members of the Party, are willing to adjust to the new ideology. Some of them appeared to be more outspokenly Marxist and doctrinaire than the official interpreters of Marx. The members of this group have continued to work in universities and school classrooms; they have been admitted to government bureaus and communication media, but not to the sensitive positions and inner councils of the Party and the State. They fill in and buttress the ranks of the ruling intelligentsia.

Still another group derives from "remnants" of the old regime, compromised by their writings, their philosophy, and their participation in former "bourgeois" governments. Despite certain official distrust, this group is a productive element in socialist society. The Party has entertained the hope that they can be "reeducated" and transformed into members of the "people's intelligentsia." Some of them have in fact reinforced the ruling class and have become known as followers of revisionism. This group includes distinguished scholars and artists who have propaganda value for their respective countries. In other words, they serve the socialist state, although they may not be trusted ideologically. Some of them have been shifted from the classroom to research institutes or have been encouraged to abandon sensitive fields of research for those in which they are less likely to expose their non-Marxist views. Nevertheless, the individuals of the "old" bourgeoisie can influence members of the "people's bourgeoisie," and often do. In purely scholarly relationships, a surprising degree of *esprit de corps* has persisted among intellectuals of divergent political camps. But the "old" intelligentsia is really old. Its ranks cannot be replenished, and the part it plays in Communist societies can be no more than temporary. Many of its characteristics, however, may be passed on to new generations of the intelligentsia.

Changing Values

While the class system has not disappeared in Eastern Europe, the social structure has undergone important transformations. Prior to 1945, each East European society was roughly divided into upper, middle, and lower classes, with subdivisions in each of these categories. The social stratification was more pronounced in some countries than in others, and in no two countries was the situation identical, although it was sometimes similar. In Hungary, Poland, and Rumania, feudal aristocracy was much in evidence. In Bulgaria and Yugoslavia (especially Serbia), on the other hand, the aristocratic class had long ceased to exist. Czechoslovakia was unique in that it contained a large and strong group of native industrialists, both Czech and German. Although the peasantry predominated everywhere, it fared worse in some countries than in others. There were large numbers of gypsies in several East European countries and thousands of pastoral Kutso-Vlachs in Yugoslavia, Bulgaria, Greece, and Albania. In Albania and Montenegro, large segments of the population had barely progressed beyond the tribal-society stage. Each East European country had large insubmissive minorities clamoring for full equality and giving impetus to extremist political movements.

The all-important industrial proletariat—the backbone of the

Communist revolutionary plan—was making substantial gains throughout Eastern Europe, but it represented real power only in Czechoslovakia, where strong Social Democratic and Communist parties were in existence. The same was true of the petty bourgeoisie, steadily growing in all countries, but representing real power only in Czechoslovakia. In prewar East European societies, economic and political power was vested in kings and their entourages, military cliques, or bureaucratic elites. The ruling element was drawn from a limited set of families and social circles, and rarely could a newcomer break into the prestigious ranks.

From the very start, the revolutionary governments of the East European states launched attacks against so-called "class enemies," a grouping that included those who opposed Communism or who might oppose it in the future. The policy was to destroy propertied classes, former top civil and military officials, and all those who opposed Communist ideals. The easily accomplished expropriation of land and the nationalization of industry and wholesale trade eliminated the "capitalist classes." The elimination of the petty shopkeeper and artisan (who subsequently were to find work in the state trade network or join artisans' cooperatives) was less rapid. The former "rulers" were socially degraded and used as scapegoats for much that went wrong (they were, for instance, first to be suspected for "wrecking activities"). Their children were also subjected to discriminatory measures. But it was not enough to reduce former ruling elements to economic and social impotence—they were expected to shed their class trappings and consciousness and to demonstrate loyalty to the new state.

The annihilation of the individualistic peasantry turned out to be an especially difficult task. The first land reforms strengthened the peasantry both economically and socially. Instead of losing land, small peasants were able to expand their holdings. Many landless peasants became landholders for the first time in their lives. But later, the collectivization of land and the regimentation of rural life encountered stiff peasant resistance. To bring socialism to the village, the Communist leaders found it necessary to destroy the well-to-do peasant by reducing his landholdings and by ruining him economically. The objective of such drastic innovations as mechanized farming, the system of line-and-staff management, and numerous tax and other financial regulations, had been to coerce the peasant into joining the farming collectives. Eventually, the peasants were expected to change into industrial workers.

Not long ago, Khrushchev echoed Stalin in saying that "agricultural labor shall be transformed into a form of industrial labor."[63] This goal is inherent in the new idea of giant farms, originating in the Soviet Union and applied to some extent in Czechoslovakia and Bulgaria. Peasants on giant farms can be more easily controlled and more firmly integrated into the total political community. Here, it is hoped, they will cease to be peasants—members of a distinct class with a specific way of life. Recent discriminatory measures in several East European countries against the remnants of the "rich" peasantry (kulaks) and against those who chose to remain outside the cooperatives are designed to accelerate the processes leading to the full socialization of the rural community.

As of 1961, according to a Communist source,[64] 98 per cent of Bulgarian agricultural land had been collectivized, 86.7 per cent in Czechoslovakia, 85.3 per cent in Rumania, and 87.2 per cent in Hungary. The 1962 reports have indicated that collectivization of agricultural land in other East European countries has also made further progress. Collectivization has increased surplus manpower for the rapidly developing industry and has also accelerated the population shift from rural to urban communities. Increased opportunities in industry lure the young people away from villages.

However impressive, the shift of population[65] to the cities has not been remarkable, except in Yugoslavia and Poland. In both of these countries, there has been a rapid transition from "a predominantly agricultural to a mixed industrial-agricultural type of economy." The percentage of agricultural population in Poland dropped from more than 60 per cent at the end of the interwar period to just less than 40 per cent in 1960. In the ten-year period 1946 to 1956, as many as 3.5 million out of a total of 14.3 million Polish peasants left their villages for towns.[66] The official Yugoslav figures are less complete, but it is expected that by 1960, the urban and rural populations will be equal.[67] Elsewhere in Eastern Europe (except in Czechoslovakia), special conditions inhibited an urbanization as rapid as that in Poland and Yugoslavia. In Czechoslovakia, the urban population before the war was only slightly smaller than the rural population and has since then exceeded it.

In the summer of 1961, I visited a village in Hercegovina. The local patriarch prefaced his welcoming speech by saying how elated he was that I could visit his village in which "No one will ever marry again!" This was his way of saying that only the old were left in the village.[68] The shift of population has hastened the breakup of rural isolation; the traditional peasant culture has begun to disappear at a rapid pace. Changes are most apparent in peasant speech (influx of Communist terminology, technological words, and urban vocabulary), diet, clothing, social habits, and artistic tastes.

The transition from rural to urban life is a slow process. While he may not enjoy the misery of the village, the peasant does not easily adjust to the impersonal life of the city. His children, however, are different. They go to the cities and try to shed all peasant trappings as quickly as they can. Whereas the urbanite may look at the village with sympathy, many a peasant youth is shamed by it. One of the most interesting phenomena is the change that has taken place in the attitude of young peasant women; they are flocking to cities for marriage and an easier life.

Traditionally, the village has been the backbone of East European societies. The peasants were the chief producers, soldiers, and taxpayers. They represented the power that made national revival in modern times possible. The peasants were the most patriotic element of each nation; they broadened their patriarchal loyalty to include the whole nation. For this reason, many of the most dedicated Communist officials, army officers, policemen, and even academicians are persons of peasant background. Among Communist defectors and political refugees, the least numerous are persons of peasant background.

The degree of transformation in rural areas differs not only from district to district, but also from one group of peasants to another, although the rate of social change is "usually proportional to the rate of development of the productive forces."[69] Although the growing "level of productive forces helps to modernize agricultural production and civilize the life of the rural communities,"

the traditional "historical instincts" (e.g., the powerful "attachment to individual farming") tend to check this advance. It is
most difficult to break these "instincts" and the peasant's way of
thinking. This is one of the reasons why Yugoslavia and Poland
were compelled to relax collectivization and to allow the peasants
to dissolve their cooperatives if they so desired.

Another problem involving the population movement that has
caused difficulties for Polish and Yugoslav planners is the high
proportion of the nonagricultural rural population. In Poland it is
estimated that this group constitutes one-third of the rural population. These are largely landless peasants and small landholders
whose principal income comes from "sources other than agriculture." Another 15 per cent of the population "supplement" their
incomes from work "outside agriculture." In round figures, there
are approximately 1.7 million people (5 million, if dependents are
included) whose chief incomes are derived from nonagricultural
sources and who are "only loosely connected with farming."[70]
One author writes that in southwestern Poland, the movement of
population from agriculture to nonagricultural occupations has
acquired such proportions that there are villages that have actually become "nonagricultural rural settlements."[71]

In Yugoslavia, the dissolution of the peasant working cooperatives in 1953, the adoption of the second land-reform law immediately after—which reduced the maximum private landhold-
ing from 25–35 acres to 10–15 acres—and the steeply progressive
tax on income from agriculture have produced a social process
comparable to that in Poland.[72] These measures produced a huge
number of uneconomical peasant farms, and efforts to convince
the peasants of the virtues of cooperation have produced minimal
results. Having a farm from which he cannot eke out a living, or
having no farm at all, the peasant (sometimes because he cannot
find housing in the city) works halfheartedly and does not care
to spend too much time in learning industrial skills. Approximately one-third of the land is held by such peasants.[73] The result is that society loses both in productivity and efficiency. Moreover, a person working in a city and living in a village is neither
a peasant nor an industrial worker. He brings the city's influence
to the village, but he slows down the process of social change be-

cause he retains a large measure of peasant psychology.

The shifts and scramblings of population in East European countries have produced a series of melting pots, which, in turn, have contributed to a lessening of national tensions and to a very significant cultural and social transformation. In order to ascertain changes in demography and social structure, the Poles have undertaken an intensive study of certain Polish areas that have been particularly affected by the "building of socialism." They believe that interdisciplinary investigations will yield important findings "for the guidance of further economic and cultural development."[74] Many of these studies, such as those directed at investigating "the occupational mobility and migration of the rural population"[75] and changes in the attitudes of rural youth toward various occupations, will be especially useful. One Polish author says that "no other aspect of contemporary rural life is so rich a field of study as rural attitudes toward the choice of occupation."[76] He maintains that these are the likely seeds of new classes. The material factors of modern life that have invaded "the social, cultural, and personal life in the countryside have replaced the traditional attitudes to work and living" on the part of villagers. He notes the change in traditional patterns of prestige, particularly the growing respect for the new rural intelligentsia—"teachers, physicians, agronomists, economists, farmwork mechanization specialists, and others."[77]

The Poles think that "the most engrossing social phenomenon" in their country has been "the formation of a new community in the Regained Territories, the re-Polonization of these lands and their integration into the rest of the country."[78] Instead of "8 million Germans who once inhabited the region there are now 8 million Poles." The new arrivals include "former inhabitants of devastated Warsaw and peasants from the overpopulated countryside in other parts of Poland. The city dwellers from Lwów and Wilno and the rural population from the Western Ukraine, Byelorussia, and Lithuania sought here a new life together with settlers who had re-emigrated from Russia and from France. . . . Here, in fact, was a melting pot: pioneers and scavengers, adventurers and the flotsam of war, the cream of the country's intelligentsia and simple workers and peasants."

A study of the social and ethnic structure of Wrocław in 1960 has revealed fascinating developments. Irena Turnau observed that "the ethos of Wrocław was so unmistakably that of Eastern Poland . . . that the myth that the total population of Lwów has been transplanted to Wrocław has been generally accepted." In fact, however, "the proportion of former inhabitants of Lwów never exceeded 10 per cent and those of Wilno barely reached 2.8 per cent." She suggested that the active part played by the new-comers from Lwów and Wilno in determining the social profile of Wrocław derived from their higher educational standards and their truly urban rather than small-town or rural way of life.[79]

Wrocław's new, once predominantly rural, population, drawn from many different regions and ways of life, has shed its charac-teristics in favor of uniformly urban mores and social relation-ships. In a few years, an aggregation of individuals whose former social loyalties were to small, dispersed groups was molded into a large urban community with a strong sense of social identity.[80]

A new ethnic policy has been used to destroy the middle classes and to remove other barriers to the Communist social structure. The expulsion of about 3 million Germans from Czechoslovakia and another 1.5 million from Yugoslavia, Hungary, and Rumania resulted in the elimination of many of the largest landowners, well-to-do business people, and professionals. The farms of the exiled Germans were either colonized by landless peasants or be-came parts of state or collective farms. The expulsion of the Ger-mans helped the East European governments to get rid of citizens who were not only of dubious national loyalty but were also "class enemies."

The liquidation of the German minority and the settlement of trusted and deserving natives on lands formerly owned by Ger-mans likewise contributed to a change in the ethnic fabric of indi-vidual states. Social and ethnic relations have been altered in Poland as a result of the Polish loss of eastern territories to the Soviet Union and the acquisition of western territories from Germany. While dispossessed Poles flocked to Poland from Rus-sian-occupied territories, millions of Germans, many of them propertied and well-to-do, were expelled or fled from territories that Poland acquired from Germany.

There were similar ethnic and social changes in other countries. More than 200,000 Turks were expelled from Bulgaria. These people were neither ethnically exclusive nor politically subversive; they were religiously conservative and socially backward and had a strong feeling of community with the neighboring Turks. Mixed with the Turks were many gypsies of Muslim faith. Similar changes were effected through the Yugoslav acquisition of Istria and the de-Italianization of Istrian cities and through the Czechoslovak expulsion of Magyars. The formation of separate administrative entities for Albanians (Kosmet) and Macedonians in Yugoslavia, and Magyars in Rumania, has likewise altered the ethnic and social relations in these countries.

Before 1945, Eastern Europe faced numerous deep-seated and complex ethnic, religious, and social problems. Chauvinism, vociferously supported by many intellectuals and government leaders, was rampant. So little did they sense the social revolution that was being unleashed by World War II, that some of the leaders of the Polish government-in-exile thought in terms of a Poland "from sea to sea," the Croats and the Serbs in their governments-in-exile were claiming the Drina and Kupa as the future ethnic borders of their respective nations, while Bulgaria was rejoicing in having acquired Macedonia and Thrace, Albania was elated over "Great Albania" created by Mussolini, and Hungary and Rumania competed for Hitler's affections so as to gain Transylvania.

Nationalism and organized religion, though the sources of much of the prewar trouble, were among the most effective obstacles to Communist social designs. The Communist governments were determined therefore to weaken or destroy these forces. The Communist governments have been partially successful. The worst features of nationalism and religious bigotry have slid into the background as the result of the rigorous application of law, along with the emphasis on "socialist morality," which diverts the attention of the young generation from nationalist issues.

The youth of Hungary and Rumania is far less stirred emotionally by the problem of Transylvania than were their parents, although this does not mean that latent passions could not again be aroused under special conditions. The animosities that once characterized Czech-Slovak and Serb-Croat relations have lost much of their intensity. Everywhere, religious interdicts and taboos have lost much of their force. The classical example of this can be seen in multinational Yugoslavia. There, marriages between persons of Muslim and Christian backgrounds and between Catholics and Orthodox, once rare, are common today. Nearly all elements of religious segregation and Muslim discriminatory practices are vanishing.

As a result of great social upheavals, ethnic stratification has ceased to be a functional social force. The opening of once closed channels (e.g., new opportunities for peasants in the towns) and the abolition of private business have removed the ground from under the old national contests. The stress on personal well-being and security within the new system seems to have made ultranationalist and religious squabbles irrelevant. But occasional outbursts of traditional anti-Semitism serve as a warning against too easily accepting the link between "ideas" and their economic and social "determinants."

At least one form of nationalism, however, continues to militate against Communist "proletarian internationalism." This stems from the national pride and the psychological remnants of old power politics that were manifested in the self-assertion of individual Communist states (Yugoslavia, Poland, Hungary, East Germany) against absolute political and economic subjugation to the Soviet Union. The Kremlin has painfully learned that proletarian revolutions and monolithic political systems neither eliminate national differences nor pave the way for supranational Communist states. They have come to realize, moreover, that the more numerous the Communist states, the greater the chances of antagonism among them.

The experiences of the East European states have clearly shown the fallacies underlying the theories concerning the withering away of the state and the classless society. The advance made toward a classless society is precarious; everywhere the disintegration of old classes has been accompanied by crystallization of new ones.

2. EDUCATION FOR COMMUNISM

MARIN V. PUNDEFF

In Soviet projections, the decade of the 1960's has been designated as the first part of a twenty-year approach to building the foundations of the next and final stage in the evolution of Soviet society—the stage of Communism. In this overriding task, education is assigned the crucial twofold responsibility of training the manpower required by the nascent technology and producing a "new Soviet man," psychologically and morally conditioned to observe the principle of contributing according to one's ability and receiving according to one's needs. To meet this responsibility, the Soviet educational system has been put through extensive curricular and "polytechnical" reforms since 1958.

The relevance of these Soviet developments to the Marxist countries in Eastern Europe lies in the convictions held by the Soviet leaders on the role of the Soviet example and the relationship between the evolution of the Soviet Union and that of the newer Marxist countries. Above all others, two concepts formulated by Khrushchev establish the framework from the Soviet point of view: the concept of the "only path" and the concept of the "more or less simultaneous entrance into Communism."* This examination of educational developments (mainly in general edu-

---

* Contrary to some notions, the Soviet leadership has never been persuaded that there are really many roads to the objectives of Marxism. Speaking in Prague in July, 1957, Khrushchev said: "What do we want? We want unity, closed ranks, and rallied forces. We acknowledge different paths, comrades. But among the different paths, there is one general path . . . the Marxist-Leninist path. This is the path on which the task of the construction of a Communist society must be tackled." The *sine qua nons* of this path were defined in a speech he made in Poland in July, 1959. The doctrine of more or less simultaneous entrance into Communism by all socialist countries was enunciated by him at the Twenty-first Congress.

cation and vocational and teacher training) will primarily seek to describe them as they have taken shape—on the whole since 1958 —in Bulgaria, Czechoslovakia, East Germany, Hungary, Poland, and Rumania; to assess the interaction between the reality, the Soviet conceptual framework, and the satellite leaders' ideas of what is desirable and possible; and to suggest some likely trends in the 1960's. In addition, it will discuss educational developments in Yugoslavia and Albania, the two countries determined and able to stay outside the Soviet framework.

I

In the totalitarian societies that, after World War II, constituted the satellite domain of the Soviet Union in Europe, education, like the politics it reflects and serves, has undergone a succession of significant changes. In the perspective afforded by eighteen years, these changes show three distinct phases: seizure of the educational apparatus and its subordination to immediate Communist political and social aims (generally 1945–48); harnessing —with attendant jolts—of facilities, programs, and enrollments to the plans for economic development and the "building of socialism" (1949–58); and total or partial adoption of the Soviet educational reforms of 1958, which are intended to prepare the human material for moving Soviet society into Communism.[1]

In the first phase, the Communists—the new ruling class—proceeding from the basic Marxist view that the educational system is simply an instrumentality used by all ruling classes to promote their interests and to perpetuate themselves, swiftly moved to grasp control of this instrumentality and use it for the entrenchment and perpetuation of their own regimes.* The new situation, created through the removal of suspect or recalcitrant teachers and administrators, the revision of curriculums and reorientation of studies, and the control of enrollments by criteria of class origin, was embodied and embellished in the new constitutions, laws

* This is one—the more immediate and pragmatic—of Marx's two basic ideas on education. The other is the humanistic idea of achieving the free, whole, noble, "true" man, through the full development of his manifold capabilities and abolition of the distinction between manual and mental work. For an elaboration, see Horst Wittig, "Marx on Education," *Soviet Survey*, No. 30, October–December, 1959, pp. 77–81.

on education, and public policy statements. These, in essence, proclaimed the principles of state monopoly of all aspects and facilities—including the all-important matter of textbooks—secularity and "scientific" atheism, unity and integration of the entire educational process, educational opportunity for all, general compulsory education up to a certain age, recognition of the educational needs of national minorities and ethnic groups, coeducation, "defascistization," and cleansing of education of "nationalistic, racialist, and anti-Soviet content" and personnel. In reality, the salient results were Communist Party monopoly (with some concessions to the Catholic Church in Poland, Hungary, and Czechoslovakia[2]) so as to pervade all education with a "Communist spirit" and to bring up the young generations in the frame of reference and values of Marxism-Leninism; creation of Communist youth organizations after the Soviet models for extramural shaping of minds, characters, and bodies; class discrimination assuring the "sons and daughters of the working class" of privilege in admissions, scholarships, housing, and other accommodations; Sovietization of theory, structure, and methodology of education through replacement of the established systems borrowed from Western Europe (for the most part mixtures of Prussian, French, Swiss, and Austrian models and experiences) by Soviet pedagogical theory (A. S. Makarenko, I. Pavlov), prototypes, and methodology; and Russification of the content of education through intensive study of the Russian language (from the fourth or fifth grade on) and culture, educational exchanges, and use of Russian texts, teaching aids, and materials.

On the other hand, this phase of transition from the old order to the new witnessed a great *élan* toward education, rapid increases in enrollments, parallel but slower expansion of facilities, and concerted drives to reduce illiteracy in the pockets of backwardness throughout the area. The educational opportunities for ethnic minorities were distinctly improved, and the often virulent nationalistic bias of traditional education was superseded by teaching in "the spirit of proletarian internationalism." In line with the orientation toward economic advancement, emphasis shifted from abstract and humanistic studies toward applied sciences, realism, and practicality.

In the second phase (1949–58), the political and social consolidation of the Communist regimes made it possible for them to proceed with economic plans for the "construction of socialism." In education, these plans produced strenuous efforts to relate enrollments and programs to the immediate needs of economic development and produce the necessary contingents of young specialists and technicians for openings throughout the economy. However, with the initial enthusiasm wearing out and enrollments leveling off, the regimes became plagued by a widespread unwillingness among young people to pursue careers in the economy and to be pressed into jobs in new industrial sites and remote areas. The traditional preference of the East European educated classes for desk jobs on the public payroll in the main cities infected both the Party functionaries and the "new toiling intelligentsia" the regimes were working to create.

Moreover, for many young people the educational opportunity did not lead to a realization of ambitions and career objectives, but rather to a multitude of frustrations, disappointments, and contradictions. Any sense of new freedom attained was displaced by an awareness of being cut off from the outside world, fed the predigested diet of a dogmatic ideology, headed for a drab existence as a cog in an enormous dehumanized machine, and destined to live the falsities of the "new freedom," "social justice," "Communist humanism," and "construction of the best society history has ever known." Far from being won over to the new order, the young people longed for liberation from its shackles and shams, restoration of the life-giving contacts with the West, and escape from the ideological bombardment via the classroom, press, radio, literature, and the arts. The alienation, unrest, and cynicism that characterized the mood of youth in Eastern Europe in the 1950's produced the combustible material that went into the fires of the Hungarian revolution of 1956.*

II

The Hungarian events taught all Communists sharp lessons; and, although profound disagreements arose among them as to the

* While much has been written on the mood of the young generation (under forty) in Eastern Europe, no coherent and comprehensive study exists. The need for one has been pointed up by the role of youth in the Hungarian and Polish upheavals in 1956.

meaning of these lessons, the deductions of Khrushchev and the
dominant faction in the Soviet Union came to control the emerging policies. Khrushchev had reached the apex of Soviet politics
after Stalin's death holding a number of basic ideas, among them
the conviction that the estrangement of the Communist elites from
the masses was a potential source of grave problems in Soviet society as well as throughout Eastern Europe. The Hungarian events
reinforced this conviction and accelerated the plans for educational reforms to bring the school closer to life, curb the contempt
for manual labor, and eliminate the bureaucratism and social
snobbishness exhibited by the classes in power.

The reorganization of the Soviet educational system was out-
lined in Khrushchev's address to the Thirteenth Congress of the
Komsomol in April, 1958, and was put into effect by his theses "On
Strengthening the Relationship of the School with Life and the
Further Development of the System of Public Education in the
Country" of November 12, 1958, and by the subsequent law of
December 24, 1958.[3] The changes, reaffirmed by the new Party
program of 1961, seek to establish an education "closely bound
up with life and productive labor" and providing "polytechnical
training in accordance with the rising level of science and engineering," in order to prepare the new generations for the coming
age of automation, atomic energy, chemistry, and space exploration and to solve "a cardinal social problem, namely, the elimination of substantial distinctions between mental and physical
labor."

The Soviet reforms extend the previous ten-year general school
into an eleven-year sequence, adding in effect the extra year to
the first seven, so as to make the general compulsory education
an eight-year course. Involvement in manual labor and practical
training in all fields of study are stressed at all levels. Specifically,
manual work is to take two hours per week in grades one to four
(plus two hours per week of "socially useful labor" on school
grounds in grades three and four), three hours in grades five to
eight (plus two hours of socially useful labor, usually off school
grounds in nearby factories and farms), and one-third of the entire instructional time in grades nine to eleven (spent in industrial
and agricultural processes of production).[4] Since the majority

of the graduates of the eight-year schools are to go directly into argicultural and industrial employment, with some opportunity for continuing their education in extended day and correspondence programs, the eight-year schools are to give them enough polytechnical preparation to make them immediately employable. In higher education the general requirement for admission is two years of employment in production. Those who do not meet this requirement must enroll in extended-day and correspondence programs until they have the two-year minimum, whereupon they may be admitted to full-time study in the day programs. The day-program curriculums, furthermore, are revised so as to reduce the "read" and "listen" time and increase the "do" time. The transition to the new system is to be completed by 1963–65.

Thus the main feature of the Soviet reforms is the reintroduction of polytechnical education, Lenin's favorite educational idea.* As defined by him and by Soviet pedagogical literature, it is the total education of man in a technological society rather than mere vocational training. It is the "familiarization of the students with the scientific foundations of contemporary production" (derivation and application of electric, thermal, and mechanical energy, mechanical processing of materials, derivation and utilization of the most important chemical substances, knowledge of machines and electronics, and plant and animal raising), familiarity with "the economics and organization of socialist production, geographic distribution of sources of raw materials, and the socialist system of organization of national economy and its advantages in comparison with the capitalist system"; "diverse practical skills and habits necessary for work in production" (skills of measuring, calculating, experimenting, drafting, processing, projecting, handling of certain most widely used machines and apparatus), as well as "skills of agricultural technology"; and acquisition of a "working technological culture and ability to organize rationally individual and collective effort."[5] Polytechnical education was attempted in the 1920's, but it degenerated into vocationalism and

---

* See *Lenin o narodnom obrazovanii* (Moscow: Izdatel'stvo Akademii pedagogicheskikh nauk RSFSR, 1957), pp. 365–66. The idea originated in Marx's belief that education should acquaint the young generation with the essentials of all production processes and train them in the practical skills of basic trades. For Engel's definition, see Bodenman, *op. cit.*, p. 35.

displacement of general education. It was abandoned in the
1930's, when the traditional "mastery of knowledge" education
was revived.

The Soviet reforms must be viewed in the context of a closed
ideology, a totalitarian system, a great-power economy, and special demographic conditions. The reforms are basically conceived
as part of the "tooling-up" reorganization of Soviet society to
prepare it for the production of plenty and to develop the "new
Soviet man," both required by the coming age of Communism.*
In their historic function, they are comparable to the Stalin reforms of the 1930's, which they are intended to supersede. Just as
the initiation of the Five-Year Plans to move the Soviet society
into socialism required basic educational changes to eliminate the
revolutionary aberrations of the "activity" school, theories of the
"withering away of the school" and slogans like "Down with the
textbook" in order to establish a new "mastery of knowledge" education, the present projections to move into the next phase of
Communism require an education that can prepare the young
generations for the new age. The abandonment of Lenin's stress
on polytechnical education in the 1930's, and the resulting ab-
stractionism and verbalism produced, as Khrushchev himself has
indicated, the alienation of the educated classes from the laboring masses, disdain for manual labor, and social snobbishness.
These "major social problems" of contradictions "between town
and country and between mental and physical labor" must be
solved if Soviet society is to be spared "the tremendous harm" that
the "separation of mental from physical labor, the conversion of
mental activity into a monopoly of the ruling classes" has brought
to other societies. Without intensive character formation to create
a "Communist attitude toward labor" and to accustom the Soviet

* Speaking before the All-Russian Conference of Teachers on July 9, 1960,
Khrushchev summed up the tasks as follows: "We are now solving two historic tasks: creation of the material-technical basis of Communism and formation of the new man. In essence, this is a single process. If we lag in forming
and educating the Soviet man, the entire work of constructing Communism
will inevitably be rendered more difficult." (*Osnovy kommunisticheskogo
vospitaniia* [Moscow: Gosudarstvennoe izdatel'stvo politicheskoi literatury,
1960], p. 10.) See also Oskar Anweiler, "Schule und Erziehung beim Über-
gang zum Kommunismus," *Osteuropa*, XII, Nos. 4–5 (April–May, 1962),
285–93.

youth to "creative and constructive work for the common good of society" as well as to self-policing in behavior and needs, the transition to Communism is deemed impossible.[6]

The Soviet political leaders, and under them the educators, recognize that moving into Communism demands individuals who not only can handle the technology of the new age, but who also possess new moral and social characteristics, and that something of a character breakthrough to convert selfishness into selflessness (or "high collectivism," as Soviet educators prefer to call it) must come from the educational system. They are ideologically committed to the propositions that human nature can be changed, that physical labor has high educative value in this respect, and that the goals of character reform can be attained.

The Soviet reforms are furthermore an attempt to diversify Soviet secondary education, which since Stalin's reforms in the 1930's has been primarily producing young people suited for university studies; to upgrade the mass of Soviet youth in both general and functional training; to raise the immediate economic usefulness of youth; and to produce enough workers in the vast varieties of competencies the Soviet great-power economy requires. In addition to these considerations, however, it should be borne in mind that the labor shortage caused by the enormous wartime losses is undoubtedly a factor behind the effort to press Soviet youth into the factories and farms on a part-time or full-time basis.

III

If the small-country economies of the satellite states have always been in plain contrast to the great-power economy of the Soviet Union, the ideas of the satellite leaders cannot be said to have so contrasted the ideas of their Soviet counterparts. In the Soviet Union as well as in Eastern Europe, Party discussions on educational problems periodically returned to the ultimates of the ideology, ambitious plans, and Lenin's injunctions about "polytechnizing" the education and uniting study with work. Sporadic experimentation with polytechnical education had even been initiated in some countries. The impetus for general change, however, came from the inauguration of the Soviet reforms. The first country to respond was Rumania, which had been experimenting with polytechnical education since the 1955–56 school year. In 1958–59, the process of conversion to such education was greatly intensified, with the Party press emphasizing that practical work was to be an integral part of instruction at all levels and that, because the majority of graduates of the seven-grade general schools were headed for immediate employment in industrial and agricultural production, it was necessary for them to "receive an education required by their future activities in life."[7] As in the Soviet Union, the transition to the new polytechnical education is to take place by 1963–65.

The structure of Rumanian education is the result of three basic enactments: the educational reform law of August 3, 1948; the joint decree of the Central Committee of the Rumanian Workers' (Communist) Party and the Council of Ministers of July 13, 1956, implementing the resolutions of the Second Party Congress; and the decree of October 7, 1961, implementing the resolutions of the Third Congress. Briefly, Rumanian education is structured as follows:

Nurseries and kindergartens take children from the age of three to six. The first eight grades (ages seven to fourteen) have, since 1961, constituted the general compulsory education and comprise the elementary school (grades one to five) and the so-called gymnasium (grades six to eight). Four additional grades (nine to twelve, ages fifteen to eighteen), known as lyceum and having two divisions in the last two grades for orientation toward the humanities or the physical and mathematical sciences, provide the complete secondary education and lead, if complemented by two years of employment and practical experience, to higher education. Coeducation was introduced in 1956–57 in grades one to eight and is being extended to the remaining grades.*

In teacher training, teachers for kindergartens and grades one to five are trained in two-year teachers' institutes, based on the lyceum, or in six-year pedagogical schools, based on the gymnasium; those for grades six to twelve are trained in five-year programs at universities and pedagogical institutes, based on the

---

* *Pedagogicheskii slovar'*, II, 290–93. Prior to 1960, the general compulsory education was four years; it was extended to seven in that year. The extension to eight, in 1961, brings it in conformity with the Soviet pattern.

lyceum or the pedagogical school.* University and institute graduates are grounded in substantive major and minor subjects so
as to be able to teach their majors in grades six to twelve and
their minors in grades six to eight.

In vocational and technical training, skilled workers and lower-
level technicians are trained in two- or three-year vocational
schools, based on the gymnasium and leading, after three to five
years of practice, to two- or three-year programs for masters.
Higher-level technicians are trained in technicums (four-year programs based on the gymnasium and leading, after practice, to
higher education), in technical schools (two-year programs based
on the physical-mathematical division of the lyceum), and in
universities and special institutes (five-year programs similarly
based).

In the rest of the satellite area, the Bulgarian, East German, and
Czechoslovak regimes appeared much more eager than those of
Hungary and Poland to follow suit. The Bulgarian leaders have
always been marked by their slavish imitation of Soviet concepts,
models, and procedures, which now include an ambitious twenty-
year projection (1961–80) for "completing the building of socialism and passing to communism."[8] Speaking before the congress of
the Bulgarian Komsomol in December, 1958, Todor Zhivkov, the
Secretary of the Bulgarian Party, echoed Khrushchev's address to
the Soviet Komsomol of the previous April and outlined the new
policy. A "basic reorganization" of the educational system was to
be made "on a polytechnical basis" and "all students from a cer-

* In 1959, there were four universities (at Bucharest, Jassy, and two—one
Rumanian, the other Hungarian—at Cluj; the latter two have since merged)
and two pedagogical institutes (at Bucharest and Timişoara). The university
professional programs and their criteria for admission are too varied to be discussed in this space. It may generally be indicated that in Rumania, as in the
other satellite countries and the Soviet Union, admission is contingent on
entrance examinations and political reliability certified as a rule by the Communist Party unit in the applicant's place of residence. Likewise scholarship,
the institutional summits of which in Rumania and the other satellite countries
are the national Academies of Sciences, is outside the limits of this discussion.
Other Rumanian statistics: In a population of 18.17 million there were about
7,000 nurseries and kindergartens with 293,257 children; 11,277 elementary
schools with 1.45 million pupils; 4,491 gymnasiums with 511,657 pupils; 454
lyceums with 181,069 students; and 40 institutions of higher education with
67,849 students (including those taking correspondence courses).

tain age on, without exception, should simultaneously study and work in production"; as to "whether it is better to permit students to learn for half a day and work for half a day, or to learn one day and work the next," he said, "the question could be discussed."[9] In April, 1959, the Central Committee duly adopted "theses" on the reorganization of education, and on July 3, 1959, the legislative body passed an appropriate law (the third since the original reform law of September 24, 1948, and the edict of November 9, 1954) on the basis of which Bulgarian education at present is structured as follows:

Provisions for preschoolers are the same as in Rumania. The previous eleven-year unified secondary school has been extended to twelve years, the extra year being added, as in the Soviet Union, to the first seven to make the seven-year general compulsory school (in existence since 1921) an eight-year program (ages seven to fourteen). Four additional grades (nine to twelve, ages fifteen to eighteen) complete the secondary education and qualify the graduates, after a period of employment, for admission to higher education. Teachers of kindergartens and grades one to four are trained in teachers' institutes (three-year programs, based on the twelve-year school); those for grades five to twelve are trained in universities (generally four-year programs). Technical talent is sifted through one-, two-, or three-year vocational schools (based on the eight-year school) and the four- or five-year technicums (also based on the eight-year school and open to vocational-school graduates as well). Technicum graduates qualify for admission to higher education in their fields of specialization. Traditional in primary school, coeducation is now extending to the higher grades. In 1959, 99.6 per cent of all children in the respective age bracket were attending the eight-year general compulsory school.* Following the Soviet model, some schools are being con-

* *Pedagogicheskii slovar'*, I, 119–21. In a population of 7.8 million, there were 6,254 nurseries and kindergartens with 285,053 children; 2,551 first- to fourth-grade schools with 622,512 pupils; 3,190 first- to seventh-grade and 113 fifth- to seventh grade schools with 397,159 pupils; and 173 eighth- to eleventh-grade and 178 first- to eleventh-grade schools with 156,810 students. In specialized education, there were 189 technicums with 72,242 students, 7 teachers' institutes with 2,472 students (a sharp drop from the peak of 14 institutes with 6,529 students in 1952), and 20 institutions of higher education with 48,880 students. Among the last-named, however, only the University of

verted into boarding schools. The reforms decreed by the law of 1959 were initiated with the 1959–60 school year and are to be completed by 1965.

An assessment of the reforms at midpoint emerged at the Bulgarian Teachers' Congress (May, 1962), which proceeded under the slogan "Closer to life, faster toward Communism." The only positive note came from statistics on growth; the weaknesses, identified by official spokesmen, were many. Polytechnical education was impeded by inadequate facilities and teachers and was taught in a "primitive" way; the urban schools were failing to train their students in the efficient operation of machines, and the rural schools were "not able to prepare pupils for highly productive labor based on modern agrotechnical methods"; academic subjects in the humanities, arts, and sciences were suffering in the overburdened curriculum; students were indifferent to their studies and assignments and susceptible to Western influences that were turning many of them into a "nylon intelligentsia"; graduates "displayed a low sense of duty" and a "negative attitude toward physical labor" and whenever possible dodged working in the field.[10]

If the teachers attending the congress had felt free to state their views, the problems undoubtedly would have been identified more sharply. Even as it was, however, the congress reflected a muddled state. Overburdened with polytechnical training and indoctrination and plagued by a shortage of good teachers, textbooks, and facilities, education seems to flounder, while the "man of the Communist society" still remains a very distant vision.

In East Germany, it would appear, the principles and objectives of the Soviet reforms have found their most meaningful implementation. Possessing the type of industrially and educationally advanced society toward which the Soviet Union is striving, East Germany is moving farther ahead in education for the new age than any of the other bloc countries. Coming closest to the ideals of the native sons, Marx and Engels, the East German educational changes require a more detailed examination.

Sofia (7,240 students) is a full-fledged university. *Statisticheski godishnik na Narodna Republika Bulgariia, 1960* (Sofia: Durzhavno izdatelstvo "Nauka i Izkustvo," 1960), pp. 289–99.

In line with Soviet procedure, the proposed changes were first
publicized as "theses" of the Central Committee and then put into
effect by a "Law on the Socialist Development of Education" of
December 2, 1959.[11] The preamble of the law noted with ill-con-
cealed pride that "In Germany, compulsory education has already
existed for more than a century,"* and that the proposed general
polytechnical school "is built on the progressive traditions of German pedagogy and corresponds to the historical experience" in
Germany. It explained that although socialist education required
the closest relationship between the school on one hand and life
and production on the other, in the past "instruction remained
isolated from life, produced one-sided, intellectualized schooling,"
and thus failed to contribute to the elimination of "the gulf between mental and physical labor and between theory and practice." Furthermore, "the rapid development of mechanization and
automation, application of modern chemical knowledge, development of electronics, and utilization of nuclear energy are changing the production processes and the nature of work"; the new
"complicated machinery and measurement and guidance apparatus can be mastered and the organization and control of the modern technological processes made possible only if the workers
possess a high-level general education" coupled with engineering-
technical knowledge. To raise the general level accordingly, the
ten-year general school (which in 1951 began to supersede the
eight-year general school) is to be "polytechnized" and made
compulsory for all in 1964. The work provisions envisage practical work lessons in grades one to six (one hour per week in
grades one to three, and two hours in grades four to six), a "day
in production" each week in grades seven to twelve (four hours,
supervised by shop teachers and factory technicians), and a new
subject, "Introduction to Socialist Production in Industry and
Agriculture," in grades nine and ten. (The total school hours in-

---

* It may be noted that in Russia, compulsory education (to the fourth
grade) did not become a statutory requirement until 1930. In popular education, Russia "was one of the most backward countries in Europe" (*Pedagogicheskii slovar'*, II, 392), even in comparison with the East European countries,
excepting Albania, where four-year compulsory education was introduced in
1946.

crease from nineteen hours per week in the first grade to thirty-eight in the twelfth.)

In addition to technological training, the new school is to instill "love for work and the working man" among the young, foster the "total development of their spiritual and physical capabilities," and teach them the "lessons of German history" in the spirit of peace and friendship among nations, "particularly friendship with the Soviet Union." The new East German school is to be the "model for the development of the school in all Germany."

In its specific provisions, the law structures education as follows:

The ten-year school (*Oberschule*) is preceded by kindergarten (ages three to five) and divided into lower grades (one to four) and upper grades (five to ten), followed by an extension of the *Oberschule* (grades eleven and twelve). There are four avenues to higher education (*Hochschule*): (1) beginning with the ninth grade, the student can select one of the three divisions of the extended *Oberschule* (natural sciences, modern languages, and classical languages), and after graduation and one year of employment appropriate to his chosen field of study, he is entitled to admission to institutions of higher education; (2) graduates of the ten-year school can continue to higher education through either the three- or four-year technicums (*Fachschule*) or the three-year vocational schools (*Berufsschule*) offering vocational training and general-education equivalent to the twelve-grade schools; (3) graduates of the ten-year school can qualify by attending factory schools, evening programs, or special courses leading to an equivalent of the twelve-year school; and (4) students who graduated from vocational schools before the reforms can continue in the so-called workers' and peasants' departments (corresponding to the Soviet *Rabfak*) attached to the universities.*

Kindergarten teachers are prepared in three-year pedagogical schools, based on the ten-year *Oberschule;* teachers of grades one

* These departments provide opportunity for workers to complete their secondary education and qualify for admission to higher education. The course of study is usually three years. On the regime in the universities, see Rudolf Reinhardt, "The Universities in East Germany," *Survey*, No. 40, January, 1962, pp. 68–76.

to four are trained in four-year teachers' institutes, similarly based. Teachers for grades five to ten are trained in four-year programs in the various departments of the universities and the pedagogical institutes, based on the twelve-year school. Specialized teachers for the extended *Oberschule* are prepared in the respective departments of the universities as well as in the Higher Pedagogical School at Potsdam. Scientific work in the field of education is coordinated by the Central Institute of Pedagogy (corresponding to the Soviet Academy of Pedagogical Sciences of the R.S.F.S.R., which has jurisdiction over methodological, administrative, and curricular problems). There is also a Central Institute for Teaching Aids. In technical-personnel training, ten-year school graduates can either go into the *Berufsschule* or, after two years of on-the-job training, continue into the *Fachschule.**

If East Germany is much better suited for polytechnical education in terms of technological progress and available facilities, it has a morale problem unmatched anywhere else in the area. The freedom and prosperity in West Germany have exerted such a magnetic pull on the people of East Germany that some 2.2 million—half under twenty-five years of age—fled to the West prior to the erection of the Berlin wall; as a result, the total population is still below the 1949 peak figure of 19 million. In addition to other valuable human resources, East Germany has lost 75,000 teachers in various categories, and those who have remained behind often prove recalcitrant and unresponsive to the political purposes of the regime. Judging from official concern, the mood of the youth presents vexatious problems; a special "Statement of the Politbureau . . . on Youth Problems" has been issued, scoring the

* See *Education in the German Democratic Republic* (Leipzig: VEB, 1962), pp. 30–160, a source effectively stating the official point of view; *Pedagogicheskii slovar'*, I, 247–52. See also *Das Schulwesen in der Sowjetzone* (Bonn: Bundesministerium für Gesamtdeutsche Fragen, 1961) and *SBZ von A bis Z: Ein Taschen–und Nachschlagebuch über die Sowjetische Besatzungszone Deutschlands* (Bonn: Deutscher Bundes-Verlag, 1960), pp. 62, 170–71, 364. In a population of 17.29 million (1959), there were 9,100 eighth-grade schools with 1.81 million pupils, 1,809 ten-year schools with 1 million students, 372 twelve-year schools with 89,403 students, 1,252 *Berufsschulen* with some 600,000 students, 307 *Fachschulen* with some 90,000 students, and 44 *Hochschulen* (of which only 6 are universities) with 82,719 students (including those in the correspondence programs and the workers' and peasants' departments).

lack of confidence between students and teachers, the widespread cynicism, hypocrisy, and doubt, and the pervasive influences of the "Western way of life."[12] The regime's principal answer to these problems has been the stock approach of the old Prussian school and army: Keep the youngsters busy at all times. A comprehensive "Program for the Political and Moral Education of School Children" has been issued, detailing methods of keeping the children busy at school during recesses, on their way to and from school, at home, and on weekends.[13]

In Czechoslovakia, a country almost as well suited for polytechnical education as East Germany, the Central Committee of the Party in April, 1959, discussed the question of creating closer ties between school and life, and a decision was reached to begin the "polytechnization" of the schools with the 1959–60 school year. The reform law, closely patterned after the Soviet prototype and enacted on December 15, 1960, provides for an extra year added to the basic eight-grade compulsory education and making the new nine-grade "general polytechnical" school compulsory for all.[14] Under the new law, the Czechoslovak educational system is structured as follows:

Children from three to five years of age attend nurseries and kindergartens. The first nine grades (ages six to fourteen) constitute the new general school (first cycle), followed by three additional grades (second cycle) encompassing training in production (eight hours per week) and qualifying the graduates for admission to higher education.

In addition to leading to the second cycle and the university, the first cycle is the basis for (1) two- or three-year programs for training skilled workers and apprentices; (2) two- to four-year technicums that entitle the graduates, after employment, to admission to schools of higher education; (3) grades ten to twelve programs (mostly evening) for workers to make completion of secondary education and admission to schools of higher education possible for them; and (4) four-year pedagogical schools for the training of kindergarten teachers. Teachers for the first cycle are prepared in three- and four-year teachers' institutes (grades one to five and six to nine, respectively), based on the twelve-year school; those for the second cycle (grades ten to twelve) are trained in the programs (usually five years) of the institutions of higher education, similarly based. The transition is to be completed by 1965, while the long-range plans there, as in the Soviet Union, are to make the complete secondary school (twelve-grade program in Czechoslovakia, eleven-grade program in the U.S.S.R.) available to the majority of the youth by the 1970's.[*]

The new Czechoslovak constitution enacted in 1960 is of more than academic interest to education. Superseding the 1948 constitution, which ushered in the people's democratic regime, the 1960 constitution proclaims that Czechoslovakia has completed the transition from capitalism to socialism[†] and sets the national goals for the years ahead as "the building of a mature socialist society" and "the creation of the material and spiritual preconditions for the transition to Communism." These goals are to be reached through "comradely collaboration" with the U.S.S.R. and the other countries of "the world socialist system," so as to move more or less simultaneously into Communism. The official ideology excluding all other viewpoints and philosophies is Marxism-

[*] *Pedagogicheskii slovar'*, II, 666–69. See also Vaclav Kristek, "L'Ecole et l'Education," *Synthèses* (Brussels), XVI, No. 188 (January, 1962), 96–110. The author, Czechoslovakia's Deputy Minister of Education and Culture, wrote this essay for a special issue devoted to Czechoslovakia. He and other Communist writers do not fail to extol the heritage of the great Czech pedagogue John Amos Comenius (1592–1670).

In a population of 13.52 million (1959), there were 6,309 nurseries and kindergartens with 262,146 children, 9,233 five-grade schools with 540,141 pupils, 2,867 eight-grade schools with 1.17 million pupils, 450 eleven-grade schools with 369,973 students, 621 two- or three-year programs for skilled workers and apprentices with 222,056 students, 715 technicums with 192,116 students, 68 pedagogical schools with 12,275 students, 9 teachers' institutes with 7,194 students, 2 pedagogical institutes (for teachers in the new grades ten to twelve) with 4,660 students, and 38 institutions of higher education with 74,896 students (including 20,903 in the evening and correspondence programs). Among the latter is the "November 17" University for Foreign Students (Czech counterpart of the Soviet "Patrice Lumumba" University), functioning since September, 1961. Czechoslovakia, it should be noted, is assigned the role of being an industrial workshop in the Communist world and supplying machinery and technological knowledge to underdeveloped countries in Asia and Africa.

[†] The Soviet Union was so proclaimed in 1936 by the Stalin constitution, which is due to be superseded as having "outlived itself." On April 25, 1962, it was announced that Khrushchev would head a commission to draft a new constitution reflecting the current "full-fledged construction of a Communist society."

Leninism: "All cultural policy in Czechoslovakia, the development of education, upbringing, and teaching, are conducted in the spirit of the scientific world view of Marxism-Leninism," on which "all education and all teaching are based" (Articles 16 and 24). The first satellite country to follow the Soviet Union into a "mature socialist society" and the transition to Communism, Czechoslovakia appears to be signaling developments in the other satellite countries.

In Hungary, the social and moral crisis that produced the revolution of 1956 has compelled the Communist regime to proceed with circumspection. While polytechnical training was introduced on an experimental basis in a number of schools beginning with 1958–59, general changes were not legislated until October, 1961. The new law on education[15] avoids the ambitious phraseology of polytechnical education and sets no time limit for conversion. Left structurally intact by the new law, the Hungarian educational system is organized as follows:

Kindergartens are provided for ages four to six. A general eight-grade school forms the foundation for (1) four-year middle school or gymnasium leading to higher education; (2) four-year technicum (industrial or agricultural), also leading to higher education in the technical professions; and (3) two- or three-year trade school for apprentices, skilled workers, and farmers. Teachers for kindergartens and grades one to eight are trained in three-year pedagogical institutes, based on the gymnasium; those for the gymnasium grades are as a rule trained in the universities, where the course of study has been lengthened to five years to provide time for work in industry and agriculture and for practice teaching.*

The law of 1961 has extended the eight-year compulsory schooling decreed in 1950 to ten years, requiring all children to attend school through their sixteenth year. In practice, this means that all children are to complete the eight-grade general school and go on to two additional years of study, which for the majority

* *Pedagogicheskii slovar'*, I, 154–56; *Osteuropa*, XI, No. 9 (September, 1961), 666–67. The approximate figures for 1960–61 are as follows: In a population of more than 10 million, some 200,000 children attended kindergarten; 1.4 million, the eight-grade school; 250,000, the gymnasium and technicum; and 40,000, the four universities and other higher institutes.

would be in trade schools and technicums. As in the other countries discussed, the reform calls for establishing the closest possible relationship between school and life, acquainting the pupils with manual work and the processes of production, and cultivating in them proper respect for labor and the laboring segments of the population. This is generally to be accomplished through the so-called five-plus-one approach—spending five days per week in classroom studies and one day in factory or farm work. Gymnasium students are to pass a graduation examination in both academic preparation and practical performance in the production processes. In admissions to schools of higher education, preferential treatment is accorded those who have been employed in industry or agriculture for at least one year after graduation. Finally, the law explicitly requires inculcation of the "Marxist-Leninist world view" and the "socialist moral commitment" in the students.

Because the reforms became general only in 1962–63, an evaluation of their application is premature. The atmosphere in which they are being applied, however, continues to show the effects of the revolution in 1956. In the face of latent conflict and widespread dissimulation, official spokesmen have pointed with concern to the continuing "contradictions between school and family" and between "official and private beliefs."

Among the countries susceptible to Soviet influences, post-1956 Poland stands out with its quietly persistent search for its own way to socialist transformation. Educational reform was discussed periodically, and the contending viewpoints crystallized in two proposals: (1) to transform the existing seven-year general school into a ten-year compulsory polytechnical school (such as that instituted in neighboring East Germany); and (2) to extend the seven-year school by one year into a longer sequence of compulsory general education leading to several alternate paths of academic and vocational preparation. The second approach was endorsed by the Central Committee of the Polish United Workers' Party in January, 1961, in three documents outlining a long-range educational policy.[16] Finding that reform was overdue in view of the rapid development of the country's economy and the changes in its technology, the Central Committee gave highest priority to beginning the transformation of the seven-year general school into an eight-year sequence in 1963–64, and completing it by 1967–68.* The slow pace of the change is justified by the shortage of teachers (especially in Russian, physics, and mathematics), buildings, and facilities. The cost of the change is to be met at least in part by voluntary public contributions to a special fund for the "Schools of the Millennial Jubilee" of the Polish state (being celebrated during 1960–65) and for the implementation of the slogan "Poland—A Country of Educated People." While the policy statements and the new law shy away from the terminology of polytechnical education and specific provisions for practical work, there is a strong emphasis on seeking harmonious and total development, improving vocational training, and fostering early specialization. One of the reasons for early specialization cited in the preliminary discussions is the "rising hooliganism" resulting from lack of vocational orientation and opportunities for such education.[17]

The Polish educational system is structured as follows:

Nurseries and kindergartens admit children between the ages of three and six. The general compulsory education is the seven-grade primary school, which leads to (1) the four-year "lyceum" (grades eight to eleven) and higher education, or (2) middle-level pedagogical or technical education, which may lead to specialized higher education. Kindergarten and primary-school teachers are trained in five-year pedagogical lyceums, based on the primary school, or in two-year teachers' institutes, based on the general lyceum and providing a possibility for higher professional education; those for the lyceums are trained in pedagogical institutes and universities, based on the lyceum and usually involving five years of study. Vocational and technical training is provided in two- or three-year trade schools based on the primary school (and leading to two- or three-year technicums) and in four- or five-year technicums, based on seven-grade schooling and leading to higher professional education.†

* An attempt was made in 1945 to extend the seven-year school (introduced in 1932) by an extra year. It was officially abandoned in 1948.

† *Pedagogicheskii slovar'*, II, 150-52. In a population of 29.5 million (1959), there were 8,356 nurseries and kindergartens with 376,549 children, 24,503 primary schools with 3.92 million pupils, 824 lyceums with 202,713 stu-

Poland thus presents, as does Hungary, an educational picture at variance with the polytechnical education reforms attempted, more or less uniformly, in the rest of the area. Poland obviously seeks to find educational patterns best suited to its economy and social conditions and grants recognition to local factors much more realistically than do the other East European countries. Two forces continue in Polish education: the Communist Party and the Catholic Church. They are in a truce made uneasy by the Party's renewed effort to press for complete secularization of the schools and elimination of contending viewpoints, which the resumption of teaching of religion after 1956 has revived. In this respect, the students' indifference to the Marxist indoctrination course "Fundamentals of Philosophy," reintroduced in 1960–61 after a four-year hiatus, has been helpful to the Church in holding its ground as an alternate system of beliefs to which Polish youth can turn. Finally, as in Hungary, there is marked silence on the subject of preparing the human material and economic conditions for moving into the phase of Communism.

IV

Yugoslavia and Albania, the two Marxist countries in Eastern Europe outside the Soviet bloc, require separate consideration, for sharply contrasting political reasons in each case. As in politics and economics, Yugoslavia since 1948 has striven to develop its own forms of education for socialism and Communism. The problems in Yugoslav education—excessive academic orientation, verbalism, impracticality, social snobbishness—were essentially the same as in the other Marxist countries, but the basic approach of solving them reflected a type of thinking diametrically opposed to that prevalent in the Soviet Union. Focusing on bureaucratization as the most dangerous vice developed by the Marxist societies, the Yugoslav leaders in 1950 started a policy of economic decentralization and local management and initiative that was gradually

---

dents, 2,950 technicums and vocational schools with 427,323 students, and 76 institutions of higher education (10 universities) with 170,330 students (including some 20,000 in evening and correspondence programs). For other statistics, see Apanasewicz and Medlin, *Educational Systems in Poland,* pp. 29–30.

extended to trim other branches of the bureaucratic growth in line with the fundamental Marxist injunction that the state should wither away under socialism. This policy became the core of the 1958 program of the League of Communists of Yugoslavia, which, in the area of education, calls for "socialist democratization of the school" and "freeing of educational, scientific, artistic and cultural life from administrative interference by state organs and from state-absolutist and pragmatist conceptions of cultural creativeness, through building and perfecting a system of social self-management in educational, scientific and other cultural institutions and organizations."[18] The program also defines an array of objectives to raise the basic education of all inhabitants in general and specialized knowledge; to link the school with the needs of society; to propagate "scientific and technological experience in order to achieve a higher economic social standard as the fundamental and all-important prerequisite of a fuller life of man"; to create "equal opportunities for every young man to choose his calling in life and, according to his abilities and interest, to continue his schooling and perfect his knowledge to the highest degree"; to introduce new social habits and narrow "the gulf between intellectual and physical work"; and to make the school boards attached to every educational institution and linked with the "Commune and economic and social organizations" the machinery for "consultation and cooperation of all interested factors: teachers, parents, youth, and the respective social organizations and state organs."

Implementing the program, the government on September 1, 1958, enacted a new general law on education.[19] On the basis of its provisions, the Yugoslav educational system has been organized as follows:

Children from three to six years of age attend nurseries and kindergartens. Grades one to eight comprise the basic compulsory education,* followed by a four-year gymnasium leading to higher education, or by vocational and technical schools (two to four-year programs) leading to advanced professional training. Teachers for kindergartens and grades one to four are trained in five-year pedagogical schools, based on the eight-grade school; those

* As of 1950; prior to that the general compulsory education was four years.

for the higher grades are trained in the universities and pedagogical institutes, based on the gymnasium. Avoiding the terminology of polytechnical education, the law stresses that "work is the basic condition of existence and progress of every individual and of society as a whole" and calls for orientation toward vocational and technical training to meet the needs of the country's changing economy. Humanistic orientation, however, is still a possible choice: The gymnasium curriculum is to have a required part and an elective part so as to enable students to concentrate on areas of their abilities and interests, and the new programs (enacted in 1959) provide for social sciences plus languages and natural sciences plus mathematics options. To utilize local initiative and funds to the maximum, all schools are placed under a regime of local self-management exercised by school boards, a method designed to free education from the centralized controls of the state apparatus and termed in the Soviet Union as an "anarcho-syndicalist attitude toward the role of the state in education."[*]

Since its estrangement from the Soviet bloc in 1961, Albania, in contrast to Yugoslavia, has not moved to eliminate the Soviet patterns and prototypes embedded in its educational system. Nor is this likely to occur, since the essential disagreement with the Soviet Union is not over domestic policy but over policy toward Yugoslavia. On the basis of the law on education of August 17, 1946, modified in 1952 and again in 1960, Albanian education is structured as follows:

Nurseries and kindergartens are provided for ages three to six. The general compulsory school is composed of grades one to eight, expanded from the seven-grade sequence and made polytechnical along Soviet lines in 1960. The general eight-year school leads to (1) four-year completion of secondary education and higher education; (2) four-year pedagogical schools for kindergarten and elementary-school teachers (grades one to four); (3) four-

---

[*] *Pedagogicheskii slovar'*, II, 746–49. See also Bora Pavlovic, "Outline of the Development of the Educational System in Yugoslavia," *Yugoslav Trade Unions*, No. 3, 1961, pp. 2–18. In round figures, in a population of 18.5 million (1959), there were 14,324 eight-grade schools with 2.47 million pupils, 741 trade schools with 124,000 students, 257 vocational schools with 76,000 students, 834 gymnasiums with 77,000 students, and 122 institutions of higher education (including 6 universities) with 96,890 students.

year technicums; and (4) three-year vocational and trade schools. Graduates of the pedagogical schools and the technicums can pursue higher professional education in Tirana University (the only one in the country, established in 1957 through the consolidation of a number of institutes).* The polytechnical reform is to be completed by 1964–65, while the new eight-year general school is expected to encompass 80 per cent of all children by that time.

The course of isolation from the Soviet bloc that began in 1961, the attendant withdrawal of bloc technicians and advisers from Albania, and the return of Albanian students studying in bloc countries have resulted in acute shortages of qualified personnel and in burdening the Albanian educational system with tasks it cannot handle alone. A depressing picture emerged in a report by the Minister of Education dwelling at length on the problems and deficiencies, which include inexperience of instructors, poor libraries and laboratory facilities, inability of instructors to read foreign literature, and a lack of translated materials.[20] By the vagaries of Communist politics, Albania, the Communist country least able to afford it, has been thrown upon its own resources in preparing for the stage of Communism.

V

Viewed in general perspective, the recent changes in education in the nine Marxist countries discussed above represent efforts, partly implemented and partly projected in laws and plans, of totalitarian regimes to adapt their educational establishments to the needs of changing economies and to the pressures of certain acute social problems. In adaptation to the needs of an increasingly industrialized and urbanized society, some of the changes are not unlike those necessitated by industrialization elsewhere in the world.[21] In fact, the extension of schooling at all levels is a world-wide phenomenon, and the new emphasis in these countries on combining maximum practical experience with study and on going to school while working has the appearance of a local variant

* *Pedagogicheskii slovar'*, I 34–35; Kemal Mandiia, "Obshcheobrazovatel'-naia shkola v Albanii," *Sovetskaia Pedagogika*, No. 3, 1961, pp. 96–101. In a population of 1.6 million (1959), there were 380 kindergartens with 17,148 children, 2,678 seven-grade schools with 219,893 pupils, 40 middle schools with some 15,000 students, and a university with 3,351 students.

of the unplanned American practice of "working one's way through school." Deviant youth behavior and educational measures to meet the problems arising from it are also developments known both in Marxist and non-Marxist countries.

However, this is as far as similarities should be pursued. Because of its subordination to a closed ideological system and state monopoly, education in the Marxist countries is marked by specificities in tasks to be discharged, problems to be met, and products to be molded that defy comparisons. The examination of common features and differences that exist within the group of Marxist countries in Europe is more rewarding. Taking into account the changes introduced since 1958, there is a degree of uniformity in the extension of general compulsory education from seven to eight years in most of the countries and in the involvement of students in manual work so as to acquaint them with production processes and prepare them for early specialization. The departures from this generalization, however, are numerous and very significant. Poland is yet to begin actual conversion to the eight-year school, while East Germany and Hungary already require ten years of compulsory education, and Czechoslovakia nine. The Soviet patterns in polytechnizing the educational process in secondary education are followed more closely in Bulgaria and Rumania than in East Germany and Czechoslovakia, while Hungary and Poland show substantial variations. Moreover, complete secondary education in the Soviet Union consists of eleven years (eight years of compulsory schooling plus three final grades), whereas in all of these countries, including Albania and Yugoslavia, it is twelve (eight-plus-four, nine-plus-three, or ten-plus-two variants). "Polyformity" and flux rather than uniformity and a steady course are clearly the general characteristics of education in the area. As the R.S.F.S.R. minister of education noted at the International Seminar on Polytechnical Education—held at Moscow on December 12–21, 1960, and attended by educators from the bloc countries—while "the unity of the principal ideas of all participants" was affirmed, "the reports and comments showed that in the individual countries of the socialist camp, and even in individual areas of a given country, there is a great variety in organization, content, forms, and methods of implementing polytechnical training and the ties of school with life."[22]

Despite the Soviet desire to exercise tutelage and promote uniformity, the evolution of the area has already produced a political and ideological "polycentrism" that cannot be reversed. In education, this tendency toward "polycentrism" is reinforced by local conditions and peculiarities in seeking diverse forms and methods which are avowedly encased in common allegiance to fundamental doctrine but which are better suited to the immediate reality. Native pedagogical ideas and attainments are emphasized through the republication of the writings of noted national pedagogues and by encouragement to study this heritage. The social malaise (or "fever," as Khrushchev chose to describe it in 1959) is recognized as a much more serious problem in the East European countries than in the Soviet Union and has compelled a more circumspect handling of sensitive social segments, especially the youth, and at least temporary relinquishment of ambitions in most countries to produce local counterparts of the "new Soviet man." In this respect, the strength of religious sentiment has been recognized in Polish and Hungarian education since 1956, and while the new laws of 1961 stress secularity, the force of this local factor will continue to be felt. The economics inherent in the different size and potential of human and natural resources also make for educational differences, as does the international division of labor agreed upon and currently implemented in the area: It is evident that the superpower economy of the Soviet Union in its present operation and future development requires technological education of a sophistication and scale out of place in the economies of Rumania, Czechoslovakia, or even East Germany. As these factors will make themselves increasingly felt, the Soviet Union will remain the vanguard of educational innovation to produce the "new man" and the "society of Communism," while the East European countries will either assert independence or as a bloc trail reluctantly and "polyformly" behind the Soviet model.

PART TWO

The Planned Economy

3. AGRICULTURE AND THE PEASANT

L. A. D. DELLIN

It has become almost axiomatic to characterize a Communist economy as able to advance beyond expectation in the military, scientific, and industrial fields, but unable to meet basic needs of the people. This is all the more astonishing because in the countries taken over by the Communists agriculture was the principal occupation and the peasant the backbone of society.

Although such generalizations necessitate corrections, their over-all validity is hardly a matter of serious dispute. The state of Communist agriculture was dramatized again, only too recently, by the Chinese debacles, by Khrushchev's repeated efforts to find the panacea for Soviet farm ills, and by reports about acute food shortages in many bloc countries, most notably East Germany, Hungary, and Bulgaria. In the light of these and past developments, little doubt should remain that Communist agriculture has been in a state of perennial crisis and that, during and after fourteen to eighteen years of Communist rule, agriculture and the peasant in Eastern Europe have been relegated to the bottom step of the Communist political, economic, and social ladder.

The following account will try to place the problem in perspective and identify the major features, causes, and consequences of Communist farm policy, on the basis of which some speculations as to probable development during the 1960's could be ventured. It should be mentioned in advance that each of the eight East European countries revealed and continue to reveal more or less specific features, so that the regional approach chosen makes some distortion unavoidable. Still, because the similarities among six of them are much greater than the differences, especially in the agricultural field, and because space is limited, only Poland, within the bloc, and Yugoslavia, the Communist stepchild, will receive separate treatment as far as their more obvious deviations are concerned.

The major sources for this article are statistical abstracts and other publications of Communist origin, with their known deficiencies, as well as United Nations publications, but a growing— although on this specific topic far from exhaustive—body of literature in the West is most helpful for the reliability of its processed data and interpretations.[1]

Background

Pre-Communist Eastern Europe was known as the "agricultural half" of the continent, and more specifically as its "granary," for its population, with the exception of Czechoslovakia and present-day East Germany, was overwhelmingly occupied in agriculture (between 50 per cent in Hungary and 95 per cent in Albania), and the area as a whole was a substantial exporter of foodstuffs, mainly grains, to Western Europe. The peasant-agricultural character of the area should not be taken as an indication that the socio-economic structure was necessarily healthy or that farming methods and surpluses were of the conventional Western type. In fact, the physical setting, with some exceptions, is none too favorable for agriculture, and rural overpopulation, primitive cultivation, and low living standards were widespread. But tradition and lack of capital and skills permitted only moderate and selective industrialization, except in Czechoslovakia and East Germany. Moreover, peasant farming was a way of life, and, in the absence of any threat of food shortages, it progressed only slowly.

A major feature, one that explains more than anything else the peasants' scale of values, often in conflict with economic efficiency, was the character of land tenure. Before the Communists took over, East European agriculture showed a marked preponderance of small family farms: About 70 per cent of the holdings were up to 12 acres in size, and another 20 per cent between 12 and 25 acres. The share of large estates (over 250 acres) in total acreage was most pronounced in Hungary (about 45 per cent) and parts of Poland, Czechoslovakia, and Albania, with Hungary registering the highest percentage (35) of landless peasants. The trend toward land concentration and capitalist farming prophesied by Marx failed to materialize; instead, repeated land reforms made excessive parceling a more serious economic problem. It was difficult to improve efficiency and increase marketable output, but the governments encouraged agglomeration and higher-value, labor-intensive crop farming and livestock-raising; more important, the peasants themselves saw merits in a growing cooperative movement that did not disturb private ownership.

In most of the countries, political parties expounding "agrarianism," an antiurban ideology based on "biological materialism" and "cooperative syndicalism," at times headed or participated in the government. The agrarians more often than not opposed the Communist parties and programs for they could not reconcile the Communist goals of a "dictatorship of the proletariat" and a propertyless peasantry with their vision of a peasant-ruled republic.

When the Communists took over, they had little to offer to a peasantry that, although eager for a better life, had a deep feeling of private property and a family-centered outlook and was not willing to participate in revolutionary experiments, least of all in their own expropriation and the building of a regimented urban-industrial society.

The Theoretical Framework

Communist agricultural policy cannot be fully understood without at least a brief reference to the place of agriculture and the peasant in Communist theory, to the "agrarian doctrine" of Marx and his followers.

It is no mystery that Communist doctrine, built around the negation of a capitalist industrial society and identifying itself with the industrial proletariat, reveals mistrust of, and even contempt for, the peasantry, and that it considers the peasantry unreceptive to the avowed Communist goals, particularly to the abolition of private property. History played an unfair trick on Marx and his disciples when rural, not industrial, Europe became the home of Communism; hence, the legacy of Marxist dogma today haunts the East European rulers, who, although aware of the deficiencies of the blueprint, are unable to redesign it. Total nationalization of the land, the conversion of peasants into agricultural workers, and the concomitant but no less important rooting out of peasant independence and outlook remain the official goals. It should thus be clear why an open or latent conflict between the Communists and the peasants is bound to persist as long as Marxist dogma colors Communist thinking and action.[2]

Communist economic theory, in so far as it affects agriculture, must also be considered in this connection. One of the priority goals is the compulsive industrialization, with emphasis on heavy industry. While few would argue against the need for and benefits of industrialization, especially in overpopulated Eastern Europe, an indiscriminate drive in an area with an inadequate resource base, and at no matter what cost, is neither the only nor the best alternative. But the blueprint requires that agriculture be neglected, although urbanization places increasing claims on farm produce, that labor be recruited *en masse* from the agricultural sector, and that the peasant pay the heaviest price for industrial achievements without obtaining benefits comparable to his sacrifice.

A second dogma is the exigency of rigid planning and control of the entire economy. Applied to agriculture—which involves climate, weather, and soil, as well as personal initiative and care, and thus requires greater flexibility and more individual responsibility than industry—central and detailed direction often works against economic rationality.

Another tenet, which at first glance seems much more plausible, involves the principle of "economies of scale." Under most conditions, integrated and large farms are more efficient, because they lend themselves to modern technology, a factor much praised by Marx and his followers. But "gigantism" per se, without corresponding capital investments in agriculture, without discrimination on the basis of specific crops, climate, and soil, and without due consideration of concrete labor-capital relationships, is of dubious value. It is obvious that beyond a given optimum size, economies may turn into diseconomies, or that large farms are to be preferred when labor is relatively scarce and capital abundant. But since the opposite conditions prevail in much of capital-deficient and overpopulated Eastern Europe, a course different from that advocated by "scientific Marxism" would appear logical, unless, as it seems, gigantism is motivated more by other than economic considerations.

All this points to the conclusion that dogmas and sociopolitical goals, even when contrary to the dictates of common sense and sound economics, mold the Communist attitude toward agriculture and the peasant. The "dictatorship of the proletariat" and the "socialist transformation of agriculture" form the ideological framework within which the peasant-agrarian society is molded to conform to an irrational concept.

The Road to Collectivization

Communist agricultural policy has passed through several stages, reflecting the conflict between theoretically dictated measures and empirical stumbling blocks, a conflict that results in oscillating tactical compromises. Yet despite such conflicts, Communist planning never abandons the goal of total collectivization with its broader concomitant aims. The Soviet example has been the over-all guide. Differences between the Soviet and the East European experiments—the fact that outright nationalization of all the land has not taken place in the satellites (even though the collectivization drive started sooner after the Communist accession to power than it did in the Soviet Union), or that the timing and intensity of collectivization policies in individual bloc countries vary, or that drastic deviations have occurred in Yugoslavia and Poland—are due not so much to a lack of enthusiasm by the Party leaderships as to prevailing international and domestic conditions that demanded different approaches.

The first phase extended from the end of the war (1945) to the time of consolidation of Communist rule (1948–49). The local Communist parties, before the seizure of power and until genuine coalitions with non-Communist parties were no longer needed, proclaimed as their goal the distribution of the land to "those who work it" and rejected any allegation that they would disturb private ownership of land. In fact, the land reforms they, jointly with coalition parties, undertook immediately after the war were mostly in conformity with their protestations, and the nationaliza-

tion of the "no man's land" in German-depopulated areas of
Czechoslovakia and of new Poland could not be used as evidence
of Communist bad faith. [The reforms affected about one-fourth
of the total agricultural area of Eastern Europe, with Poland
leading in the redistribution (43 per cent) and Bulgaria trailing
(2 per cent), but in every instance the state kept about one-third
of the expropriated land.] Still, the general arbitrariness, the excesses, the discrimination against the large landowners (a relative term meaning different things in latifundic Hungary and in
dwarf-household Bulgaria), as well as the beginnings of collectivization here and there, were like warnings of a gathering storm.
The end effect of this initial land reform was, in fact, a further
breakup of farm land, a further increase in subsistence holdings
(farms now averaged 12–25 acres per family throughout the region), and consequently a reduction in marketable surpluses.
This, of course, ran counter to Communist economic theory and
goals, but was found expedient in political terms, eroding as it
did the strength of the medium and large farmer and neutralizing
the peasantry.

It should be pointed out that this phase coincided with the
nationalization of industry and the period of economic reconstruction, so that, when the end of the decade was approached, long-
range planning could be undertaken within a regimented nonagricultural sector and attention could be devoted to regimenting
the agricultural sector as well.

The about-face in Communist policy came almost unexpectedly
and abruptly, although Bulgaria and Yugoslavia had started
modest collectivization as early as 1945. As it became known
later on, the decision to push ahead at the fastest pace possible
was made at the June, 1948, meeting of the Cominform and implemented with great vigor in the early 1950's, until Stalin's
death. The priority goals were: in the political field—to do away
with the peasants' independence; in the economic—to subject agriculture to strict government planning and control, so as to extract
forced savings from the peasant majority for industrial investment, to shift manpower to industry, and (as a professed long-
term objective) to provide the basis for large-scale modern farm-

ing. That this objective played a subordinate role is evidenced by the fact that more efficient farming could have been encouraged by methods not affecting private ownership, especially since planned state investment in agriculture almost nowhere exceeded 10 per cent (and was actually much lower), and private investment could not be expected to be forthcoming in any appreciable degree.

In view of its motivation, the collectivization drive had to rely on force and drastic economic measures rather than on persuasion. Opponents were branded "kulaks" and treated accordingly. The exceedingly discriminatory economic measures used against them included higher compulsory delivery quotas, steeper tax rates, higher interest, and higher charges for the use of machinery, seeds, and fertilizers. As if conscious of the unpopularity of their policy, the Communists avoided using the term "collective" at all, preferring instead the traditional designation "cooperative," and enacted statutes extolling the "voluntary" and "democratic" character of the new institutions. In most countries, more than one and up to four types of "cooperative farms" were organized: the looser forms (types I and II), in which joint work did not affect property, and the advanced types (types III and IV), where collective property became the rule. It goes without saying that the regimes pressured toward the latter group, and the peasants, when given a choice, preferred the former.

The end of this hectic period saw collectivization embrace over 50 per cent of the agricultural land in Bulgaria, and 20 to 40 per cent in Czechoslovakia, Hungary, and Yugoslavia (excluding the looser cooperatives). The remaining countries were about 10 per cent collectivized, but if the state farms' area is added (which was most prominent in Hungary, Poland, East Germany, and Rumania), the joint "socialist sector" comprised from one-fifth (Poland) to two-thirds (Bulgaria) of the cultivable land, except in Albania, in which about 10 per cent was collectivized. The average collective farm ranged from 370 acres (East Germany) to 2,200 acres (Bulgaria) and included up to 200 former individual farms.

It is evident that the results of this first pull were neither total nor the same in each of the countries. This divergence was due to differences of individual Communist regimes—different degrees of subordination to Soviet leadership and different national characteristics resulting in different methods. But the underlying motives and trends were similar (with the exception of Yugoslavia, where a reappraisal was already indicated), and so were the results.

At the time of Stalin's death, an appraisal of this first round of collectivization revealed a serious setback in agriculture and near despair among the peasants. Aside from the inadequacy of available capital and skills for such a rapid and drastic transformation, the price and procurement system and the discrimination against the private sector destroyed personal incentive and cut into farm income and production. The compulsory delivery quotas set for all major crops and livestock based on acreage and type of ownership were irrationally large, and prices disproportionately low (at least one-half and down to one-fifth of the prices paid by the state for above-quota deliveries, not to mention free-market comparisons), and thus acted as a severe tax on farm income. On the other hand, prices of goods sold by the state were purposely set high (including "turnover" sales taxes and profit markups), thus further reducing the farmers' purchasing power. Furthermore, payments by private farmers to machine-tractor stations —the monopolists of farm machinery—were set three to four times higher than those required from collective farms. It is, therefore, not surprising that the rural areas were depressed and that, while industrial output doubled over the prewar level, agricultural production fell way below. (The average grain and potato crops in 1948–52 were at least 15 and as much as 25 per cent lower than in 1934–38). What was surprising was that the abused and shrinking private sector (including individual plots of members of collectives) continued to contribute most of the agricultural output and about three-fourths of the marketable grain (except in Bulgaria), while the collectives, especially the state farms, had to be heavily subsidized. There was little doubt that the collectivization and agricultural policies in general would ultimately lead to a dead end.[3]

The phase initiated after Stalin's death (everywhere except in Yugoslavia) can be divided into approximately four subphases, closely corresponding to the over-all changes in the Soviet leadership and policy. It reflects a mixture of tactical retreats from above and strong to violent reaction from below and a renewed collectivization drive, one more rational and empirical, more heedful of local diversity and tolerant of "deviations," fairer to agriculture and the peasant, but yet still burdened with many of the old organic defects and inadequacies.

At first, the "Malenkov line" (1953–54) was reflected in Eastern Europe by a temporary halt in collectivization and by promises of greater attention to the agricultural sector. Gradually, some positive measures were initiated, such as an increase in the absolute and relative shares of investment in agriculture (and consumer-goods industries), greater reliance on "voluntarism" rather than compulsion in joining collectives, and favorable adjustments in prices of farms goods, delivery quotas, taxation rates. Some collective farms were even permitted to dissolve, which, especially in Hungary and Czechoslovakia, reduced the share of collectivized land by one-third and one-eighth, respectively. However, there as in the Soviet Union, the promised trend was soon reversed, with heavy industry resuming its priority and total collectivization reaffirmed as the proximate goal. Thus, 1955–56 witnessed a return to the familiar, although somewhat mitigated, agricultural policy.

Then came the unexpected events culminating in the Poznan revolt and the Hungarian revolution. If there were still any doubts as to the peasants' attitude toward collectivization, they were certainly dispelled by the happenings of October, 1956, and their immediate aftermath. Poland, where collectivization never made much headway (affecting less than 10 per cent of the agricultural land), witnessed the almost complete disappearance of the collectives (four-fifths of them were dissolved, leaving their share at about 2 per cent); also, many state farms were liquidated and the land leased or even sold to private farmers. In Hungary, despite the immediate drastic reprisals, more than 60 per cent of the collective farms of the advanced types chose dissolution, reducing their share to less than 10 per cent of the agricultural land. Many state farms were also dissolved. In both countries a nucleus was left intact, although their subsequent policies varied substantially. It is indicative that the abandoning of collectivization was one of the principal demands of the Hungarian and Polish peasants, and that the pronouncements of the new Gomulka and Nagy governments supported the peasantry by acknowledging the many wrongs of the previous Communist regimes and extolling the "worker-peasant alliance."

During that period, collectivization was pursued in the remaining bloc countries. Bulgaria continued to lead in this area, but Albania and Czechoslovakia stepped up the pace in 1957, each surpassing the one-half mark in collectivized land.

After 1958, all the bloc regimes, with the sole exception of Poland, felt ready to undertake the final drive toward collectivization. Khrushchev's policy and reforms began to be felt throughout most of the area, although to a lesser degree than in the Soviet Union, and long-term (five to seven years) as well as "perspective" plans suggested over-all coordination, to be effected also in agriculture. In 1959 and 1960, Bulgaria, Czechoslovakia, and Albania were joined in mass-collectivization waves by the "laggards," Hungary, East Germany, and Rumania, so that the state and collective farms finally occupied the overwhelming part of East European farm land. East Germany, in particular, witnessed a collectivization fury in 1960, increasing the share of the collective sector from 38 to 84 per cent in the course of about one year. However, there as well as in Rumania, the looser types of farm associations accounted for about 30 per cent of the collective sector. Rumania expropriated all land not directly cultivated by the families that owned it and began pushing the peasantry into the "advanced" collective farms. In 1962, it was announced that collectivization had been completed three years ahead of time and that the share of the looser farm associations had fallen to about 18 per cent of Rumania's arable land. Czechoslovakia, in this respect the first country outside the U.S.S.R., started dissolving its machine-tractor stations and selling their stock to the collectives. During the closing years of the 1950's, compulsory deliveries gave way in most of the countries to "contractual" ones, average investment increased, uniform and higher prices for farm goods were introduced, taxes and prices of farm inputs lowered, and plans outlined for more machines, fertilization, and irrigation. But the stress was still on increased use of labor and greater labor productivity, clearly denoting the capital shortage. Bulgaria in particular mobilized much unskilled peasant labor in 1959, with questionable results, and urban dwellers were drawn into field work at crucial periods elsewhere, too.

The trend toward gigantism became evident as collectivization neared completion. Here, too, Bulgaria led the way, becoming the country with the largest average farms in Europe (over 10,000 acres). Stepped-up plans aiming at unusually high targets for farm output, especially in Bulgaria (the "big leap forward" plan of 1958–60) and Rumania, however, fell far short of the goals, and the 1961–62 performance on the whole was below previous modest records.

The early 1960's find agriculture in Eastern Europe (except in Poland and Yugoslavia) virtually collectivized, with attention given to private plots and privately owned livestock. Variations from country to country are confined to minor aspects, such as the ratio between state and collective farms, the type and size of the collectives, and other secondary features reflecting specifics of agricultural policy. "Socialized agriculture" has finally 'triumphed," but in performance it has failed to produce the promised bonanza.[4]

The Results of Collectivization

The economic results of Communist agricultural policy in the collectivized countries of Eastern Europe have been disappointing. A precise evaluation of farm output is not feasible because of deficiencies in data and in methods of computation, which are further distorted by the inflated figures of Communist statistics; yet taking even these statistics at face value, total output, although increasing by about 10 to 30 per cent in the late 1950's over the low levels of the early 1950's (due to increased investment and other correctives), has barely surpassed prewar figures. The smaller producers—Albania, Bulgaria, and Rumania—claim the largest increases, Hungary shows little progress and Czechoslovakia a decline, while East Germany withholds much pertinent data and prefers not to make any comparisons with prewar years. Per capita output, furthermore, still lags behind, due to the population increase, and agricultural imports have become the rule rather

than the exception. A most embarrassing indication of the performance of socialized agriculture is that in relative terms the
private sector is generally faring better.*

Unlike the Soviet Union, Eastern Europe had little unused cultivable land, so that any meaningful increase in output had to
come from greater productivity. This has not been the case. In
fact, the sown area has decreased, for a variety of reasons, among
them mismanagement and lack of incentive. The traditional
grains still remain the major crops, but the trend that began during prewar times, i.e., devoting more land to fodder and industrial
crops, has been emphatically pursued at the expense of grain
cultivation. In particular, the area sown with bread grains has
declined everywhere, but since output failed to meet the targets,
some reversals became necessary in 1960, as in Albania (which
plans to extend the area under wheat by a whooping 43 per cent)
and Czechoslovakia.

During 1956–59, the reported total grain output was only 4 per
cent higher than the prewar average, with declines in Czechoslovakia and especially East Germany. Production of potatoes, an
important staple in the northern countries, was no larger than
before the war. According to Western sources, it is doubtful that
the output of grains and potatoes has surpassed the prewar
mark. Be that as it may, over-all grain and potato production is
deficient by any standard. The area under industrial crops, expanded by about one-third since the war, has led to an obvious
increase in output; production of sugar beet reportedly has doubled. Compared with prewar figures, per-acre yields are considered higher for the priority crops—sugar beet and corn—less so
for the bread grains, and possibly lower for potatoes and several
other crops of minor importance.

There are, of course, more or less pronounced differences
among the individual countries (the more advanced northern part
leads in labor productivity, whereas the more backward southern
part registers the greatest relative advances), but a comparison

* The latest available official figures show that 1962–63 agricultural production was about 5 per cent higher than the prewar average, while per-
capita output was 5 per cent lower, all countries except Albania considered.
(See U.S. Department of Agriculture, *The 1963 Eastern European Agricultural Situation,* Washington, D.C., April, 1963.)

not only with the prewar period, when output was low, but also with the corresponding performance of Western Europe since the end of the war, puts agricultural output in Eastern Europe in a distinctly unfavorable light. Thus, while total output in Eastern Europe has increased only a little since before the war, Western Europe has registered an average increase of about 25 per cent, the much more advanced base notwithstanding. Even during the best East European period—1956–59—per-acre yields in Western Europe were twice as high for wheat, barley, and corn, and on the average up to three times higher for sugar beet, and the per-capita gap is widening.

The livestock sector is hardly in a better position, despite special efforts to raise animal production. The number of cattle has not surpassed the prewar level and in some countries—Bulgaria, for example—has declined by as much as one-fifth. Instead, the number of hogs has almost doubled, with great fluctuations from year to year. Sheep have not increased in number, and goats show a drastic decline. Meat output, reported in live weight (a defective measure), has allegedly increased by about one-third over prewar figures, a questionable although unimpressive gain. Milk output, which includes that fed to calves and, in many countries, ewe's and goat's milk as well, is reported increased by only 6 per cent over prewar years, a most serious shortcoming. Comparisons with Western Europe in this field are even less favorable for the area than in plant agriculture.

Most revealing is the output comparison between the socialist and the private sectors. It should be kept in mind that with the exception of Yugoslavia and Poland, independent private farms nowhere exceed 10 per cent of the agricultural land and usually account for much less, and that the private plots of the collective-farm members (included by the Communists into the collectivized sector) also average 5 per cent of the land. The livestock is also increasingly concentrated in the socialist sector (70 per cent in Bulgaria and Czechoslovakia and around 50 per cent in the remaining collectivized countries, with the exception of Rumania). Still, it is the private sector which turns out most of the livestock and poultry, as well as a substantial amount of various crops, out of all proportion to the limited area involved. Thus in 1959, Bulgaria, which has the lowest share of sown area under private cultivation (9.5 per cent, if individual farms and private plots are added together), attributed 16 per cent of the total crop production and 40 per cent of the animal production to the private sector. In Hungary, at the other extreme, the individual holdings alone, with about 10 per cent of the land, contributed over 60 per cent of total agricultural output in 1961, and the private plots supplied the collectives with all their meat, 90 per cent of the potatoes, 65 per cent of the animal fodder, and all the fruit and vegetables, an almost unbelievable situation. Even in per-acre yields, which tend to understate the contributions of the private sector, they outstrip the collectives in several labor-intensive and high-value crops in some countries. Moreover, differences in yields of crops in which the socialist sector is leading, like the major grains, are so small that the higher input of machinery (and other preferential treatment) makes the contrast in the performance of the two sectors even greater.

Another indicator of the disappointing performance of agriculture in the collectivized countries is the foreign trade situation. Thus, one-fifth to one-fourth of Czechoslovakia's and East Germany's imports consists of foodstuffs (one-fourth of their grain requirements and much of their meat comes from abroad), and the rest of Eastern Europe also has increased imports of food to a surprising extent. It should be kept in mind that, in view of the restriction on consumption and the need to pay for industrial imports, much of the domestically short agricultural products are exported while only essentials are imported.

All in all, one may conclude that agricultural production in Eastern Europe has responded almost inversely to the degree of collectivization and that reports of the early 1960's reveal stagnation and even decline under practically completed collectivization.*

* Detailed information on output is contained in the annual United Nations economic surveys of Europe, especially in the *Economic Survey of Europe, 1960* (Geneva, 1961) and *Economic Survey of Europe, 1961* (Geneva, 1962); and the Food and Agricultural Organization's *1960 Production Yearbook*. Latest information indicates that in 1961, only Albania (besides Poland) made progress, while everywhere else total farm output fell below previous levels— 10 per cent in Rumania and Yugoslavia and much more in East Germany. East

A Survey of Current Features

INSTITUTIONAL STRUCTURE

The "socialist sector," which, except for the two "deviationists," occupies at least 90 per cent of the agricultural land in each country, consists of state farms and cooperative farms of various types, primarily the collectives and their private plots.

State farms, owned and operated by the governments, correspond to the sovkhoz in the U.S.S.R. All workers are salaried state employees. This type is considered the ultimate goal, but for the time being is meant to serve as a model of the advantages of state ownership and large-scale production. The state farms are also supposed to aid the collectives and the private farms with their agricultural machinery, seed, purebred stock, etc. Their main features are their mammoth size (4,500 to 7,200 acres) and the preferential treatment given them by the regime, but their performance is unimpressive and they are heavily subsidized. They occupy between 3 and 6 per cent of the agricultural land in the socialist sector in Bulgaria, Czechoslovakia, and East Germany, and up to 16–18 per cent in Hungary and Rumania.

The collective farm of the kolkhoz or artel type is the basic institutional unit. Since the land in Eastern Europe is not nationalized (except for state farms), collectivized land should be *de jure* private, rather than public, property. The official term used is "cooperative property," but the regime includes the collectives into the "socialist sector," thus brushing aside theoretical and juridical objections. The only vestige of "private" land property in the collectives is the claim to rent, but no-rent collectives are being extended continuously. The "cooperative property" includes land, capital, and livestock contributed; the net income is distributed entirely or overwhelmingly (at least 75–80 per cent) on the basis of the work done. This is calculated by applying "labor-

Germany's production dropped below 1960 figures by as much as 24 per cent in grain, 37 in corn, 43 in potatoes, 32 in sugar beets, 46,000 head of cattle, and 1.3 million hogs. Adverse weather was given as the major general cause. In 1962, for much the same official reason, net agricultural output declined further throughout the area and food shortages became widespread. (See U.S. Department of Agriculture, *The 1963 Eastern European Agricultural Situation.*)

days," accounting units credited on the basis of the type and length of work performed primarily in "permanent production brigades" of the members. The new 1961 statute of Czechoslovakia's collectives as a rule attempts to introduce guaranteed money wages. An innovation in Hungary, termed temporary, involves the division of the collective land among the members who work their piece by family and even employ outside help, a Communist variety of the "odious" sharecropping of latifundic days.

The organization of the collectives is governed by "model statutes," which are patterned to varying degrees on the Soviet prototype and stress voluntarism and democracy, albeit on paper. A general meeting of all members "elects" the executive council, headed by a chairman (usually a Party member), who has broad powers locally in implementing the state production plan by assigning tasks, controlling their fulfillment, rewarding, disciplining, and distributing the income. The hierarchical ladder leads to a ministry of agriculture, except in Rumania, where a Supreme Council of Agriculture replaced the familiar setup in 1962. The Party apparatus is also involved at all levels. Except in Czechoslovakia, the chairman's range of activity is limited by the independent machine-tractor stations, which serve as powerful supervisors over the affairs of the collective. Even there, however, bureaucratic procedures and other controls, such as the recent reversal to centralized scheduling of deliveries, stifle any creative independence of leadership and members. It seems that only in Hungary has management been granted more leeway and the general meeting more prestige.

According to the statutes, withdrawal from a collective does not entitle the former member to the same but to an "equivalent value" of his contribution. The right to sell, divide, bequeath, or donate, even with regard to the small private plot of the collective-farm member, is officially limited, and even more restricted in practice.

There are considerable differences in detail within the statutes of the various "advanced cooperatives," including such peculiar features as reduced rent payment if members do not meet their labor-day quotas, different shares of the distribution in kind as against cash, provisions for part-time work and absentee ownership, and prohibitions against diminishing the size of the collective. However, almost all types may be subordinated to three basic models: the statute of the Bulgarian labor-cooperative farms (TKZS), as amended in December, 1957; the statute of the Rumanian collective farms, as amended in May, 1953; and the 1961 statute of the Czechoslovak collectives. Except for the fact that the collective land is not state property, the model statutes of the no-rent type of East European collectives are close replicas of the Soviet kolkhozes; the limited and shrinking rent type is organized along similar lines, except for the rent feature.

The size of the kolkhoz-type collectives has grown considerably as a result of amalgamations (between 700 and 10,000 acres in East Germany and Bulgaria, respectively) and is to be further enlarged.

The second type of "cooperatives," the TOZ variety, involves primarily joint-tillage operations and recognition of private ownership of land and capital. The amount of work of each member is proportionate to the size of his land. These units are viewed as transitional and are now insignificant, except possibly in East Germany. Even there, however, a 1962 statute for reshaped type-II farms approximates quite closely the "advanced" type arrangements.

Privately owned independent farms, dominant in Poland and Yugoslavia, are the exception in the rest of the area, occupying an insignificant share of the total agricultural land and being reduced to dwarf size. The private plots of the collective farm members are greater in number. Their typical size varies between .5 and 1.5 acres, and their owners are allowed to keep small implements, one to three head of livestock, and an unlimited number of poultry. Theoretically incompatible with Communism, these vestiges of private initiative are permitted and even encouraged in times of food crises, because of their surprising viability. Hungary's leadership has given repeated assurances in this respect and has extended government support so as to enable the private-plot owners to continue to supply the population, primarily with animal products. Still, they are subject to pressures and economic discrimination, and the new Czechoslovak statute tries to restrict or abolish them altogether. Special efforts are devoted also to increasing the share of the socialist sector in total livestock, which meet with expected resistance.

The astounding performance of the private plots, despite the general policies, is ascribed to the fact that the members of the collectives (and their families) devote as much time as possible to their own plots at the expense of the collective. This best of all exemplifies the peasants' attitude toward land ownership.

Another institution that is inseparable from agriculture are the machine-tractor stations. They enjoy a monopoly over agricultural machinery (outside of the state farms) and perform a double task —to aid as well as to control agriculture. They are state-owned and operated, and their work is paid for by the farms in kind and in cash. Although their discrimination against the private sector has been modified, their main service is performed on the collective farms. The Soviet policy of dissolving the stations in order to eliminate the "two bosses on the land" has not been followed, except in Czechoslovakia and, more cautiously, in Bulgaria.

No drastic changes are expected in the present institutional setup, with the possible exception of the dissolution of the machine-tractor stations. The collective farm is expected to remain the basic unit, with trends indicated toward further amalgamation, transition to "advanced" types, and possible extinction of the private plots.[5]

Economic Correctives

Having decided to lean on a collectivized agriculture with the "unavoidable evil" of the private plots, the regimes have taken steps to remedy the two major economic defects of their agricultural policies—the insufficiency of farm investment and of "material incentives" for the peasants—so as to make the collectives more viable and attractive.

Investment has reached an average of about 15 per cent of the total, which, although a marked increase over the Stalinist years, is still far from sufficient. The machine-tractor stock (whose number is given in average horsepower units) is reported almost tripled over the early 1950's, as is the supply of chemical fertilizers.

But, in view of the low starting levels and the necessities of the large-to-giant farms, as well as the poor quality of machines and technical personnel, much more capital and skill is required in order to achieve the needed drastic improvements, let alone approach the capital-intensive agriculture of Western Europe. Per-acre use of draught power and chemical fertilizers is still very low, except in East Germany and Czechoslovakia, which report 134 and 166 acres of arable land per 15 hp-equivalent tractor, and 135 and 170 lbs. of plant nutrient per acre, respectively. The remaining countries service three to four times more acreage per tractor and apply three to six times (Rumania and Albania even up to ten times) less chemical nutrients per acre. Draft horses (especially in Poland) and even cattle are still a familiar sight, and, though adding to draft power, they deplete available produce still further. All in all, farming in most of Eastern Europe remains labor-intensive and backward, and the regimes' effort is inadequate to attain their goals.

Centralized, bureaucratic, partly incompetent management is another feature that has been remedied only partially by a degree of decentralization, adaptation to local conditions, and intensified training of specialists.

More important changes have occurred in the "material-incentive" field. The pricing and procurement system now relies mainly on contractual deliveries (compulsive deliveries are in force only in Albania, East Germany, and Poland) and higher, more uniform, prices—all intended to remedy the extremely low, highly unequal farm income.

The contractual-purchasing agreement does not differ much in substance from the compulsory-delivery arrangement; in both cases the farmer is expected to supply quantities determined by the state. The difference is that the new system does not set quotas as high as before and does take into consideration specific crops and conditions. The uniform, higher prices for all government purchases have proved the best of all the new incentives and have not only improved the terms of trade for the peasants but lessened the inequalities within the farm sectors. As a result, peasants' real incomes have undoubtedly increased substantially, although no reliable figures are available and average peasant labor-day income is estimated to be at only about one-third to one-half the wage level of the average industrial worker.

Other alleviative measures includes tax reductions, reductions in prices of farm-purchased materials, introduction of bonuses for overfulfillment, "advance payments" for farm work, and greater reliance on payment in cash rather than in kind, as well as eligibility for old-age pensions and other social-security benefits. The new statute in Czechoslovakia introduces all-embracing social-security features for collective farmers, but ties the benefits to the degree of plan fulfillment and gradual abolition of private plots. In July, 1962, Bulgaria again followed in the footsteps of Soviet price adjustments by increasing prices of livestock products—passed on to the consumer—by as much as 25 per cent for meat, and by reshaping its price-tax-pension system, so as to stimulate output and level off income inequality. Hungary added to its labor-day system of remuneration a profit-sharing plan under which part of the produce is distributed in kind for each labor-day performed. At the same time, restrictions on free-market sales were reported from Hungary, as was the outright abolition of surplus-good sales in Czechoslovakia, in order to assure state deliveries and check the farmers' preference of disposing as much of their produce as possible on the market at the prevailing higher prices there, even at the expense of contractual obligations. In East Germany, Hungary, and Bulgaria, various forms of rationing of several food items were introduced.

On balance, material incentives have substantially increased throughout the area, but the peasant still fails to respond commensurably.

The Human Element

Although it is difficult to know and interpret the present attitude of the peasant with full accuracy, all comprehensive information points to the conclusion that the majority of the East European peasantry remains averse to Communist philosophy and practice. This should not be surprising in view of the peasant's long quest for and attachment to his land, his clinging to traditional values, his independence, or his mistrust of the "town people" and foreign-imposed patterns—all of which run counter to Communist goals and policies and denote a basic conflict. The economist, for his part, trying to measure efficiency and alternatives, cannot fail to notice the inadequate performance of agriculture and will not be able to explain the "whole truth" without taking the human element into account. Communist sources themselves have admitted repeatedly, to quote the Czechoslovak *Pravda* (November 15, 1960), that the "decisive factor in agriculture, where every attempt and bona fide effort breaks down, lies elsewhere [and not in the know-how and pure economics]." This "elsewhere" is clearly the peasants' negative attitude toward Communism in general and Communist agricultural policies in particular. An alien-inspired and imposed dictatorship, armed with an antipeasant ideology, cannot generate much following, no matter what its specific policies. But for the peasant, Communist policy has perhaps been more onerous than for other social groups. It is he primarily who is paying the price for industrialization. He has been deprived of his most treasured possession—his land. He has been driven out of his world. He has been promised an easier and better life under collectivization, but this has not materialized.

Left on his own, the East European peasant has reacted in various ways: by open revolts, as in northwestern Bulgaria in 1951; by his solid support of the Hungarian revolution; by mass escape, as in East Germany. More often, he has resorted to indirect sabotage—slaughtering livestock, burning fields, chopping down fruit trees, concealing produce. Due to the lessening of overt force and pressures during the post-Stalin period, the immovable advent of collectivization, the various economic correctives, as well as the small hope for radical change, the enormous tension of the Stalinist period seems much reduced and confined mainly to the future of the private plot to which the farmer devotes his free time while avoiding work on "his" collective farm— a practice he seems prepared to defend. Collectivization, rightly or wrongly, stands compromised in his eyes, and it will take some doing to win back his confidence, let alone the spontaneous cooperation of this "greatest passive resister in history."

Poland and Yugoslavia

Deviating from the Soviet model to varying degree, Poland and Yugoslavia exemplify the disenchantment with collectivization. Although collectivization has not been abandoned as an official goal, it has been laid to rest; and to the small extent that it has been revived, it appears in new, more rational and palatable, forms.

After collectivization proved a failure and ties with Moscow were either severed (Yugoslavia) or reshaped (Poland), most of the collective farms were disbanded (1952–53 in Yugoslavia and 1956–57 in Poland). Since then, the private sector has been by far the largest and most important one and now accounts for nearly 90 per cent of the arable land. The mass dissolution of the collectives (much more numerous and important in Yugoslavia than in Poland) was accompanied by a series of supplementary measures, such as the abolishment of compulsory deliveries in Yugoslavia, and the use of state farm land to enlarge the private sector in Poland, besides the familiar price, fiscal, and other correctives in favor of the now dominant private sector. In both countries the state farms occupy by far the largest share of the land in the socialist sector, with kolkhoz-type collectives accounting for only about 1.5 per cent thereof. The emphasis is now laid on an intermediary form, the "general agricultural cooperatives" (OZZ) in Yugoslavia and the "agricultural circles" (*kolka rolnicze*) in Poland. Although the OZZ are included in the socialist sector, whereas the circles are not, they have much in common and exemplify the desire of the deviationists to combine private ownership and social paternalism.

The Yugoslav general cooperatives are the monopolists in the purchase and distribution of grains and the main suppliers of investment funds, loans, and machinery to the private owners. Moreover, they promote cooperative working of all land, whether owned by them or by individual farmers, sharing the proceeds. In 1960, the more than 4,800 cooperatives performed various kinds of farm work on about 20 per cent of the private holdings and serviced, in one form or another, about one-half of all private farms. However, the expected growth in collaboration has failed to materialize in the early 1960's, so that the regime is pressing to incorporate part-time farmers, who allegedly hold 35 per cent of the total arable area, into the socialist sector.

The Polish agricultural circles also rest on joint state-private effort. Their distinguishing feature lies in the fact that the state, through its Agricultural Development Fund, guarantees the circle a large contribution (75 to 85 per cent) from the state's profit on the resale of the compulsory deliveries toward the purchase of farm machinery of common ownership. The circles act also as cooperative purchasing organizations and are continuously broadening their tasks, such as the recent inclusion of the operation of their own model farms. Thus far, 25,000 such circles in 60 per cent of Poland's villages have been established and their membership includes every fifth private farm. They account also for about 10 per cent of total farm investment.

It is evident that both institutions, drawing on historical parallels, substantially depart from the pattern in the rest of the area, in that private property is recognized and voluntarism is basically observed. But pressures, in the shadow of the powerful Party and state machine, are there, no matter how subtle and indirect. The official line is to convince the peasant of the benefits of mechanized farming, and in 1959, Yugoslavia legalized the requisition of improperly tilled land; machines and other favoritisms are granted the farmer who consents to adhere to government policies. Poland followed suit in 1961 by authorizing the expropriation of uneconomical private farms and placed restrictions on bequeathals to nonfarmers.

Several strings also were attached to the conversion to private farming. Farm sizes are limited to 25 acres in Yugoslavia and to about 100 in Poland (the actual average is about 12 acres), which handicaps the farmer from the very outset and is indicative of the halfhearted approach to private farming. Furthermore, price, procurement, loan, and investment policies still discriminate against private units, although to a much smaller degree than in the rest of Eastern Europe, the pragmatic quest to raise output being stronger than theoretical prejudice.

The production results of the deviationist type of Polish and Yugoslav agriculture, relying overwhelmingly on restricted private holdings plus more viable state and collective farms, have in many ways been superior to the Soviet-type agriculture of most of Eastern Europe. In 1959, Yugoslavia claimed an increase in farm output of 50 per cent over 1956, becoming self-sufficient in wheat for the first time since the war; and Poland reported a corresponding increase of over 20 per cent, and an additional 10 per cent in 1961 alone, with per-acre yields in the individual farms increasing in everything except grains and milk. The two countries also achieved the highest increase in per-capita production of the major grains over prewar years and registered the only substantial advancements in crops and livestock products in Eastern Europe during the latter part of the 1950's. Peasant incomes rose also to the extent that Poland felt it necessary to increase land taxes and Yugoslavia to check food-price rises in order to alleviate inflationary pressures. It should not be forgotten that foreign aid, including substantial quantities of wheat, primarily from the United States, has been available to boost the economy of the two countries.

The problems are by no means solved and difficulties will continue to beset the two deviationists, but as of now no other East European countries can claim better agricultural performance and a less dissatisfied peasantry. The crucial question is whether, in the prevailing climate, coexistence with an overwhelmingly state-owned and controlled economy will be feasible in the long run.*

Present Problems and Future Prospects

At the beginning of the 1960's, the Communist balance sheet in East European agriculture shows a stagnation in farm output at about prewar levels, while the area's population grows by about 1 million annually, thus confronting the increasingly industrial-

* For recent studies on Yugoslavia, see George W. Hoffman and Fred W. Neal, *Yugoslavia and the New Communism* (New York: Twentieth Century Fund, 1962), chap. xv. On Poland, see "Organizing the Polish Peasant," *East Europe,* December, 1960. During the early 1960's, Poland reported record levels of output, interrupted in 1962, while Yugoslavia experienced some of the worst results since 1958, thus exemplifying the precarious nature of the halfhearted policies. Still the current output of both countries is much higher than during the Stalinist years. Up to 1962, Yugoslavia had received the equivalent of more than $650 million in U.S. farm products, and Poland the equivalent of $400 million, under Public Law 480.

urbanized society with a serious problem. The reasons for this are not physical limitations (its food potential is estimated at least one-third higher than it is under present conditions), as much as the over-all Communist bias against the agrarian-agricultural society, the imperative of collectivization, the low economic priority given to agriculture, the erroneous application of Communist economic principles to East European farming, and the lack of adequate incentives to the peasantry.

Presently, Communist agricultural policy is plagued by numerous self-defeating contradictions that tend to create a vicious circle. On the one hand, it has been proved that the peasants perform best on their own land and when left alone; but collectivization and centralized government control exclude such a course, and even in Poland and Yugoslavia the private farms are restricted to an anachronistic size, thus forfeiting the virtues inherent in the existence of a private sector. Moreover, the private plots and the privately owned livestock, both relative assets, are threatened rather than encouraged. On the other hand, large-scale collectivized farming fails to supply the desired substitute, due to the insufficiency of current technology and the lack of incentives. Under these circumstances it would be expected that greater reliance be placed on labor-intensive farming; instead, farm labor has been pushed away from the land to the extent that Czechoslovakia and East Germany suffer from severe labor shortages; and the rest of the area, which is still overwhelmingly rural (between 45 and 75 per cent of the gainful population depend on the land) continues to lose manpower to the cities without adequate substitution of nonlabor inputs, thus leaving the countryside with an aging labor force working on huge farms with inadequate technology. The average age of the farmer in most countries is between forty and fifty years, and "back-to-the-farm" measures, including redistribution of farm specialists, are being attempted in most of Eastern Europe, albeit with limited success and conviction. As to the professed modernization, labor alone certainly cannot do the job, but its release from the villages should now be preceded by larger investments in agriculture. The truth of the matter is, however, that such investment, in spite of the substantial increases during the post-Stalin period, is still very much wanting. It thus seems that present Communist policies work at cross purposes, aiming at larger output to be based on modern farming methods without providing the *sine qua non* for its realization, while at the same time pulling the rug from under the more rational utilization of resources available under the circumstances.

The regimes, although not unaware of the problem, try to improve agricultural performance within the present framework. Their "catch-up" long-term plans (until 1965) call for self-sufficiency in basic foods with constantly rising living standards, better diets, and, in some cases, increased exports. Even if this could be achieved (desired rates of increase in agricultural output have not even been aproximated in comparable past periods), only Czechoslovakia and East Germany will approach present West European standards. How this will be done, however, is not too clear, because neither the share of investment (set mostly at about 15 per cent of the total but actually leveling off below 15 per cent), nor incentives are to be appreciably increased in the years to come. Some of the countries unveiled 1980 targets calling for twice (Czechoslovakia and Poland) and two and one-half times (Bulgaria) the agricultural output of 1960, without indicating any drastic changes of the underlying factors, so that the targets cannot be considered as more than unrealistic promises made and broken too often in the past. Under the present and proposed measures, some progress is to be expected as the full impact of the post-Stalinist modifications works itself out. Also, the virtually completed collectivization may have a stabilizing influence, save for the uncertainty with regard to the private plots and privately owned livestock. But the over-all performance will have to remain erratic as long as some of the built-in defects are not eliminated, or at least substantially altered.

The most that can be hoped for in the more remote future is that in the collectivized countries the trend of the late 1950's will be pursued with much more vigor, so as to make the collectives more viable, productive, and responsive. This is not too likely, however, if for no other reason than that heavy industry will again receive top priority, and increased Party and Government control over agriculture and the peasant seems to be in store, if the Soviet example is followed. But, unless the regimes realize that a modern technological society—let alone a humane one—cannot be built solidly on one limping leg, that a lasting industrial revolution presupposes an agrarian one, and that human needs and aspirations cannot be disregarded for ever, agriculture will remain stationary, will tend to retard industrial advancement, and act as a brake on over-all economic and military power.*

The 1960's pose the agricultural and peasant problem, and its implications, with growing acuteness. It remains to be seen whether the Communist rulers will find the foresight to break the vicious circle on their own initiative, for sooner or later drastic adjustments may be imposed upon them.

* United Nations economists contend with justification that agricultural performance has been mainly responsible for over-all economic expansion in Poland and for the slowing down of economic growth rates in most of the other East European countries, thus substantiating the above point. (*Economic Survey of Europe, 1961*, Part 1, chap. ii, pp. 1, 2, and *passim.*)

4. INDUSTRY AND LABOR

Stanley J. Zyzniewski

Intensive industrialization radically altering the economies of Eastern Europe has been an outstanding ramification of Soviet ascendancy. The drive toward industrial maturity continues. Current economic plans, most of which are scheduled for completion in 1965, will mark two decades of Soviet tutelage. Simultaneously they reflect a new stage in the region's economic development. The earlier patterns of industrialization were notoriously painful and erratic, but, as the decade of 1960 unfolded, greater vigor and calculation for more efficient growth has been evident among bloc members. Revisions of past premises, changes in tempo and method, and more complex relationships have modified characteristics of East European industrialization. The recent adjustments and innovations form a suitable bench mark by which to measure past trends, present conditions, and more immediate portents.*

Initially, wartime destruction and the expansion of Soviet power imposed Herculean strains upon the region, although some countries fared worse than others. Concomitants of Soviet expansion included a drain of assets and the rapid structural reorganization of each economy. The large flow of unrequited exports to the Soviet Union in the early years stemmed from a variety of now-

* Any generalized treatment of East European industrialization is obviously subject to various limitations: diverse conditions and singular exceptions, gaps in data and standardization, upward biases of official computations. Nonetheless, mutually shared pressures and problems, as well as common achievements and shortcomings, permit a useful degree of regional characterziation which at least conveys orders of magnitude and salient trends. Paucity of information and the relative insignificance of Albanian developments prompt only infrequent references. One summary of that state's development is available in *Economic Survey of Europe, 1960,* chap. ii. Yugoslavia's successful defection from lock-step patterns of the bloc prompts a separate addendum.

familiar devices (war-booty clauses, reparations, "special" agreements, and mixed-stock companies). The stream eastward has been estimated to have been between $15 billion and $20 billion in postwar prices, constituting 10 per cent or more of gross fixed investments that primed Soviet reconstruction. A smaller Soviet intake of these assets continued after Stalin's death as well, while trade agreements, often highly disadvantageous, complemented the flow of goods into the Soviet economy. The deleterious impact of these practices upon satellite economies in the early postwar years was enormous.[1]

Institutional reorganizations for "socialist construction," meantime, varied in scope and pace throughout Eastern Europe. Cumulatively, the nationalization of "industry proper" (i.e., excluding local industry and handicrafts) was virtually completed by 1949. The share of the value of gross output of manufactures attributed to the socialist sectors that year ranged from 85 per cent in Rumania to 94 per cent in Czechoslovakia and Poland. Private sectors contracted further thereafter.[2]

The intensity of both wartime damage and Soviet spoliation generally determined the pace of reconstruction in each country. Prewar levels of output were attained or exceeded by all states between 1948 and 1950, with the exception of East Germany, which reached this level only in 1953.

Regionally, East European industry reached or exceeded prewar production in 1949, particularly in the capital-goods sector. Moreover, the ratio of investments to national income in most states had surpassed prewar norms, and from 32 per cent to 47 per cent of each country's investments had been channeled into industry. The deliberate restructuring of industrial output also shifted the ratio of production of consumer goods to capital goods. The latter commanded a larger share of total output.

Industrial labor during the period of reconstruction likewise underwent changes. Although the proportion of the labor force to total population of the area approximated prewar levels, a dearth of trained workers was common among these countries, and the need for training cadres was urgent in the more devastated states. Although there was no significant numerical increase in industrial labor at this time, a marked increase in the employment of women was evident. In some countries, the transition to postwar conditions was initially marked by the emergence of workers' councils temporarily assuming control of production. Their authority proved ephemeral as new regimes appointed administrators to direct rehabilitation.

Inasmuch as the economies still retained a somewhat mixed character, trade unionism, granted advantages by the new regimes and given authority to oversee health and welfare benefits, expanded during these years. Paralleling political developments, however, trade unionism also experienced greater Communist infiltration, and by the end of 1948, all unions throughout the area fell under the control of Communists.

Industrial Drives

Postwar recovery was still incomplete when the ensuing polarization of world politics led to additional strains. Stalin's reactions to the more vigorous posture of the West included the determination to intensify Soviet hegemony over Eastern Europe. The decision to consolidate the "socialist bloc" was subsequently manifested in the attenuation of contacts with Western markets and in a program to maximize the rates of economic growth among bloc members. A determined implementation of "the law of the predominant increase in the output of producer goods" would harness East European growth to Soviet strategic considerations.

The immediate objective of rapid industrialization required adjustments in economic relations. The planned expansion of heavy industry to provide a base for rapid economic growth had to contend with the inadequacy of natural resources in Eastern Europe. Some Soviet priming of accelerated industrialization was inevitable, and, in the face of continued isolation from the West, a larger flow of intrabloc trade was mandatory. Consequently, between 1948 and 1951, Soviet credits in excess of $790 million were extended to some of these states. Agreements for greater cooperation and trade were likewise negotiated among them. Consonant with the new orientation, a supranational Council for Mutual Economic Assistance (CMEA or COMECON) was organized in 1949. Ostensibly set up to expedite coordination, this agency remained ineffective for several years, serving merely as a symbol.

Summarily, the expansion of the industrial base in each country as the key to rapid economic growth meant that an inordinate concentration was made upon those industries regarded as crucial for increasing potentials, among them mining, building materials, iron and steel, machine-building. Natural resources above those required to maintain subsistence levels were applied to the growth of these and other, complementary industries. The earlier Soviet policies were emulated as reductions in levels of consumption were planned to increase margins available for such investments.

In view of the staggered pace of reconstruction, the new developmental plans of the region were not simultaneously adopted.* Nonetheless, as international tensions deepened in 1950 and 1951, all the regimes were impelled to revise upward the already high goals of vital industries, as well as to allocate additional resources to armaments, thereby decreasing further the levels of consumption.

Under these operating principles, member countries exhibited similar patterns. Continually higher rates of annual investments were drawn from national incomes until 1953. In that year the ratio of gross fixed investments to national income ranged from 19.5 per cent in Bulgaria to a high of 29 per cent in Rumania. Simultaneously, successively larger increments were allocated to heavy industry and construction, so that in 1953, more than 38 per cent of each state's investment was pre-empted by these sectors, reaching 53 per cent in Rumania, which, with Poland and Hungary, experienced the sharpest increases. A methodical stress was maintained upon the metallurgical and machine-building industries; from 1950 to 1953, their combined share of the investments assigned to heavy industries ranged from one-fifth to more than two-fifths in each country.[3]

This single-minded focus upon heavy industry was rooted to each state's pursuit of autarchy. The avowed aims of COMECON were ignored. Neither were any of the plans concerned with a correlation between the level of development and the shares of

---

* The Czechoslovak Five-Year Plan ran from 1948 to 1952, while that of Bulgaria was started in 1949. Poland began a Six-Year Plan in 1950; Hungary started a Five-Year Plan that same year. Albania, Rumania, and East Germany began Five-Year plans in 1951.

investments designated for heavy industry: All were geared to relatively crude, quantitative drives for larger industrial output. Under such circumstances, the industrial position of a member country vis-à-vis another would ultimately be preserved.

Out of this preordained intensity, the sharp rises in industrial production naturally followed during the early 1950's. Viewed regionally, the official indexes appeared impressive in the year of Stalin's death. The combined industrial production of six countries (including East Germany but excluding Albania) had risen 114 per cent above that of 1949. Results in heavy industry appeared even greater during the three years ending in 1952. Excluding East Germany (because of continued reparations), the five remaining states had increased their annual output of capital goods on the average of 20 per cent or more, with Rumania and Hungary achieving a 40 per cent increase in 1950 and 1951, respectively. Among these five states, the output of capital goods to the end of 1953 outstripped total industrial growth, the 1953 level being 134 per cent above that of 1949. Consequently, the share of industry in the gross national income of each country exceeded 50 per cent, whereas capital goods constituted more than 60 per cent of the group's total industrial production. Despite inflated statistics resulting from calculations on a "gross" basis, the rapidity of this expansion was evident. The fastest growth naturally occurred in the engineering or machine-building branches, many of which were newly established.

Emulation of Soviet policies also developed in the employment and labor policies of the East European regimes. The dynamic push of these years brought a considerable absorption of unskilled workers from rural areas and among the urban unemployed. The attrition of private sectors and the deliberately depressed wage scales likewise contributed to a larger proportion of women employed in industry. In less than four years, from 1950 to 1953, the influx of new labor reached enormous proportions in the building, transport, and industrial branches of the economy. The labor force for these three branches in Bulgaria was increased by only 130,-000; highly advanced Czechoslovakia absorbed slightly more than 200,000. Among the remaining states, however, absorptions ran from 400,000 in Hungary to 800,000 in Poland. Much over-employment, of course, existed. Low wages, along with unconcern for the upkeep and replacement of capital stock, permitted temporarily cheap increments to the growth of production even from the marginal productivity of the unskilled newcomers in industrial labor.

The nadir of proletarian fortunes developed in these years of rapid sovietization. As one-man management in enterprises was strengthened, most governments introduced labor codes by 1950 modeled upon previous Soviet legislation. Although enforcement of these did not reach the point of earlier Soviet stringency, drastic regulations were nonetheless applied. Centrally planned systems of low wages and high norms, anchored in schemata of piecework bonuses, naturally led to hardships. Living standards throughout the region plummeted downward by 17–20 per cent; absenteeism and labor turnover increased. To combat the latter, new legislation restricted movement and provided for compulsory job transfers, among other practices. Trade unions, having been purged of independent leadership before 1950, merely acted as links between the workers and governments striving to maintain discipline and surpass production norms.[4]

Crises

The outward appearances of impressive achievements could not mask the growing strains that had also appeared by 1953. Unequal in magnitude and not identical in each country, the various pressures arising from defects of planning, management, and productivity were nonetheless ominous and required adjustments. Stalin's fortuitous death and the initiation of the "New Course" by his successors soon encouraged the East European authorities to address themselves to the threatening imbalances.

Technical miscalculations and a lack of synchronization among sectors were among the outstanding defects that compounded the original strains of inordinate plans in Eastern Europe. Over-optimistic projections of rates of growth and the relative costs involved had often brought additional expenditures, yet in some cases such measures still failed to place new projects on an operating basis. Megalomanic targets set for manufacturing branches had not been matched with adequate investments for industries producing raw materials, fuels, and energy. Soviet exports of primary commodities had initially nourished industrial expansion, but as requirements rose rapidly, a steady flow at increased tempo could not be maintained. The inattention to proper balances among industrial branches caused bottlenecks in supplies: Fabricating industries were forced to operate below capacity and even experienced stoppages.

Furthermore, policies of "enforced savings" intensified the situation throughout the area. Depressed living standards soon affected labor productivity. Agricultural output, for the most part unable to attain quotas or prewar levels, brought on food shortages at a time of increased urbanization. Along with a lack of consumer goods, these conditions fostered inflationary trends as both real wages and per-capita consumption declined. Consequently, a decreasing rate of expansion in per-capita productivity in industry was felt. The rates of increase fell by more than 5 per cent in 1953. The nonfulfillment of quotas became a common problem in all states and with other ominous trends hampered further growth. Modifications in the crudely quantitative onslaught appeared mandatory.*

The major revisions introduced by East European authorities by the end of 1953 led to three broad trends: a slowing in the rate of industrial growth, some reallocation of investments to reduce imbalances within and among sectors, and a slight amelioration in living standards. All countries curtailed the rate of industrial expansion by more than 50 per cent, the most drastic cuts occurring in Hungary and Czechoslovakia. Manufacturing was scaled downward for closer coordination with the output of basic materials, so that the production of capital goods in 1954 increased less than or only as much as that projected for gross industrial output—a reversal of trends prevailing since 1949. Investments for sectors related to consumption were increased generally up to 5 per cent.

These palliatives could not resolve a fundamental problem con-

---

* The 1953 cost-of-living index rose 28 per cent above the 1949 level in Poland, but real wages declined to 88 per cent of the 1949 level. The impact upon productivity was dramatized by the example in Polish coal mining; planners had projected a 37 per cent rise in per-capita output but were confronted in 1954 with productivity below that of 1949. (United Nations, *Economic Bulletin for Europe,* IX, No. 3 [1957], 26 and 35.)

fronting the bloc. Ambitious industrialization, unable to be sustained by domestic sources, depended upon the Soviet Union as the chief source of supplies. Yet the very pattern of earlier Soviet industrialization, and one imitated by bloc members, had emphasized the expansion of sectors producing capital goods, while nonfabricating branches developed at a slower pace. The more advanced development of the former had reached a point where shifts in the relative costs of production worked to the disadvantage of nonindustrial and nonmanufacturing branches. It evolved at a time when the need for a faster output of raw materials within the Soviet economy itself was more apparent if the desired pace of industrial growth were to be maintained. The increased disparity in the growth and costs of production of basic materials and those of industrial-processing sectors preoccupied Soviet authorities. Eastern Europe's dependence upon, and emulation of, the Soviet Union added a graver hue. The autarchical orientation of each country expanded the needs for primary commodities when greater exploitation and rationalization of resources grew increasingly desirable.

Confronted by this irrationality, the Soviet conclusion that individual self-sufficiency was ill-conceived and fatuous soon appeared in press campaigns deploring "harmful parallelisms" and advocating the international division of labor among the East European members.[5] COMECON acquired a greater vigor by 1954. The fourth and fifth council meetings held that year in Moscow stressed the virtues of coordination, and at the meeting in Budapest the following year, *ad hoc* commissions for various branches of the economy were set up for this purpose. Following Khrushchev's reaffirmation at the Twentieth Party Congress of the Soviet Union in 1956 that intrabloc specialization would free considerable resources for other purposes, the COMECON meeting in East Berlin that year initiated steps to institutionalize the thesis. Temporary commissions became permanent, aimed at calibrating specialized production. Reportedly, more than 150 types of production in different branches were to be redistributed among member countries.

As the first period of the industrial drives in Eastern Europe drew to a close amidst these rising redefinitions, the summary

results still appeared significant. The gross industrial output of
the area at the end of 1955 was more than 150 per cent above
1949 levels, the highest gains being made in metallurgy, machine-
building, and related industries. But serious defects marred
achievements, and major gaps in fulfillment indicated the un-
steady tempo of growth. Two outstanding imbalances made the
disequilibrium dangerous: an insufficient flow of basic materials
and fuels, and an inadequately leavened increase in consumption.
Throughout 1954 and 1955, annual rates of growth for both per-
capita productivity and gross industrial output kept falling, the
latter by 5–6 per cent in Czechoslovakia and East Germany, by
9 per cent in Poland, and by 19 per cent in Hungary. In all of
these four states, the rates of increase in labor productivity fell
4 per cent or more.

The deceleration of industrialization was obviously hinged to
the poor showing among the extractive industries. Planned targets
for the output of iron ore, coal, and petroleum were considerably
short of realization in all but two countries, the sharpest dis-
parities between goal and performance occurring in the more
industrialized countries. Moreover, the increases planned for consumption as part of the "New Course" proved ephemeral, as
Khrushchev subsequently insisted that priority for heavy industry
be maintained. Improvements in living standards were barely
perceptible.

Disruption and Revisions

Plans for the second quinquennium in 1956 reflected an increased awareness of continuing pressures. The focus upon heavy
industry remained and production goals were still ambitious, but
a slower rate of growth was formulated as investments were
scaled down by 3–7 per cent throughout the region. The planned
rate of industrial growth was further reduced by 29–55 per cent
(most sharply in Poland and Hungary), whereas the expansion of
capital goods output was generally projected at half the rates of
previous years. Planning directives stressed the completion of
projects rather than initiation of new ones. Sectoral reallocations
of investments anticipated improvements in consumption.[6]

These modifications proved inadequate. The impact of tensions interacting with noneconomic grievances led to the 1956 dramas in Poland and Hungary. The workers' councils, which reappeared spontaneously, played a major role in raising Gomulka to power and contributed to an armed showdown between Hungarian and Soviet forces. In addition to the ideological and political ramifications of their activities, these organs in both countries reflected the deep alienation of industrial labor—a reaction to depressed living conditions, gross abuses of officialdom, and the hypocritical role of trade unionism. Widespread and entrenched, they had to be recognized by the new regimes even after the immediate crises, but their pretensions toward independent action were short-circuited once immediate dangers had subsided. Legislation in the following year transformed them into "conferences" or "factory councils," with membership widened to include management, trade unions, and Party personnel—a technique for re-establishing governmental control. Their activities were redirected to the examination of grievances, discussion of production problems, and other nonexplosive issues.*

Dangerous as the political implications of the Polish and Hungarian developments were, the portents of wider economic disruption throughout the bloc obviously prompted authorities into quickening earlier, more modest readjustments in planning and intrabloc relations. The rescue operations by the Soviet Union in 1956 and 1957 spotlighted the chronic shortages of raw commodities and fuels. Nearly two-thirds of more than $1.2 billion in Soviet credits and loans extended at this time went to Poland, Hungary, and East Germany, and about half of these involved foodstuffs and basic materials. A large proportion of Soviet payments for East European exports during this period was made in convertible currencies—an uncommon practice that permitted bloc members to patronize extrabloc sources and implied strains upon Soviet capabilities. As a result, relatively spectacular increases in imports

* Reportedly, 1,492 of 1,936 enterprises in Poland had workers' councils functioning in the autumn of 1957. Further details on the genesis and fate of these bodies are in Zbigniew K. Brzezinski, *The Soviet Bloc: Unity and Conflict* (rev. ed.; New York: Frederick A. Praeger, 1961); Frank Gibney, *The Frozen Revolution* (New York: Farrar, Straus and Cudahy, 1959); *The Revolt in Hungary* (New York: Free Europe Committee, 1957); Jiri Kolaja, *The Polish Factory* (Lexington, Ky.: University of Kentucky Press, 1960); *East Europe*, VIII (1959), Nos. 1 and 3.

of primary commodities were registered by the East European states in 1957.[*]

Concomitantly, although the magnitude of disproportions varied among them, the East European governments also strove to reduce tensions and obstructions in industrial pipelines. Ratios of gross fixed investments to national incomes were scaled down further in 1957, as were allocations to heavy industry. Decreases in outlays for metallurgical and engineering branches accompanied increments for industries producing basic commodities. The efforts at stabilization included reapportionment of investments to speed up the output of consumer goods over that of heavy industry. A marked increase in durables, textiles, and processed food resulted in 1957.

By 1958, the cumulative effect of these and similar measures enabled the East European governments to surmount immediate dangers. Imbalances remained, and the problems of productivity persisted when output targets were scheduled for that year. Slightly higher rates of investments were set, and the relatively moderate raises in industrial production were aimed essentially at expanding inventories and eliminating bottlenecks. Most states maintained an equal rate of growth for both heavy and light industries. In the following year, all but Hungary refocused sights upon an investment drive, with increases of 14 per cent or more being registered (the largest being 32 per cent to spark the Bulgarian "leap forward"). Bulgaria reported an exceptional increase of 25 per cent in gross industrial output for that year, while remaining states generally duplicated the comparatively moderate rates of the previous year. Poland reported a 9 per cent increase in output, and the increase reported by the remaining members ranged from 11 to 12 per cent. However, as some bottlenecks were eliminated, the production of capital goods again rose at a faster rate than that of consumer goods, reaffirming the shibboleth of

[*] The share of raw materials and fuels constituted about 57 per cent of Soviet exports to Eastern Europe in 1955; by the end of 1956 it had gone up an additional 8 per cent. Additional material on Soviet rescue operations is in *Economic Survey of Europe, 1956*, p. 18; *ibid., 1957*, chaps. i, vi; *ibid., 1958*, chap. i; *World Economic Survey, 1960*, p. 120; *Promyshlenno-Ekonomicheskaia Gazeta*, November 4, 1959; *East Europe*, IX, No. 4 (April, 1960), 9; *ibid.*, XI, No. 8 (August, 1962), 3 ff.

expansion and again widening the comparative rates of growth between the two sectors, which had been temporarily narrowed. Nonetheless, the output of cosumer goods increased at a faster rate than before, so that, despite shortages, living standards continued to improve.

A reduction in investments followed in 1960, partly induced by adverse trade balances. However, Rumania amalgamated the last year of its old plan with a new Six-Year Plan, and increased investments by more than 20 per cent that year, as did Bulgaria. Regionally, gross industrial output continued to rise relatively moderately, compared to the early 1950's. All but East Germany (with an increase of 8 per cent) reported rises of 10 per cent or higher (Rumania reporting 14 per cent). A speedier expansion of heavy industry continued, but targets for consumer goods were attained at slightly higher levels, and there were no indications that a reversion to Stalinist practices was being contemplated.[7]

The annual, post-1956 readjustments were essentially ameliorative responses to immediate pressures. They reduced disproportions and raised targets in the tradition of trial-and-error procedures. The need to establish stable, long-term expansion at relatively rapid rates was of more crucial importance. The *coûte-que-coûte* orientation had initially uplifted the bloc economies to a more advanced stage, but the costs had become prohibitive and stultifying trends had developed. The stress upon quantitative results had reached a point of diminishing returns and had preoccupied Soviet authorities even before the near-debacle of 1956. Autarchic emulation by Eastern Europe further taxed Soviet resources. It was increasingly apparent that the growing complexities of the bloc economies made them more vulnerable to wasteful practices, unbalanced structures of output, and social pressures of consumption.* Consequently, 1957 and 1958 were pregnant with reappraisals of economic policies.

Confronted by more subtle challenges of growing maturity, Soviet economic thinking questioned previously sacrosanct premises in planning and management. The 1957 industrial organi-

* Officially, the industrial share of the gross economic product in 1957 ranged from 64 per cent in Rumania to 75 per cent in the Soviet Union and 85 per cent in East Germany. (*Sotsialisticheskii Trud*, No. 10, 1958, p. 55.)

zation, the superimposition of the Seven-Year Plan (1959–65), and the introduction of broad goals over a fifteen-year period were among the major manifestations of refurbished principles operating in the Soviet Union. These gradually brought alterations in the procedural character of planning and management in Eastern Europe, albeit the timing and details varied, and continue to do so, among the member countries. Broadly speaking, the 1956–57 crisis made dramatically apparent the need for efficiency, sectoral correlation, and popular incentive. The responses, particularly among the four northern, more advanced bloc members, whose production constituted about seven-eighths of Eastern Europe's industrial output, included decentralization, searches for new planning criteria, and stricter economic accounting.

The redefined functions of central planning were at the core of innovations emerging after 1957. The devolution of management as a revitalizing agent for rationality and flexibility necessitated more specific delineations between operational and planning sectors, with a consequent limitation placed upon the managerial powers of central planning authorities. A clearer separation between industrial operations and planning coordination evolved. Decentralization in decision-making also appeared. Central plans, previously rigid in determining both quantitative targets and product-mixes for lower echelons, acquired a more aggregative character as regional and local initiative in formulating output goals was encouraged. Concurrently, changes in planning practices brought forth formulations of "perspective" plans, long-term targets of ten to fifteen years (subsequently raised to twenty years) calculated for certain important branches of industry. These, along with the goals of the Five-Year, Six-Year, or Seven-Year plans, were less rigidly paced, because of the tendency to relate them to current performance and such factors as the state of industrial pipelines and balance of payments. It permitted upward or downward revisions to be made more efficiently in response to existing conditions.*

---

* The Polish, Czech, and Hungarian successes in surpassing relatively moderate goals in 1960, for example, brought upward revisions in outlays and growth for plans beginning in 1961, while the disappearance of earlier buoyancy led to downward revisions in East Germany. Czech anxieties over slackening expansion and underfulfillment in engineering branches since 1961 led

Meantime, greater attention to sectoral correlation brought re-interpretations of planning principles. Earlier growth, predicated upon excessive priming of "leading industries" regarded as keys to expansion, led to gross imbalances. The concept was implicitly modified by growing insistence upon analyses of all relevant factors in the establishment of planning goals. As the previous focus upon "leading industries" was rooted in the concept of "material balances," it had precluded any precise calculations of relative advantages or efficiency of investment alternatives. Although the concept was not wholly scrapped, it acquired different hues in so far as the idea of maximizing investments for "leading industries" had become outmoded.

The dual concern for balance and efficiency spawned a still-continuing search for investment criteria permitting greater precision. Price reforms appearing in recent years and the various campaigns for realistic accounting practices continue to reflect this penchant. The absence of uniform pricing methods still precludes successful formulas, but these efforts do underscore the concern among East European authorities for a better utilization of resources within and between sectors and industries.[8]

On the operational level, decentralization led to the organization of intermediate agencies linking central and local levels either as territorial subdivisions or as groups of industrial associations. This stratum has acquired diverse authority, both in the formulation of specific targets and in the disposition of resources within the central matrix of national planning. Correlative extensions of such latitude have likewise been conferred upon local authorities and geared to systems of incentives promoting greater productivity and economy: *Inter alia,* enterprises retain larger shares of profits and broader discretion in disposition of funds. Incentives for technical progress and profitable innovations have been given increased attention.

Summarily, reactions to previous traumata of wastefulness, imbalances, and social pressures have been expressed by interrelated remedies appearing since 1958. The desideratum of a relatively

in turn to the August, 1962, announcement that the Five-Year Plan had been dropped and a Seven-Year Plan would begin in 1964. (*East Europe,* XI, No. 10 [October, 1962], 34.)

rapid but less erratic rhythm of industrial growth brought forth discernible shifts of emphases in planning and management: from maximum to optimum rates of growth, from material-intensive operations to labor-intensive, from the unqualified guide of "leading industries" to improved sectoral balances, and from "enforced savings" to improvements in consumption.

As one decade ended and another unfolded, the ingestive process of East European revisions was evident. The greater diligence toward rationality in production and growth constitute the over-all design for revitalizing the industrialization process. Of course, varying environmental factors also prompted adoptions of expedients for surmounting obstacles that sometimes appeared contrary to general trends. Chronological differences among the national plans also persisted: Some states adopted new versions after 1958; others revised existing targets. With the exception recently announced in Czechoslovakia, bloc members established goals for 1965 as their immediate targets. Common among them was the initial decision to formulate levels of anticipated output for major commodities in 1975, which, in turn, were superseded by the 1961 decision to submit "perspective" plans for 1980. Consequently, though individual peculiarities affected and continue to affect the details and timing, within the diversity a common effort to facilitate a smoother yet relatively rapid pattern of industrial growth is discernible.*

---

* Lax practices and disruptive tendencies growing out of earlier changes, for example, led to a significant amount of recentralization in Poland. Chronic failures in East Germany were presumably responsible for the announcement that far-reaching administrative changes were to be instituted. The Czech explanation in 1962 that the current plan was dropped included references to the unrealistically wide assortment in the product mix of engineering industries in the light of recent progress toward integration. For the most part, greater similarity in developmental trends exists among the four, more industrialized, countries in the north. At the same time, the ideological theses of "equalization" and "all-around" development appear cogent to the spurts of industrialization manifested in the two Balkan states. The Bulgarian drive of 1959 was a divergence from the more moderate pace of others. Major gaps in fulfillment and defects arising from the purely quantitative drive soon impelled authorities to consider costs and quality as well, so that the rise in gross industrial output in 1961 declined to a saner level of less than 10 per cent. A recent summary is in J. Kalo, "The Bulgarian Economy," *Survey*, No. 39, December, 1961. Neighboring Rumania continues its industrial expansion at the fastest

Current Plans

It is obvious that the "heroic" period of industrialization has passed, and the East European regimes, chastened somewhat by the perils of unqualified drives amidst increasingly complex conditions, have become more sensitive to economic realities. Keeping a steady flow in industrial pipelines, intensifying the uses of capital, and raising labor productivity are among the major concerns of current plan fulfillment. The more realistic sectoral balances and improvement in consumption schedules have simultaneously led to declines in annual rates of growth and greater emphasis upon efficiency as a partial compensation for the decline. More weight has been given to better utilization of resources and capacity, to more precise accounting methods, to the modernization and upkeep of capital stock, and to those decentralizing techniques that can be geared to both incentive and control so as to spur per-capita productivity. Notwithstanding the spectrum of variations, continuing refinements are directed toward these broad silhouettes of similar problems and aims.

Current plans call for increases in gross fixed investments to 1965, with none of the erratic spurts of the past. Regionally, the shares assigned industry during this period are proportionally lower than those set a decade ago, and, in as much as investment considerations extend beyond mere growth (e.g., replacement of obsolete capital stock), the annual growth rates for gross industrial output have also been set below those of a decade ago and deviate little from the recent past. The primacy of heavy industry remains; throughout the area its expansion is to be more rapid than increases in either total industrial output or output of consumer goods. The rates of consumption, however, are not to be depressed to previous levels as the ameliorative, post-1956 trends continue, with larger outlays projected for consumer durables.*

---

rate in the bloc since 1960, anticipating a 110 per cent increase in 1965 as the average annual rates of growth continue to be pegged at more than 13 per cent. Cf. *Economic Survey of Europe, 1961*, chap. ii, p. 2.

* Bulgaria, Hungary, and Poland will complete their Five-Year plans in 1965, when Rumania's Six-Year Plan and East Germany's Seven-Year Plan are also to be completed. Czechoslovak planning has been reoriented to 1970. See Appendix II for the general figures.

Particularly notable among the current plans are the modifications in the production profiles of heavy industry, apparently induced to a certain extent by persistent shortages of basic materials. In all countries a more intense exploitation of remoter and less rich sources of fuels and raw materials is being pressed. Along with nonferrous ores, available supplies of fuels and energy are to be expanded markedly. The output of brown coal is to rise 80 per cent by 1965, and the production of coking coal is to increase by more than 53 per cent. The cumulative increase in East European fuel production, which totaled the equivalent of 277.6 million tons in 1958, is scheduled to raise the level to 381 million tons in 1965. Nonetheless, the region's output of both fuels and many vital raw materials will continue to lag behind the demands; the gaps are to be filled by imports.

Directly related to these problems of shortages are the construction of intrabloc pipelines and the expansion of industrial chemistry, which have been emphasized. Besides facilitating a shift to petroleum sources of fuel and power, the pipelines are to spur the growth of chemical industries. Each country is stressing the exploitation of basic materials for this branch, although international specialization will guide the advanced fabricating processes. In addition to supplying fertilizers to ailing agricultural sectors, the projected expansion of chemical production to three times the output of 1959 is also anticipated to permit replacement of metal input with synthetic products in engineering branches.

The emphasis upon industrial chemistry has reduced the priority previously enjoyed by the engineering industries, although these are still scheduled for considerable expansion to provide new equipment for the production of chemical products. Moreover, reflecting greater coordination, bloc countries appear more concerned in producing machinery having greater export capabilities. Finally, the building-materials industry is the third sector receiving high priority in current planning.

At this more advanced stage of industrialization, East European planners have directed more attention to per-capita productivity. Previously, the absorption of surplus, nonindustrial population (even beyond actual needs) facilitated increases in gross output even with inefficient labor. Changing demographic trends discourage such practices now, as do the factors that brought shifts from materials-intensive to labor-intensive operations. Larger contributions to industrial growth are currently expected from rises in labor productivity. Also, outlays for replacement of obsolete equipment are larger than ever and constitute correlatives aimed at increasing output, while "carrot and stick" legislation that has appeared since the late 1950's reflects official concern. This preoccupation has included efforts to enforce stricter discipline, upward revisions of work norms, attacks upon duplication of labor, and more severe punishment of violations. Apparent stimuli have included wage reforms raising minimum levels and a de-emphasis of the unreasonable standards of piecework.*

Bloc Coordination

The emphasis upon economic rationality demonstrated in recent years by individual members has been strikingly projected on an intrabloc level. The revitalization of COMECON, reflecting the effort to avoid past errors and surmount new obstacles without an extensive reduction in the pace of expansion, has gathered greater momentum since the 1956–57 crisis. Interrelated considerations have accelerated the integrative process under its auspices. Avoiding any recurrence of area-wide scarcities, reducing wasteful duplication of production, increasing capital efficiency, promoting multilateral standardization—these are among the major concerns that have added new dimensions to COMECON activities and have led to a proliferation of its subunits. After several years of a more or less symbolic existence, COMECON has acquired a more meaningful identity and its authoritative character has been more precisely defined as Eastern Europe advances into the 1960's.†

* Efforts to enlist labor's cooperation include the recent appeal in Poland that plans be drawn up in time to permit factory "conferences" (emasculated successors to earlier workers councils) to review and discuss goals on the enterprise level. (*East Europe*, XI, No. 4 [April, 1962], 45.) Statistical details related to East European labor, its output and wages, are in Appendix II.

† In the wake of the 1958 decision of Communist Party leaders to effect greater coordination, both the number of specialized organs within COMECON and the frequency of their meetings markedly increased. New permanent commissions for coordinating major sectors on an area-wide basis were created in 1958, to which three more were added in 1962. Headquartered

In the months immediately following the East European crisis, COMECON units were preoccupied with improving fuels and raw-material supplies. Previously modest gestures at coordinating plans had to be abandoned for the most part. The May, 1958, meeting of Party leaders was heralded as a landmark for the more dynamic renewal of bloc coordination. Agreements to synchronize individual plans on a fifteen-year basis and to expedite multilateral arrangements were announced. Thereafter, COMECON representatives exhibited greater energies in deliberations over unsolved problems.* As three general sessions of COMECON were convened between the summers of 1958 and 1959, the bloc's press carried on campaigns to emphasize the bright prospects for living standards that would materialize with the elimination of duplications in planning and output.[9]

---

in various capitals of the bloc, these seventeen permanent commissions strive toward coordination in the following fields: coal, oil and gas, electric power, ferrous metallurgy, nonferrous metallurgy, chemicals, transport, machine-building, building materials, light and food industries, agriculture, atomic energy, foreign trade, economic problems, standardization, coordination of research, and statistics. After eleven years of existence, an organizational statute was finally adopted for COMECON in April, 1960, stating over-all purposes and requiring unanimous concurrence for decisions to be effective. A greater sense of urgency and an increase in authority materialized after a June, 1962, meeting of Communist Party leaders, when an Executive Committee was created within COMECON consisting of deputy premiers of member states. Below these upper echelons function subcommittees, specialized groups, an institute for standardization, and periodic technical conferences for planning and production within branches of the bloc's economies. Other organizational details are in *Izvestiia*, February 15, 1956; *East Europe*, IV, No. 4 (April, 1957); *ibid.*, VIII, No. 7 (July, 1959); *ibid.*, XI, No. 6 (June, 1962); *ibid.*, No. 7 (July, 1962); *ibid.*, No. 9 (September, 1962); *ibid.*, No. 11 (November, 1962); *Vneshniaia Torgovlia*, No. 7, 1961; *Mirovaia Ekonomika i Mezhdunarodnie Otnosheniia*, No. 4, April, 1959; *Economic Bulletin for Europe*, XI, No. 1.

* More than sixty meetings of COMECON units were estimated to have been held between October, 1956, and April, 1958. U.S. Department of State, *Notes: Soviet Affairs*, No. 223 (June 18, 1958). Sessions devoted to methodological problems, held in 1958 in Warsaw and 1959 in Berlin, aimed at facilitating intercountry comparability of national accounting. No full reports appeared and the continued preoccupation with techniques of comparability indicates slight if any achievement at this time. Some recent observations about methods of national accounting within the bloc and the problems of comparability are in *Economic Bulletin for Europe*, XI, No. 3, 52 ff.; M. Hoffman, "How to Read National Income Statistics," *East Europe*, XI, No. 11 (November, 1962), 11 ff.

Despite apparent advantages, impedimenta of a nontechnical nature were encountered, in addition to existing problems. Innately nationalistic hindrances had to be confronted. Previous autarchy had been costly, but it also had fostered pride in the industrial progress achieved. New industries, however inefficient their performance, were viewed as objects of achievements, endangered by a logical pursuit of intrabloc specialization. Moreover, the less advanced countries could be relegated to roles as suppliers of basic commodities without attaining industrial maturity.

The effort to reconcile these apprehensions with integration was evident in the pronouncements that followed another meeting of Communist Party leaders in May, 1959. It was affirmed that the "all-around" development of each state's economy would enable all members to reach the stage of Communism at the same time. This ideological elaboration in effect averred that major industrial branches in a member country would not be sacrificed upon the altar of specialization, but that coordination would develop among similar industries in the area as a whole (the Soviet Union, of course, preserving its autarchical prerogatives). The expansion of sectors regarded as indispensable for industrial maturity would continue—notably, power, building materials, machine-building, and some light industry.

Subsequent avowals of this thesis of a "more or less simultaneous transition" attested to the persistent apprehensions among some circles that supranational coordination presaged dubitable rewards for some participants. In the light of continuing press assurances and criticisms, other nuances or variants of this apprehension continue to linger.[10]

Notwithstanding such impedimenta, the process of integration has been spurred since 1958. The scope of specialized production has been broadened and a greater interdependence upon sources of supply has developed.

As early as 1955 and 1956, COMECON had designated more than 140 types of machine, chemical, and agricultural products for specialization. Subsequent events prevented implementation of many of these policies, but a vigorous resumption of delineating specialized production occurred at the eleventh session held in

Tirana in 1959. Primary attention was focused upon the engineering industries and a considerable elimination of duplicated output was announced. This "socialist division of labor" at the end of the previous decade reportedly had affected the production of about 600 products involving iron pipes, rolled steel, machine-building, and chemicals. The Budapest meeting of COMECON in 1961 deepened the process by adding about twenty-two types to the lists for specialized production—machines for the chemical, sugar, paper, and meat industries in the region. This trend continued at the Warsaw sessions of COMECON in December, 1961, at which it was announced that 1,000 additional products (mostly in chemical industries) were being considered for specialization. Greater attention was also apparently directed both to capital-intensive production and to branches where future growth could be achieved rapidly.

Lack of detailed information precludes a comprehensive analysis of the patterns of specialized production among member countries (whether operative or projected). Official claims indicate that some 1,500 individual products may have been designated at the end of 1961, and, apparently consonant with emphases of current plans, the majority are in engineering and previously neglected chemical industries. Projected increases of 200–400 per cent in the output of industrial chemistry are scheduled for 1965.[11]

The broader outlines of the specialization profile can be discerned. As might be anticipated, the larger share of this has been assigned to one or two countries among the more industrially advanced.*

---

* Machine tools for the bearings industries, for example, have been apportioned among East Germany, Czechoslovakia, and Poland. The same states appear to have been assigned the lion's share of producing machinery for the chemical industries and for rolling mills. Wire-drawing machinery, precision instruments, and tele-communications are to be emphasized by Hungary. Rumania is to concentrate upon the manufacture of oil equipment, while Poland is to focus upon shipbuilding and papermaking machines, among others. Power tools and power machinery appear to be largely the preserve of Czechoslovakia and East Germany; both have been designated as major sources of machines for heavy industry. In addition to specialization in raw materials, Bulgaria has been designated for the output of chemical products and equipment for light industry. Specialization has not deterred Bulgarian authorities from stressing an ambitious expansion of metallurgical production during the

Specialization in the final analysis is tied to the problem of inadequate resources in the area for meeting the ambitious plans of expansion. Behind the greater stature attained by COMECON runs the steady thread of concern for the flow of basic materials needed to meet rising requirements.[12] As early as 1958, COMECON efforts to relieve shortages brought on a multilateral agreement to construct two oil pipelines tapping Soviet sources, one running through Poland to East Germany and the other through Czechoslovakia to Hungary. Further cooperation along these lines appeared at the eleventh session of COMECON in 1959, with the decision to link the electric-power grids of the area into a network anchored to Soviet stations in the Ukraine and the northwest. Preoccupation with providing a steady flow of fuels and raw materials was further reflected in the 1960 COMECON agreement to specialize in commodities vital to the rapid growth of chemical industries (e.g., sulphur in Poland, potash in East Germany, oil and gas in Rumania).*

This continuing concern has also fostered practices perhaps more portentous for the regional interdependence that is materializing. Various developmental projects have been pursued on a joint-aid basis recently. Bilateral and multilateral projects of "joint construction" have become more common since 1957, whereby neighboring aid is usually to be compensated by deliveries from the expected output of new projects.†

---

current plan; steel output has been scheduled to rise from 79,000 tons in 1962 to more than a million tons in 1965. (*East Europe*, XI, No. 3 [March, 1962], 44 ff.)

* Completion of the oil pipelines into Poland and Czechoslovakia was reported at the end of 1961, and in the following year the electric-power grid network linked East Germany, Czechoslovakia, Poland, and Hungary. The network is expected to be in full operation by 1965, after extensions connecting Rumania and Bulgaria with the Ukraine are completed. Meantime, during 1961, more than 120 million kilowatt hours were reportedly exchanged between East Germany and Czechoslovakia, serving either to redress breakdowns or to exploit temporarily excess capacities. (*Neues Deutschland*, March 2, 1962, as reported in *East Europe*, XI, No. 5 [May, 1962], 36–37.) The grid network is expected to save about 65 million rubles for the bloc in 1965. (*International Affairs*, No. 11, 1962, p. 56.)

† Rumania, for example, is receiving aid from Poland, Czechoslovakia, and East Germany in the construction of a cellulose combine whose future production will supply the paper industries of these states. Czechoslovak aid for a Rumanian woodworking combine will be compensated with wood products;

The trend toward capital mobility among member states remains somewhat embryonic. In its relation to the development of raw-materials sources, it has also been a matter of concern to the less industrialized members. The faster development of extractive sectors highly desirable to meet the demands of growing industrialization has posed investment problems. When compared with manufacturing sectors, more capital formation is required and a longer investment cycle develops. It takes longer for a smaller increase to be registered in the national product. Concurrently, the more industrialized economies are the major users of these raw materials. Consequently, increasingly more vocal proposals have been made for the more advanced states to assume larger investment burdens for developing raw materials in neighboring countries, even as much as in proportion to their future needs. This has not yet elicited a wide response, although a limited flow of capital has crossed borders since 1957.* The coordination of investment efforts to expand sources of primary materials remains an important problem, although bloc planners have agreed in principle that, in return for such aid, the recipient country must undertake to cover the needs of its allies. The pressures upon capital resources in each state apparently has limited capital mobility within the bloc. The absence of a broader intramural program of this nature tends to cast suspicion among some upon the thesis of the "simultaneous transition to Communism."†

Rumanian electric power will serve the same ends for aid in erecting power plants using natural gas and cheap coal. The joint Czech-Hungarian effort in building hydroelectric units on the Danube and Rumanian-Hungarian projects for a chemical combine have been programmed along these lines.

* The more obvious admonitions for larger mutual investments have come from Polish authorities and have been obviously directed at East Germany and Czechoslovakia. In 1957 and 1958, Czech and German credits approximating $160 million were advanced to expand Polish coal mining and to exploit brown-coal deposits, with much of the repayment to be made in future deliveries. Reiterated Polish demands have been apparently responsible for additional advances made in 1961. East Germany extended about $64 million in credits for the installation of the Polish section of the oil pipeline from the Soviet Union, while Czechoslovakia has committed some $300 million to 1967 to support the Polish exploitation of copper deposits in Lower Silesia.

† The heavy responsibility of the Soviet Union in supplying its rapidly industrializing partners has extended the mutual-investment concept in still another direction, as recently reported in Poland. Development of new mines and processing facilities in Estonia, in order to meet the greater need for phos-

Beyond the range of these more immediate steps promoting greater coordination and interdependence, COMECON authorities have also given greater impetus to the basic precondition of complete integration—synchronization of planning. While harmonizing short-term features of national plans, efforts to coordinate major targets over longer periods of time are increasingly evident. The establishment and enforcement within a generation of a centrally directed scheme for the whole region is the final aim.

Developments in this direction first appeared following the meeting of party leaders in 1958 when the COMECON session in Bucharest in June of that year announced an intention to correlate the major national-plan targets for 1975. Oblique evidence has indicated that a division of opinion existed within the bloc between proponents of cooperation among individual economies and the adherents of a more rigid, supranational planning procedure that would increase COMECON powers.[13]

At the thirteenth meeting of the organization held in Budapest in July, 1960, members agreed to the submission of new "perspective" plans set for 1980 and reference was made to COMECON's future role in determining the major guides of economic expansion within the bloc. Subsequent communiqués emanating from the fourteenth and fifteenth meetings of 1961 gave little more than platitudinous assurances that such work was progressing. This trend toward supranational planning seemed to grow more emphatic in 1962, when another meeting of Party leaders resulted in the creation of an Executive Committee within COMECON consisting of deputy premiers from member countries empowered to make fundamental decisions. Information on the subject remains meager and no statement at the end of 1962 was made about the previously announced evaluation of "perspective" plans scheduled for that year. Attainment of supranational planning is still confronted by serious technical obstacles, which, it has been asserted, are to be overcome by 1970. Thereafter, under new operating principles, the formulation of a single plan for the whole of Eastern Europe is anticipated to be within the realm of reality.[14]

---

phates in Eastern Europe, has created a situation "in which the interested countries participate in covering the cost of the investment." (*New York Times,* November 11, 1962.)

Outlook

Under a system commanding top priority for rapid industrialization, Eastern Europe is in the midst of a transition necessitated by painful achievements and past follies. The industrial expansion has been considerable; but, confronted by threats to growth prospects from the previously simplistic drive, the bloc has been impelled toward reorientation. Many of the innovations or refinements of recent years are still in the process of implementation, thus not yet subject to precise assessment. But other crucial, still unsolved problems persist.

Barring gross miscalculations and extensive revisions that may come from noneconomic pressures, current targets in many sectors of the national plans are not unduly ambitious.[15] However attainable the 1965 goals, the various prognoses that the region's industrial output will increase at least sixfold by 1980 optimistically assumes that major obstacles will disappear. However, the current unevenness of the industrial picture indicates that this disappearance is still problematical.

Within the context of the sharper focus upon rationality, a variety of interrelated considerations are given stronger emphasis at the present time, among them, smooth-flowing industrial pipelines, reductions in output costs, technical improvements, more efficiency in planning and operations, quality and assortment in production, etc. Juxtaposed are such hindrances as the difficulty of providing larger industrial investments in the face of adverse trade balances, the penchant of bloc planners to raise targets following short-term fulfillments that often threaten to reintroduce bottlenecks, and the persistent lag in the area's output of fuel and raw materials.*

Out of the diversity of efforts taken to improve the rhythm and

---

* Increasing dependence upon Soviet supplies will continue despite the economies arising from regional coordination. About 63 per cent of Eastern Europe's iron-ore requirements are being met by imports, and the Soviet Union is committed to increase its deliveries by about 12 million tons by 1965. Estimates for 1972–75 place the total deficit for East European industry at approximately 3.4 million tons in crude-steel equivalent. (*Long-Term Trends and Problems of the European Steel Industry* [Geneva: United Nations, 1959], p. 166.)

maintain the speed of industrial growth, two chief ingredients that have been projected as solutions for some of the bloc's problems may be cited: per-capita productivity and economic integration.

Throughout the bloc, a higher industrial output per man is among the major priorities of current planning.* It is anticipated that from 70 per cent to 80 per cent of the increases scheduled for industrial output in 1965 will be derived from greater labor productivity, with largest increments coming in the vital branches of metallurgy, fuel, industrial chemistry, and engineering. These projections, of course, are closely related to employment policies: Per-capita increases reduce the need to recruit new labor in order to achieve quantitative norms of output. Concurrently, labor incentives to stimulate increases cannot be ignored. Recent trends and earlier depressions of living standards nonetheless cast serious doubts as to whether such targets for labor productivity will be attained.

In 1961, most bloc members were unable to maintain the correlated patterns of these "per-capita" goals. While East Germany and Czechoslovakia fell behind the planned rates for increasing labor productivity, Poland, Hungary, and Rumania exceeded the quotas that had been set for new employment (in part due to the shorter work week enacted).†

In the final analysis, these goals must contend with the fundamental reality that stimulates the will and skill of the industrial worker—living standards. Although the regimes have shown greater awareness of this factor, the initial momentum of the post-1956 ameliorations has slackened recently. Cumulative increases in industrial real wages from 1954 to 1958 ranged from

---

* Using 100 as the base figure for 1950, the indexes of per-capita increases in labor productivity among member countries in 1962 were as follows: 141 in Hungary, 174 in Bulgaria, 197 in Rumania, 199 in Czechoslovakia, 209 in both Poland and East Germany; the Soviet Union's index was 187. (*Magyar Nemzet*, July 17, 1962, as quoted in *East Europe*, XI, No. 9 [September, 1962], 41.) Labor productivity in 1965 is expected to surpass that of 1960 by 44 per cent in Bulgaria, 32 per cent in Hungary, 40 per cent in Poland, and 43 per cent in Czechoslovakia. It is to be 85 per cent higher than 1958 levels in East Germany and 60 to 70 per cent above 1959 in Rumania. (*International Affairs* [Moscow], No. 8, August, 1962, pp. 102–10.

† Hungary and Poland reported similar shortcomings in mid-1962.

14 per cent in Czechoslovakia to 40 per cent in Poland. In 1959, the increases averaged from 4–5 per cent in the area, and in 1961 real wages have been estimated to have risen from 2–5 per cent. These increases, however, have not eliminated the enormous backlog of consumer demand; and, although more attention has been given to the production of durable consumer goods, the planned investments for this sector are inadequate for a rapid or marked improvement in living standards. Neither do the current plans provide for any rapid improvement in the housing situation. Throughout 1962, in fact, authorities in the more advanced states of the bloc uttered warnings that a greater austerity was probable in the near future.

For the most part, real wages have not been permitted to rise as rapidly as the planned or actual increases in per capita output; and, as long as the intense priorities given heavy industries retard faster increases in living standards, the planning goals of labor productivity in East European industry will remain in jeopardy.[16]

On an intrabloc basis, greater momentum given to economic integration has been an outstanding feature of recent years. The incapability of domestic resources to sustain planned rates of expansion continues to heighten the tempo of COMECON activities and a crucial period also unfolds for that organization. Its authority requires further elaboration if some of the technical and practical problems are to be resolved.

Stimuli for greater coordination stem simultaneously from innate attractions, external challenges, and Soviet pressures. Maximum standardization and serial production nurture greater efficiency and economy, which, when related to the avowed aim of leveling differences in development among member countries,* hold obvious attraction and advantages for the region. Moreover,

---

* As a probable reflection of the "simultaneous transition to Communism" thesis, the trade targets of current plans project a four-to-fivefold increase in Bulgarian and Rumanian exports of machinery within the bloc, as compared to a twofold increase of such exports for the other members by 1965, a time when machinery exports within the bloc will constitute 36 per cent of intrabloc trade, in comparison to the 28 per cent that machinery pre-empted in 1958.

although the Soviet Union is capable of maintaining deliveries of vital materials to prime the industrialization of its allies, it is also apparent that it would prefer to reduce proportionally the costs of this role with greater bloc coordination. A more businesslike posture in its relations with Eastern Europe has emerged.* Furthermore, the development of the Common Market in Western Europe has become an added factor; its success will create economic difficulties for the bloc and compound the problems of industrial growth.† Consequently, these and allied considerations will continue to press bloc authorities into the search for solutions to problems presently preventing COMECON from being the supranational agency supervising integrated economic expansion.

Although the East European regimes have agreed in principle to a radical pooling of resources and energies, serious deterrents remain. Among the more significant are the shortcomings in cost-price relationships, the absence of multilateral standardization, and the persistence of centripetal tendencies.

Unless pricing methods permit comparisons of alternatives within and among economies, international specialization must remain arrested. Little guidance for comparability now exists in the domestic prices of member countries, divorced as they are from external markets. Notwithstanding the search for formulas without rejecting ideological dicta, comparative costs are still inadequately reflected in prices of products. This impediment to comparability permits only a crude determination of production specialization, and bloc authorities have indicated their aware-

* By 1965, Soviet exports of oil are to be trebled to 15 million tons, while, on the other hand, its imports of machinery, chemicals, and consumer goods will probably be 2.3 times greater than in 1957. Recent Polish statements reported in *The New York Times* of November 11, 1962, indicate that Soviet delivery of investment goods is leveling off and that Soviet credits at low interests will not be as readily available to Eastern Europe.

† Throughout the latter part of 1962, the Common Market was a frequent object of the bloc's attention, and despite the numerous strictures, the real concern was the anticipated effect upon the bloc's trading position. Regional autarchy of Eastern Europe is intended to be a response to the challenge, yet intrabloc trade has not kept pace with COMECOM trade with the West. Consequently, a sense of greater urgency for integration has emerged from the standpoint of this consideration alone. Cf. pertinent sections in the monthly issues of *East Europe* for 1962.

ness that optimum division of labor is impossible without a practical basis for comparison.*

Bilateralism, therefore, retains its prominence in the bloc's economic relations. Serving as an instrument to facilitate the balance
of accounts in the absence of reliable prices, it likewise constitutes
a barrier to any steady, continuous flow of materials and capital
across borders.[17] Consequently, seasonal fluctuations in production and supplies still plague the economies. These bilateral patterns will continue to prevent refinements in the distribution and
development of resources fundamental to bloc integration.

The heterogeneous systems retarding multilateral standardization—industrial classifications, national accounting, measurements,
etc.—compound the problems created by the absence of valid
indicators and attendant practices that forestall integration. Such
technical standardization, a precondition of operative integration,
must evolve before mutual planning as well as advanced specialization in production can be effectively implemented. Developments in 1962 reflect the growing concern among COMECON
authorities over these problems.†

These two basic technical shortcomings alone prevent COME-
CON at this time from becoming a truly supranational institution empowered to enforce broad planning, regulate investments,
and assign patterns of production. Other, less prominent, defects
further complicate the task of integration. Furthermore, despite
the ideological shibboleth of brotherhood, centripetal tendencies,
reflected in the niggardliness of capital mobility and in the pro-
crastination that has attended some efforts at specialized production, persist among bloc members. The lack of developmental and
qualitative uniformity among member countries, vestigial psychological apprehensions, and technical hazards and shortcomings
still beset the planners for a single economic system in Eastern
Europe. Their claim that economic integration will be a reality

---

* Plans were announced in 1961 that estimates would be made of output
levels in the bloc by re-evaluating *in rubles* some 200–300 major types of output. (*Problems of Economics*, IV, No. 11 [March, 1962], 61.)

† The sixteenth session of COMECON in June, 1962, established two permanent commissions for standardization and statistics, as well as a research
institute for advancing common systems for the bloc.

by 1980 is rather tenuous. The multilateral program of East European industrialization under COMECON still faces enormous tasks.[18]

Appendix I: Yugoslavia

The evolution of a Yugoslav form of socialism represents perhaps the most ironic of postwar developments in Eastern Europe. Initially avid in its emulation of Stalinist patterns, the Titoist regime subsequently was impelled toward practical reforms and ideological redefinitions. These radically altered the process of its industrial growth and have evoked alternating rebukes and toleration from its former allies within the Soviet bloc.

Among the least industrialized of prewar states in Europe, Yugoslavia lost more than one-third of its meager industrial base during the war. The new regime, however, displayed little moderation in its drive to abolish the old order and to spur industrial expansion. While nationalization virtually eliminated the private sector in all but ownership of land by 1948, the goals of reconstruction and industrialization were ambitiously incorporated into the First Five-Year Plan, adopted in 1947. Under highly centralized direction, megalomanic targets epitomized the Stalinist principles of economic growth in Eastern Europe.

Summarily, the plan scheduled approximately 27 per cent of national income for new fixed investments, and about half of these were allocated to the industrial sector. Anticipating a 223 per cent increase in the gross value of industrial production, Yugoslav planners put particular emphasis on capital-goods production, scheduling an increase to 57 per cent of gross industrial output. Enormous projections of this program, estimated to require $5 billion, presupposed attainment of extraordinary output levels in vital branches: steel production was to be tripled, that of pig iron quintupled, and all metal industries were to produce seven times the 1939 output. Metallurgy, chemicals, and electric power were to dominate the production picture.

Under ordinary circumstances the gross unrealities of the plan inevitably would have resulted in major shortfalls. Yugoslavia's expulsion from the Cominform and the subsequent economic

blockade by its erstwhile allies rapidly complicated and intensified strains in the economy. Soviet commitments of $800 million
in aid quickly evaporated after only $130 million had been ex-
tended. On the other hand, geopolitical considerations motivated
the West (notably the United States) partly to fill the breech with
$500 million up to 1956. In any event, as the 1950 decade began,
an impending crisis of catastrophic proportions loomed. The deep-
ening imbalances of fanciful planning, an agricultural slump, and
traumata related to reorientation of economic relations were
among the factors portending major failures in plan fulfillment.
The disheartening effects of forced-draft industrialization further
heightened tensions. The irrational practices of a centralized and
inflexible bureaucracy, along with an unenthusiastic (even apa-
thetic) population, likewise took their toll. The Stalinist pattern
of growth had become prohibitively expensive, from the standpoint of both resources and the human factor.

Briefly, the Tito Government first addressed itself to the problem of economic rationality and popular incentive (later to pre-
occupy Soviet bloc authorities in varying degrees), while last-ditch
efforts were made to attain some of the targets. Legislation introduced somewhat falteringly with the establishment of Workers'
Councils in enterprises in June, 1950, strove to eliminate Stalinist
dross and energize growth under new institutions and policies.
Meantime, the extension of the plan period to 1952, and the ac-
celeration of investments, continued in the effort to reduce the
disparity between plan and fulfillment.* Nonetheless, as late as
1953, the output levels of almost all major branches lagged behind goals initially established for 1951. It was increasingly obvious that reallocation of resources to other sectors was mandatory
if intolerable disproportions were to be corrected.

The core of Titoist innovations in the industrial sector was of
a pragmatic character, although new considerations and conditions attending successful defection from the bloc gave impetus

---

* In 1953, fixed investments for industry rose to about 64 per cent of gross
investments, pre-empting 18 per cent of the national income. These were for
the most part channeled into metallurgy and industrial chemistry, which, combined, absorbed more than two-thirds of industrial investments. Naturally,
output of capital goods rose rapidly, by 13 per cent annually. Cf. *Economic
Survey of Europe, 1959*, chap. vii, pp. 25 ff.

to ideological soul-searching and reinterpretations. Decentralization of planning and management constituted the moving spirit. The attempt to promote greater initiative among lower echelons and advance rationality without challenging the broader aims and ultimate control of the Titoist regime gave the reforms of the early 1950's a trial-and-error appearance. The instability brought by institutional and policy changes naturally precluded realistic, long-term planning, so that to 1957 (when the Second Five-Year Plan was adopted), only annual plans were formulated, and these, too, were often revised. The impact of decentralization, however, was not abrupt. Workers' Councils initially were granted only a consultative status in local enterprises. Later legislation expanded stimuli for local efficiency with profit-sharing features and subsequently broader roles in the formulation of local planning goals.

Stripped to its bare essentials as they affected the industrial sector, the decentralizing enactments have been anchored to financial inducements and safeguards.[19] On the one hand, decentralization has brought a restructuring of the industrial hierarchy: Central ministries have been replaced by coordinating councils, and economic associations for the various industries exist as intermediate organs linking the center with local enterprises. Central planning has also acquired a changed character. Legislation in 1951 stipulated that the central plan be of a global nature, setting "basic proportions" to determine the magnitude and direction of industrial growth, but passing on to lower echelons (down to individual enterprises) the task of defining the details.

Concomitantly, however, the ramifications of decentralization went beyond planning and management. Economic rationality could not be served without realistic standards of price and cost, commonly absent in a command-type economy. Consequently, supply and demand as a basis of local decision-making was given increased recognition by authorities. But, although the regime has permitted facets of the market mechanism to operate in some areas, a totally free market is out of the question. Both fiscal and monetary policies and systems have been reorganized in order to enable authorities to curb deleterious trends and to safeguard "socialism." The application of these various inducements for promoting efficiency and growth has been accompanied by the

114   *The Planned Economy*

central retention of legislative and financial restraints to keep
industrial growth consonant with ideological commitment. The
levers of control include, among others, certain areas of price-
fixing, a determination of investment priorities, dictation of financial prerequisites for enterprises, control of foreign trade, and
powers of taxation. These operate alongside permissible facets
of the market mechanism, financial incentives, and some latitude
in setting output targets: instruments encouraging efficiency and
expansion.*

Absence of a long-term plan in the mid-1950's did not alter the
fundamental character of industrialization, though some of the
extremist tendencies were modified or abolished. Industrial production rose annually at an average of 9 per cent and, characteris-
tically, the output of capital goods increased at a faster pace than
that of consumer goods and global production. By 1957, gross
industrial production was 89 per cent above that of 1952, while
the output of capital goods had risen 93 per cent. Steel output at
the time surpassed 1 million tons, more than double the amount
available in 1950.

Nonetheless, the need to alleviate previously bred disproportions was responsible for some reallocation of resources for other
sectors, leading to a smaller share for industry: Industrial investments in 1952 constituted 64 per cent of gross investments, but
pre-empted only 36 per cent in 1957. All in all, while considerable
growth was registered during the first decade following the adoption of the First Five-Year Plan, industrial maturity was still on
the far horizon: Only 40 per cent of the gross national product in
1957 originated in industry.

The adjustment of past imbalances and improved decentralization did prepare the ground for the implementation of the Second
Five-Year Plan in 1957. The relatively low levels at which it was

* Among safeguards is the flexible application of the turnover tax, which, in
influencing prices, affects supply and demand. Also, for example, 30 per cent
of all investments in 1960 were allocated by central authorities. Some recent
analyses of the economic system include that of C. Dupont and F. Keesing,
"The Yugoslav Economic System and Instruments of Yugoslav Economic Policy," *Staff Papers* (International Monetary Fund), VIII, No. 1 (November,
1960), while Yugoslav explanations include those of J. Stanovik, "Planning
Through the Market: The Yugoslav Experience," *Foreign Affairs*, XL, No. 2
(January, 1962).

effected and the greater capacity made available by prior reallo-cations permitted significant increments and enabled authorities to declare plan completion in four years. Gross investments were less than planned, but total industrial output increased 69 per cent (the plan scheduled 70 per cent) above 1956 levels, and capital-goods production rose by 84 per cent. The average annual rate of expansion was 14 per cent, thereby raising the share of industry in the gross national product by an estimated 3–5 per cent. Consequently, the Third Five-Year Plan was declared opera-tive in January, 1961.

The unprecedented spurt of industrial growth at the end of the previous decade reinforced Yugoslav confidence in the pursuit of comparable targets under the new plan and encouraged them to legislate extensions of those stimuli that had initially animated the boom. But unanticipated shortfalls and unforeseen difficulties, which leavened serious imbalances during 1961 (the first year of the new plan), spurred Yugoslav authorities into rescinding some of the liberalizing adjustments and reintroducing degrees of cen-tralization.

The current plan has projected industrial investments to be 53 per cent of gross fixed investments, a rise of 3 per cent over past years. Thus primed, industrial production has been scheduled to grow annually at an average of 13 per cent, with continuing em-phasis upon capital goods and with the metallurgical, chemical, and construction branches still retaining top priorities. Greater attention has also been given to the improvement of less advanced regions, e.g., Macedonia and Montenegro. Having raised the econ-omy from the depths of underdevelopment, Yugoslav planners also have striven for greater labor productivity, calling for an average annual rise of 6.4 per cent in per-capita productivity, compared to the 5.4 per cent of the previous plan. Yugoslav op-timism has also reasoned that maintaining the present rate of industrial growth over the next two decades will lift the economy to the level of industrialization currently enjoyed by the more ad-vanced states of Western Europe.

This prognosis, however, immediately met with serious chal-lenges. A sweeping reform of 1960 virtually removed restrictions on wages, apparently in the belief that this measure would stimulate a rise in productivity without unduly disrupting the pattern of growth. In 1961, import restrictions were removed. Both these and related facets of greater liberalization reflected the desire to advance rationality and increase incentives without slowing industrial growth. Toward the end of 1961, it was apparent that serious flaws marred Yugoslav anticipations.

Summarily, this expanded liberalization set loose excessive demand and nurtured a serious inflationary spiral. Projected increases in exports failed to offset the drain caused by increased imports. Nominal wages rose three times faster than per-capita output, but prices spiraled even faster, so that real wages declined sharply. Industrial output plunged: The 1961 increase was only 7 per cent, as compared to more than 15 per cent in 1960 and the planned rate of 12 per cent. The inflationary spiral brought an 18 per cent rise in the cost of living.[20]

As the second year of the new plan evolved, the Yugoslav economy was again faced with a series of fiscal and administrative changes. While new wage and price controls were hastily reintroduced, restrictions on imports were likewise re-established. In addition to the fiscal measures enacted to meet the crisis, authorities also addressed themselves to other reform projects within industry to stabilize a rapid growth and stimulate efficient production; i.e., subdividing an enterprise into smaller units to promote competition, with financial identity and some autonomy being granted to the lower echelons.

At the end of 1962, Yugoslav economic difficulties continue. Tied to the central threads of economic rationality and continuing expansion at relatively rapid rates, the interrelated refinements of recent economic policies prompted by recent deleterious trends appear to include a comprehensive overhaul of the monetary system in partial adjustment to the world economy; re-establishment of tighter controls on credits, wages, and prices to curb inflationary trends; and some changes in the relationship between enterprises and local governmental organs intended to reduce administrative obstacles while encouraging local investments for growth purposes.[21]

Consequently, the flux of economic readjustments continues more than a decade after its start in Yugoslavia, and current developments indicate that the regime itself seems to be in a state of relative uncertainty now that it has been made more sensitively cognizant that decentralization and fiscal liberalization do not offer panaceas. At the present time the pendulum appears to be swinging to some degree of recentralization.[22] Therefore, the drive to industrial maturity and a "planned and free" economy still carries with it as yet unresolved problems that also embody sociopolitical implications. Although the relatively salubrious effects of decentralization and its attendant departure from the previous pattern have been evident, further success in sustaining industrial growth at the desired pace (ideological rationalizations notwithstanding) is contingent upon resolving facets of the ostensible contradiction between governmental planning and the free market.

A. Shares of gross fixed investments for industry

	Years	Per cent
Bulgaria	1949-58	44.9
Czechoslovakia	1949-53	55.0
	1961-65	45.6[a]
East Germany	1951-55	53.8
	1959-65	42.0
Hungary	1950-54	51.8
	1961-65	39.0
Poland	1950-55	45.4
	1961-65	40.1
Rumania	1951-55	57.7
	1960-65	58.8

[a]An announcement was made in 1962 that the Plan had been dropped and that a Seven-Year Plan was to begin in 1964.

B. Average annual rates of growth of gross industrial output (in percentages)
    A=heavy industry   B=light industry

	1951-55	1959	1960	1961	Plan 1962 — 1965		A	B
Bulgaria[a]	10.4	20.5	13.4	9.9	9.9	11.2	—	—
Czechoslovakia	11.2	10.9	11.7	8.9	9.9	9.3	11.2	6.0
East Germany	13.6	12.6	8.3	6.2	—	9.5	10.0	8.5
Hungary[c]	14.9	10.8	13.4	12.0	8.0	8.3	8.7	7.4
Poland	19.1	9.2	11.1	10.5	8.4	8.7	9.5	7.6
Rumania[b][c]	9.8	10.2	16.9	15.6	13.5	13.2	14.1	12.3

[a]10.4 per cent applies to years 1953-58.
[b] 9.8 per cent applies to years 1954-58.
[c]Socialized industry only.

C. Employment and per-capita output in industry (percentage increase over
    previous year)   E=employment   O=output

		1954	1955	1956	1957	1958	1959	1960	1961	1965 (Plan)
Bulgaria	E	6	2.0	8.0	14.7	6.9	17.0	10.4	1.9	
	O	2	4.6	7.0	-.2	5.6	5.9	2.6	4.4	7.6
Czechoslovakia	E	2	2.0	3.0	3.9	3.4	3.5	4.5	3.6	
	O	2	7.9	6.8	5.9	7.4	7.9	6.9	5.1	7.4
East Germany	E	5	—	1.0	3.6	2.1	2.1	.1	—	
	O	6	7.5	10.5	3.9	8.9	10.0	8.2	—	9.2
Hungary	E	4	2.0	—	.8	4.1	5.2	7.0	3.7	
	O	-1	6.1	-10.2	10.4	8.0	4.2	6.0	8.0	5.8
Poland	E	3	5.0	4.0	3.4	1.0	1.8	.5	2.9	
	O	8	6.5	4.6	5.9	8.7	7.4	10.7	7.4	7.0
Rumania	E	4	3.0	2.0	.2	4.0	3.0	4.5	4.0	
	O	3	9.3	8.7	8.2	5.8	7.0	12.0	—	8-9

D. Annual increases in real wages in industry (in percentages)

	1955	1956	1957	1958	1959	1960[a]	1961[a]
Bulgaria	11.4	10.9	4.9	2.9	4.2	8.7	—
Czechoslovakia	3.9	5.7	2.4	2.1	4.6	5.1	2.5
East Germany	5.9	3.7	3.6	4.9	9.2	—	—
Hungary	5.6	7.2	17.6	1.0	4.3	-0.9	1.5
Poland	6.5	11.8	13.2	3.5	3.7	-1.6	3.0
Rumania	—	12.2	—	—	—	—	—

[a]Real wages as reported for the economy as a whole.

E. Monthly earnings in manufacturing industries

	1953	1957	1959	1960	
Bulgaria	588	700	745	793	(lev)
Czechoslovakia	1,100	1,248	1,296	1,338	(koruna)
East Germany	—	469	546	567	(mark)
Hungary	994	1,486	1,551	1,577	(florint)
Poland	1,051	1,578	1,782	1,822	(zloty)

F. Production of pig iron and ferrous alloys (in thousands of metric tons)

	1948	1953	1957	1960
Bulgaria	1	6	54	192
Czechoslovakia[a]	1,645	2,781	3,563	4,696
East Germany	182	1,078	1,663	1,995
Hungary[b]	384	735	837	1,264
Poland[a]	1,134	2,359	3,682	4,563
Rumania[b]	186	448	686	1,014

[a]Excluding ferrous alloys in electric furnaces.
[b]Excluding ferrous alloys.

G. Production of crude steel (in thousands of metric tons)

	1948	1953	1957	1960
Bulgaria	—	13	159	253
Czechoslovakia	2,621	4,366	5,166	6,768
East Germany	305	2,163	2,894	3,337
Hungary	770	1,543	1,375	1,885
Poland	1,955	3,604	5,304	6,681
Rumania	353	717	864	1,806

H. Production of radios and television sets (in thousands)
   R=radio   T=television sets

		1953	1957	1960
Bulgaria	R	22	108	157
	T	—	—	—
Czechoslovakia	R	182	255	230
	T	12	79	263
East Germany	R	729	653	810
	T	38	55	416
Hungary	R	158	454	212
	T	—	6	140
Poland	R	268	646	623
	T	—	16	171
Rumania	R	23	113	167
	T	—	—	—

Sources: United Nations publications.

5. NEW PATTERNS OF TRADE

Jan Wszelaki

This study is largely based upon the official trade statistics issued by the eight East European countries and the Soviet Union. This material is not always complete and, especially in the case of East Germany and Albania, is published with much delay. Hence it has not been possible to collect all information necessary for the discussion of trade in 1960; data pertaining to 1961 are provisional. There are inexplicable discrepancies between data furnished by the Soviet Union and those of other bloc countries, and information on some important fields of trade, such as uranium ore, is not available at all. Despite these drawbacks, the picture that emerges from the available material is clear enough and allows the researcher to present the main features and trends. Yugoslav trade statistics are, on the whole, satisfactory.

To avoid unnecessary repetition, the region comprising Bulgaria, Czechoslovakia, East Germany, Hungary, Poland, and Rumania is often described as "six countries," or "seven countries" or "the area" if Albania is included. Trade with the Soviet Union is discussed on the basis of Soviet data. "National" data pertain to the six or seven countries. Quotations and footnotes are limited to matters of controversy. Figures in tables are rounded and therefore do not always add up to the totals given.

The literature of the subject is limited and dispersed. Apart from the official yearbooks and periodicals, a great deal of information is periodically issued by the United Nations in the *Economic Bulletin for Europe,* published in Geneva. This source, however, must of necessity refrain from discussing the sensitive aspects of the problem. The many Soviet studies are too permeated by propaganda to be accepted as sources of objective information. The only comprehensive book on the trade under examination is Professor Bruno Kiesewetter's *Der Ostblock-Aussenhandel* (Berlin, 1960), which includes hundreds of statistical tables. Among the other writings are studies by Horst Mendershausen, Samuel Pisar, and Curt Zinnemann, all of whom are quoted below, and by Alfred Zauberman. Information may also be found in *East Europe* (New York), in *The World To-day* (London), and in the many pamphlets published by semi official French study centers and by the U.S. Department of Commerce.

Trade Development and Industrial Transformation

Two concurrent basic factors have shaped the present pattern of East European foreign trade. One of them is the gradual structural transformation of Eastern Europe as a whole into a predominantly industrial area. The second, no less important, factor is the continuing Soviet control over the economic policies of the six countries. Because of autonomous economic causes, the first development is irreversible. The second, imposed on the area by the spreading Soviet empire, also seems to be a constant, at least within the foreseeable future.

It is true that, just as the Yugoslavs did in 1948, the Albanian leaders liberated themselves from Soviet control in 1961 without abandoning the Communist system of government. The case of Hungary in 1956 shows that a similar occurrence in any of the six countries directly or indirectly adjacent to the Soviet Union is most improbable. At the outset of the 1960's, it was evident that the two above-mentioned factors will continue to influence the direction and the character of Eastern European trade in the years to come.

Between the two world wars, free East European governments, seeking to modernize their countries, generally promoted industrialization. During World War II, it could easily be forecast that this program would be forcefully promoted regardless of the political system of the area after its liberation, and that, because of war damage and capital shortage, industrialization would involve a large measure of state control and nationalization. After the Communist takeover of the area (including Yugoslavia and East Germany), such a program was ruthlessly implemented, at enormous social cost, through multibillion investments in state-owned industry. The planned structural alteration was by and large realized by the end of the 1950's. East Germany and the Czech part of Czechoslovakia, already in possession of a large industrial capacity prior to 1939, rose to the level of such highly industrialized countries as Belgium or West Germany. The industrial development of Hungary and Poland in 1960 could be compared to that of France before 1939, and Rumania did not lag far behind. The Yugoslav and Bulgarian per-capita industrial output equaled that of Spain. In other words, in so far as industrial development was concerned, the gap which in 1939 separated Eastern Europe—except Eastern Germany and Bohemia—from the advanced countries of Western Europe has perceptibly narrowed and to all evidence will narrow still more in the future.

This transformation inevitably was accompanied by profound changes in the foreign trade of the six countries. Prior to 1939, the preponderantly agrarian parts of Eastern Europe exported their real or apparent surpluses of foodstuffs, fuels, and raw materials; they imported machinery, consumer goods, and basic materials in short local supply. At the end of the 1950's, most local raw materials were no longer available for export. The area is still capable of exporting a limited, and gradually diminishing, volume of fuels, and very little else. On the other hand, because of its expanded industrial capacity, its demand for industrial raw materials has tripled. How to check the further increase of these requirements through local production of substitute materials, such as plastics, synthetic rubber, and synthetic yarns; where to obtain the required metallic ores, metals and minerals, petroleum and petroleum derivatives, cotton, wool, rubber, and other raw materials; and how to pay for all these imports, has become the paramount foreign-trade problem of the six countries. Moreover, they are still faced with the necessity of importing technologically advanced equipment for the steel, chemical, and light industries, which the six countries still cannot—or cannot yet—produce themselves or import from the Soviet Union.

East European trade difficulties are further complicated by the Soviet-imposed collectivization of farming—except in Poland—and its direct consequence, agricultural stagnation. The area's growing population and the increased food requirements of its urban population of more than 45 million have created a demand that can no longer be covered by home production. Despite the fact that food exports from Bulgaria, Hungary, and Rumania still exceed imports, the area as a whole had an adverse trade balance in foodstuffs to the value of about $175 million in 1960: It imported $418 million worth of foodstuffs, especially grains, from the Soviet Union, and about $370 million worth from the West. Trade in foodstuffs can only be balanced in the rare cases of bumper crops extending over the entire area. Yugoslavia has similar problems and is dependent upon imports of American farming surpluses—as is Poland. The shortage developed during a decade when Western Europe, traditionally dependent upon imports of foodstuffs, materially increased her own output of cereals, dairy products, and meat.

The Soviet Union supplies about 40 per cent of joint East European imports of raw materials and foodstuffs—about $2.29 billion worth in 1960, out of a total of $5.63 billion, and much more than 50 per cent if mutual intraregional deliveries are not taken into consideration. These massive imports have resulted in a far-reaching dependence of the six countries on the Soviet Union as their principal supplier and, since imports must be paid for, as their main customer.

Quite apart from the political and military control exercised by the Soviet Union, the fact that it accounts for some 37–40 per cent of the joint trade of the six countries has an immense impact upon their economies. Entire branches of industry have been or are being developed or contracted all over the area because of the changing trade requirements of the big customer. Thus, for example, Bulgaria's horticulture and garment industry are being forcefully extended because of the Soviet demand for fresh vegetables and clothing, while petrochemical industries are being en-

larged in the four northern countries in part because of the growing Soviet surplus of crude oil.

International labor division in industry, and in part, also in agriculture—unheard of in the autarchic Stalinist period—is being
sought by the Soviet bloc in Europe through the instrumentality
of the Council of Mutual Economic Aid, known as CEMA or
COMECON. Relatively inactive until 1954, this body, which includes the Soviet Union and its European dependencies, promotes
the specialization of output in the countries best qualified for a
given type of industrial and farming production. While the Soviet
Union is supposed to produce all types of goods, its European
wards will divide their output of basic and finished products, especially equipment and machinery, in accordance with their resources and skills. The aim is to manufacture these products in
large series and thus at minimal cost. Many hundreds of types
of industrial products have already been allocated to individual
East European countries that are extending—or, inversely, reducing or even relinquishing—their output of specific goods. Thus, for
example, the manufacture of oil-drilling equipment is being concentrated in Rumania, of telephone equipment in Hungary, and of
passenger automobiles in Czechoslovakia; Bulgaria is specializing
in the manufacture of small electric motors, and East Germany
and Poland in large-scale shipbuilding. Surpluses of such products
over the local requirements are delivered within Eastern Europe
and, in particular, to the Soviet Union.

Thus, industrial labor division acts as a stimulant to trade
within the Soviet bloc and even more so to intraregional trade
within Eastern Europe. At its present, initial stage, its main bene-
ficiaries are East Germany and Czechoslovakia, the countries able
to sell the more lucrative specialized equipment, and the Soviet
Union, the principal purchaser of such machinery.

Until the end of the Stalinist era, roughly speaking, the Soviet
Union regarded East European trade with the non-Soviet world
as politically undesirable, and it shrank to a minimum in the early
1950's. This attitude underwent a reversal under Khrushchev.
Provided that its import requirements from Eastern Europe are

fully covered, the Soviet Union encourages sales to Western Europe in exchange for modern plant equipment—an economically justified and necessary trade. Again, since the launching of the Soviet drive in underdeveloped, formerly colonial countries, Eastern Europe is not merely encouraged but in fact forced to sell its merchandise to the "new" African, Asian, and Latin American markets.

The aims of this drive are political. The Soviet Union does not possess sufficient capacity to produce consumer goods for export; moreover, its foreign-trade apparatus is cumbersome and incapable of acting with the required speed. In view of their prewar knowledge of these distant markets and the capacity to manufacture most consumer goods, the six countries can rapidly deliver their various products to the "sensitive" parts of the world. They are also more capable than the Soviet Union of processing the materials they obtain in exchange for their exports. Egypt, Indonesia, and Iraq in the recent past, and Cuba, Ghana, and Guinea in the early 1960's, all of them actively or potentially oriented against the West, have been won at least in part by East European trade and thus indirectly opened to Soviet economic and political penetration.

Dynamics and Commodity Breakdown of Trade

The joint exports and imports of the seven dependent countries represented about 6 per cent of 1960 world trade—that is, more than that of France and the Soviet Union, but less than that of the United Kingdom and West Germany, and about 45 per cent of that of U.S. trade. By European standards it was not very high, especially when it is taken into consideration that some 27 per cent of this turnover was formed by intraregional trade. However, it amounted to some $155 per capita—that is, three times as much as in the Soviet Union. In addition, it showed a strong ascensive tendency.

From a total of $15.5 billion in 1960, the seven countries' joint trade rose to more than $17 billion in 1961—that is, to about 205 per cent of its 1954 volume. As shown in Table 1, the rate of growth was unequally distributed among the individual countries. Not unnaturally, the trade of the less advanced countries—includ-

TABLE 1

DYNAMICS OF FOREIGN TRADE: 1954-61
(in billions of current dollars and percentages)

Country	Turnover 1954 $	Turnover 1960 $	Increase %	Turnover 1961 $	Increase %	Exports 1954 $	Exports 1960 $	Increase %	Exports 1961 $
Albania	.045	[.149]	[231]	—	—	.017	.048	182	—
Bulgaria	.428	1.205	183	1.327	210	.233	.572	145	.661
Czechoslovakia	1.938	3.810	96	4.124	113	1.005	1.994	98	2.120
East Germany	2.376	4.361	84	—	—	1.280	2.191	77	—
Hungary	1.038	1.850	76	2.054	88	.525	.874	67	1.029
Poland	1.773	2.850	59	3.192	80	.831	1.325	59	1.505
Rumania	.688	1.365	98	1.596	132	.350	.717	105	.798
TOTAL	8.286	[23.876]	[87]	—	—	4.241	7.721	82	—
Yugoslavia	.579	1.394	142	1.458	152	.240	.567	136	.557
Soviet Union	6.250	11.191	79	11.712	87	3.125	5.562	78	5.738

Sources: National statistics. Data in brackets are provisional or estimated.

TABLE 2

PLANNED DEVELOPMENT OF FOREIGN TRADE: 1958-65
(in billions of dollars and percentages)

Country	Turnover 1958 $	Planned increase %	Planned 1965 $	Turnover 1960 $	Increase %	Turnover 1961 $	Increase %
Bulgaria	.727	200	2.180	1.205	33	1.327	41
Czechoslovakia	2.870	90	5.450	3.810	36	4.124	49
East Germany	3.560	70	6.050	4.361	32	—	—
Hungary[a]	1.310	77	2.320	1.850	53	2.054	73
Poland	2.286	80	4.115	2.851	21	3.192	50
Rumania	.950	120	2.090	1.365	36	1.596	57
TOTAL	11.703	90	22.205	15.442	34	—	—
Soviet Union	8.647	50	12.970	11.191	59	11.721	71

[a]The originally planned 90 per cent increase in Hungarian foreign trade, to $2.46 billion in 1965, was subsequently reduced to 77 per cent and $2.32 billion.

ing Yugoslavia—was growing more rapidly than that of the more mature ones, though the rate of expansion of Czechoslovak trade (up 210 per cent from 1954 to 1961) was indeed remarkable. The slower Hungarian performance could be explained in the light of the temporary retrogression of the Hungarian economy in 1956–57, while the moderate development of Polish trade was a consequence of Poland's relatively high self-sufficiency in such primary goods as hard fuels, timber, and most foodstuffs.

Judging by the 1961 achievements, the area's target of an average 90 per cent trade increase between 1958 and 1965 (see Table 2) may be expected to be realized as planned, perhaps even ahead of time. A reservation may be made with respect to East Germany, whose economy was subject to critical shortages and stresses after the Berlin events of 1961. However, the large emergency credits the Soviet Government granted that country early in 1962 are supposed to ensure an uninterrupted supply of raw materials and foodstuffs and thus result in a further extension of East German industrial output for export. In the rest of the area, growing shortages of basic materials, the constantly increasing availability of exportable industrial products, and the predictable extension of intraregional trade in machinery may well result in an average annual foreign-trade increase of 10 per cent.

Tables 3 and 4 show the distribution of East European trade by four major groups of commodities according to COMECON classification. Some of the figures quoted are merely close approximations. However, the picture that emerges from the tables is clear enough. In 1960, the East European area, excluding Albania, had a net balance of more than 1 billion dollars in machinery trade alone, and almost 2 billion in finished industrial goods. This was a characteristic feature of areas with a high level of industrial development. In the same year, the six countries' adverse trade balance in basic goods and foodstuffs reached about $2.3 billion.

The tables confirm the industrial character of the East German and Czechoslovak national economies. It is striking to note that the machinery exports of East Germany, a country with 17 million inhabitants, equaled those of the Soviet Union, the world's second

TABLE 3

PERCENTAGE DISTRIBUTION OF EAST EUROPEAN TRADE, BY GROUPS OF COMMODITIES

Commodity	Albania 1959	Bulgaria 1959	Czecho-slovakia 1960	East Germany 1960	Hungary 1961	Poland 1961	Rumania 1960	Yugo-slavia 1960	Soviet Union 1960
Exports									
Machinery	0	12.1	45.1	48.4	36.6	28.0	17	9.9	20.5
Raw materials	[83]	39.7	29.3	32.1	22.9	39.1	[67]	57.6	63.7
Foodstuffs	—	33.7	5.2	3.5	19.4	21.5	—	28.1	13.0
Consumer goods	—	14.5	20.4	15.0	21.1	11.4	—	4.4	2.8
Finished industrial goods	[1]	26.6	65.5	63.4	57.7	39.4	[20]	14.3	23.3
Primary and basic goods	[99]	73.4	34.5	36.6	42.3	60.6	[80]	85.7	76.7
Imports									
Machinery	47	37.2	21.7	12.3	24.5	29.1	[35]	28.5	29.8
Raw materials	37	42.5	53.0	58.8	59.8	49.7	—	56.7	42.6
Foodstuffs	2	7.8	21.9	23.6	10.8	15.3	—	8.1	11.5
Consumer goods	14	12.5	3.3	5.3	4.9	5.9	—	6.6	17.7
Finished industrial goods	61	49.7	25.0	17.6	29.4	35.0	[38]	35.1	46.9
Primary and basic goods	39	50.3	75.0	82.4	70.6	65.0	[62]	65.8	53.1

Source: National and Soviet yearbooks and publications.

Figures in brackets are estimates based upon various sources and indications. According to the COMECON goods classification. machinery includes industrial equipment, industrial and office precision goods and instruments, and transportation means. Raw materials include basic semimanufactured commodities, such as rolled steel, tubes, cable, chemicals; and timber, coal, and oil derivatives. Foodstuffs include beverages and cigarettes, but not tobacco. Industrial consumer goods include textile yarns and fabrics, clothing, footwear, furniture, medicines, cosmetics, bicycles, cameras, and sundry house appliances, as well as publications.

industrial power, with a population of 210 million. The tables also show that the Hungarian economy is assuming an industrial character, as is Poland. In 1961, Polish machinery exports reached 28 per cent of all exports and amounted to $421 million—i.e., four times as much as in 1954, when they amounted to $104 million; for the first time in history, Poland's exports of finished industrial products exceeded her imports. This in itself was a milestone in her economic development. Finally, the tables show that in this sector Rumania and Bulgaria as well as Yugoslavia are far behind the area's four northern countries, and that they cannot achieve industrial self-sufficiency before the end of the present decade.

Basic data pertaining to the division of East European trade among the world's several geographical and economic areas are presented in Table 5. The reader will observe the general stability of this division between 1958 and 1960. The two more important trends are the absolute and percentual growth of intraregional trade and a stagnation in trade with the four Asian Communist countries. More detailed comments on East European

TABLE 4

EAST EUROPEAN TRADE IN FINISHED INDUSTRIAL GOODS: 1960
(in millions of dollars and percentages)

Country	Machinery and Equipment			All Finished Industrial Goods		
	Exports	Imports	Balance	Exports	Imports	Balance
Bulgaria	70	259	-181	104	297	-193
Czechoslovakia	870	394	476	1,264	454	810
East Germany	1,139	250	889	1,489	321	1,168
Hungary	331	261	70	490	310	180
Poland	325	403	- 78	474	485	- 9
Rumania	122	226	-104	143	254	-111
TOTAL	2,857	1,793	1,072	3,964	2,121	1,845
Per cent of total	38.0	22.6	—	52.7	27.0	—
Yugoslavia	56	236	-180	71	290	-219
Soviet Union	1,141	1,675	-534	1,302	2,658	-1,356

Note: Figures for Bulgaria, East Germany, and Rumania are the author's estimates.

trade with the world's six major divisions are also presented in
Table 5.

Trade with the Soviet Union

In 1960, the commercial turnover with Eastern Europe con-

TABLE 5

REGIONAL DISTRIBUTION OF EAST EUROPEAN TRADE: 1958-60
(in billions of dollars and percentages)

East European trade	1958 $	1958 %	1959 $	1959 %	1960 Provisional $	1960 Provisional %
Intraregional	3.020	25.8	3.626	26.7	4.245	27.3
With the U.S.S.R.	4.340	37.0	5.443	40.2	5.807	37.5
Total—COMECON countries	7.360	62.8	9.069	66.9	10.052	64.8
With Asian socialist countries	.770	6.6	.793	5.8	.770	5.0
Total—intrabloc trade	8.130	69.3	9.862	72.7	10.822	69.7
With Yugoslavia	.230	2.0	.197	1.5	.265	1.7
Total—all socialist countries	8.360	71.3	10.060	74.2	11.087	71.5
With the rest of the world	3.360	28.7	3.500	25.8	4.413[b]	28.5
Of this: with industrial countries[a]	2.445	20.9	2.620	19.3	2.946	19.1
with primary producing countries[a]	.915	7.8	.880	6.5	1.227[b]	8.0
GRAND TOTAL	11.720	100.0	13.560	100.0	15.500	100.0

Sources: National statistics and Economic Bulletin for Europe.
[a] The Asian socialist countries are Mainland China, Mongolia, North Korea,
and North Vietnam. Trade with industrial countries includes that between East
and West Germany, and that with Western Europe, Japan, the United States,
and Canada. However, primary producing countries include Greece and Turkey.
[b] Figures of the Value Series, U.S. Department of Commerce for 1960. According to this source, East European trade with the non-Communist world
added to $4.173 billion in 1960. The provisional figure derived from the national
statistics seems more complete. Should it be accepted, East European trade
with primary producing countries would amount to $1.467 billion in 1960, or 9.4
per cent.

stituted 53.1 per cent of the entire Soviet trade; it rose to 54.9 per cent in 1961. The two major Soviet trade partners were East Germany and China, which, however, was surpassed by Czechoslovakia in 1961 and also by Poland in 1962. Conversely, the turnover with the Soviet Union represented 37.5 per cent of the entire East European trade in 1960, and 51 per cent of the seven dependent countries' trade outside of their mutual exchange of goods. The Soviet Union was by far the most important trade partner of every East European country.

The striking figures of the trade in question, presented in more detail in Tables 6–9, testify to the extreme importance it has come to play in the economic relationship between the Soviet Union and Eastern Europe and to the significant degree of their economic interdependence. Because of the various developments within the Soviet bloc in Europe and the control the Soviet Union exercises over central planning, the two areas have gradually become economically complementary.

Let us first consider the economic relationship from the East European point of view. If at present the area's industry were cut off from Soviet deliveries of basic materials, a large part of it would come to a standstill. Even if such materials could be imported from other sources—an undertaking that, for a variety of reasons, would be very difficult—many industrial plants would have to close if the Soviet Union discontinued its purchases of the six countries' industrial products. Within the six-year period 1954 to 1960, the Soviet Union delivered to Eastern Europe 23.67 million tons of grain, 1.61 million tons of cotton, 30.34 million tons of oil and oil products, 68.51 million tons of iron ore, 8.39 million tons of rolled steel, and 1.29 million tons of nonferrous metals (copper, zinc, lead, tin, and aluminum), in addition to correspondingly large volumes of timber, coal, phosphate rock, and other basic raw materials. Moreover, within the same period, the Soviet Union delivered to the seven countries $1.78 billion worth of machinery, mainly heavy equipment for metallurgic, basic chemical, and machine-making plants. Scores of such plants in Poland, Rumania, and Bulgaria could not have been built without Soviet equipment (sometimes sold on credit) and Soviet technical aid.

TABLE 6

SOVIET TRADE WITH EASTERN EUROPE: 1960 AND 1961
(in millions of dollars and percentages)

Country	Exports 1960	Exports 1961	Imports 1960	Imports 1961	Turnover 1960	Turnover 1961	Per cent of all Soviet trade 1960	Per cent of all Soviet trade 1961	Balance 1960	Balance 1961
Albania	44	20	24	22	67	42	0.6	0.3	20	− 2
Bulgaria	329	357	299	326	628	682	5.6	5.8	30	31
Czechoslovakia	632	653	652	698	1,284	1,350	11.5	11.5	− 20	− 45
East Germany	1,052	1,209	929	876	1,981	2,085	17.7	17.7	123	333
Hungary	311	359	248	327	559	686	5.0	5.8	63	32
Poland	491	531	387	477	878	1,008	7.8	8.5	104	54
Rumania	261	291	280	341	541	632	4.8	5.4	− 19	− 50
TOTAL	3,120	3,420	2,819	3,067	5,938	6,485	53.0	54.9	301	353
TOTAL: 1959	2,950		2,519		5,470		52.4		431	
Per cent of trade: 1961	57.1		52.3				54.7			
Per cent of trade: 1960	56.1		50.1				53.1			
Per cent of trade: 1959	54.2		49.9				52.4			

Source: Soviet statistics.

Since Soviet exports to the seven countries are constantly mentioned and extolled in the Soviet and national press for rendering

TABLE 7

SOVIET TRADE WITH EASTERN EUROPE, COMMODITY BREAKDOWN
(in billions of dollars and percentages)

	Exports			
	1960		1961	
Commodity	$	%	$	%
Machinery	.414	13.3	.459	13.4
Consumer goods	.075	2.4	.060	1.7
Total—finished industrial goods	.489	15.7	.519	15.1
Fuels	.413	13.2	.486	14.2
Ores and metals	.791	25.4	.874	25.6
Other raw materials	.557	17.8	.622	18.2
Foodstuffs	.526	16.9	.429	12.5
Total—primary and basic goods	2.287	73.3	2.411	70.5
Goods accounted for	2.776	89.0	2.930	85.6
Goods not accounted for	.344	11.1	.490	14.4
GRAND TOTAL	3.120	100.0	3.420	100.0
	Imports			
Machinery	1.209	42.9	1.245	40.6
Industrial consumer goods	.500	17.7	.569	18.5
Total—finished industrial goods	1.709	60.6	1.814	59.1
Fuels	.216	7.7	.198	6.5
Ores and metals	.196	6.9	.218	7.1
Other basic materials	.247	8.8	.303	9.9
Foodstuffs	.170	6.0	.252	8.2
Total—primary and basic goods	.829	29.4	.971	31.7
Goods accounted for	2.538	90.0	2.785	90.8
Goods not accounted for	.280	9.9	.281	9.2
GRAND TOTAL	2.818	100.0	3.066	100.0

fraternal aid to the "younger" members of the bloc, their scope is easily ascertainable. The reverse side of the picture, discussed only in little-read special publications, is not so well known, but it is equally impressive. To offset the figures quoted above, it may be sufficient to cite the following selected Soviet imports from Eastern Europe in 1955–60: 20,167 metal-cutting machine tools (78 per cent of all Soviet imports in this category); 27,095 miles of power cable (63 per cent); 7,663 railroad coaches (98 per cent); $1.22 billion worth of ships (73 per cent); and 54 million pairs of leather shoes (71 per cent). During this six-year period, Eastern Europe delivered to the Soviet Union machinery, equipment, and means of transportation worth $5.22 billion (Soviet data), i.e., three times the value of machinery imports from the Soviet Union, and almost exactly three-quarters of all Soviet machinery imports during that period. Finally, on the basis of Soviet statistics, it may be assumed that Soviet imports of uranium ore from all the East European countries except Bulgaria may well

TABLE 8

SOVIET TRADE IN MACHINERY WITH EASTERN EUROPE: 1955-61
(in billions of dollars)

	Exports	Imports	Balance
Albania	.115	—	.115
Bulgaria	.488	.173	.315
Czechoslovakia	.367	1.413	−1.076
East Germany	.184	3.249	−3.065
Hungary	.256	.769	− .513
Poland	.485	.685	− .200
Rumania	.339	.139	.200
TOTAL	2.234	6.428	−4.224
1955	.304	.733	− .429
1956	.218	.656	− .438
1957	.221	.714	− .493
1958	.248	.862	− .614
1959	.368	1.040	− .672
1960	.415	1.209	− .795
1961	.459	1.245	− .786
TOTAL	2.233	6.459	−4.227

Source: Soviet statistics of foreign trade.

TABLE 9

SOVIET TRADE WITH EASTERN EUROPE
COMMODITY BREAKDOWN: 1960

Commodity	Exports	Imports
Cereals (in thousands of tons)	4,910	101
Butter "	36	0.3
Meat and products "	59	4
Sugar "	0	219
Tobacco "	0	40
Fruit and vegetables (in millions of dollars)	0	66
Cigarettes (in billions of units)	0	6
Cotton (in thousands of tons)	300	0
Natural and synthetic rubber "	47	25
Coal and coke "	9,381	5,234
Oil and oil products "	9,100	3,247
Ferrous ores "	15,526	0
Pig iron "	927	0
Rolled steel "	2,080	85
Steel tubes "	129	273[a]
Nonferrous metals "	215	47
Cement "	0	797
Sawn wood (in thousands of steres)	1,426	265
Uranium ore (in millions of dollars)	0	212[a]
Power cable (in kilometers)	799	7,963
Complete plant equipment (in millions of dollars)	76	0
Metallurgic equipment "	7	34
Hoisting equipment "	0	40
Generating and electrical equipment "	18	88
Food-industry equipment "	2	110
Cement-industry equipment "	0	65
Light-industry equipment "	6	23
Chemical-industry equipment "	4	61
Farming equipment "	31	7
Tools and instruments "	8	52
Ships and equipment "	0	274
Rolling stock "	0	190
Automobiles and equipment "	62	47
Tractors (in units)	4,549	0
Metal-working machine tools	1,023	6,925
Cotton fabrics (in millions of meters)	37	40
Woolen fabrics "	0	10
Linen fabrics "	0	8
Clothing (in millions of dollars)	0	180
Furniture "	0	64
Medicines "	3	21
Leather shoes (in millions of pairs)	0	15
Sewing machines (in thousands of units)	0	208
Television sets "	103	0
Watches "	3,760	0

[a]Estimated figures.

have amounted to $1.38 billion during the six years in question.*

In connection with Table 7, it should be added that Eastern Europe's net balance in industrial consumer goods amounted to $425 million in 1960 (exports, $500; imports, $75 million, according to Soviet data), and, in 1961, to $509 million (exports, $569 million; imports, $60 million), while her adverse balance in foodstuffs, fuels, metals, and the remaining raw and basic materials (such as cotton, timber, chemicals) amounted to $384 million, $197 million, $595 million, and $310 million, respectively.

Thus, the conclusion must be drawn that, during the 1950's, Eastern Europe has become a workshop processing Soviet basic materials into finished goods for export to the Soviet Union, China, and noncommitted countries of interest to Soviet foreign policy. Whether this development has been planned or could be foreseen in 1945, when the Kremlin imposed its rule on Eastern Europe, may be doubted and is at present immaterial. What is material is the fact that the area's present economic role vis-à-vis the Soviet Union has been the outcome of several concurrent, partly autonomous, processes whose joint effect can only increase in the years to come.

The ratio of population, natural resources, and political power between the Soviet Union and Eastern Europe being what it is, the trade between them is of lesser significance to the Soviet Union than vice versa. It would be a gross error, however, to underestimate its significance. Generally speaking, the six countries have assumed, or more properly have been assigned, the task of supplying the Soviet economy with a large part of its requirements of ships and rolling stock; of equipment for several important sectors of Soviet industry, especially the food-processing, textile, cement, and chemical industries ($1.01 billion worth of equipment deliveries for these industries in 1955–60, Soviet data); and of most finished consumer goods (see Table 9). Endowed with a surplus of most raw and basic materials, the Soviet Union is able to obtain these and other products from Eastern

---

* $131 million in 1955; $231 million in 1956; $301 million in 1957; $287 million in 1958; $216 million in 1959; and $212 million in 1960. The annual value fluctuations reflect the increase of the world price of uranium ore since 1957, as well as the gradual exhaustion of East European, especially Czech, ore deposits.

Europe on barter—i.e., without spending foreign currency—and to reduce the allocation of capital for the manufacture of these products at home. This, in turn, enables it to concentrate its investments and skilled manpower on the extension of industrial branches of critical importance for its world position, such as heavy and precise-goods industry, and the production of rockets and other ultramodern armaments. Were it not for the services rendered it by Eastern Europe, the Soviet Union would have to reduce some of its world power activities, such as space exploration. The advantage of possessing dependencies that, in a sense, can be described as industrial colonies, is even more evident in light of the conditions presented in the next section of this study.

Pricing in Trade with the Soviet Union

An analysis of Soviet commerce with Eastern Europe would be incomplete without an inquiry into the terms of this trade. What are the prices at which the Soviet Union sells its products to Eastern Europe, and vice versa?

The study of this all-important problem has been possible since the publication of Soviet and national foreign trade statistics was resumed after the blackout of the Stalinist era. On the basis of this public data it has been established conclusively that the Soviet Union has been systematically overcharging Eastern Europe for most of its primary and basic goods. Scores of identical or comparable commodities are sold to Eastern Europe at substantially higher prices than to Western Europe and other parts of the free world. In 1958, the average difference between the two sets of prices—international prices in the sales to the West and inflated prices in the sales to Eastern Europe—amounted to 11.2 per cent, based on the joint value of 48 comparable commodities sold to Eastern Europe and constituting over 60 per cent of all Soviet exports to that area. In 1960, the same ratio with respect to fifty-three comparable commodities reached 20.6 per cent. Between 1957 and 1960, Eastern Europe had to overpay for her imports from the Soviet Union by $1 billion. Detailed figures pertaining to this discrimination are shown in Tables 10 and 11.

The validity of this calculation, and indeed of the entire method of studying the Soviet Union's flexible pricing policy, has been

TABLE 10

PRICES CHARGED BY THE SOVIET UNION FOR FORTY-ONE BASIC COMMODITIES SOLD TO EASTERN EUROPE: 1958-60
(The average price charged to non-Communist countries equals 100.)

Commodity	1958	Price 1959	1960
Wheat†	105	120	118
Rye	110	105	131
Barley	121	114	127
Oats	114	113	104
Maize	114	98	118
Meat, fresh	—	—	114
Butter*	—	71	90
Roundwood	134	136	131
Softwood timber*	121	132	117
Cellulose	145	143	136
Cotton†	103	153	129
Flax	124	153	129
Coal*	120	142	146
Anthracite	116	120	157
Coke*	146	155	158
Crude oil†	142	167	163
Gasoline*	99	97	118
Kerosene	117	163	123
Fuel oil	145	143	153
Diesel fuel*	128	124	144
Lubricants	241	228	115
Iron ore†	78	93	95
Manganese ore	97	119	117
Chrome ore	123	152	176
Pig iron*	108	154	140
Rolled steel†	137	168	137
Zinc	134	101	94
Lead	136	160	136
Tin	107	98	91
Aluminum	121	117	112
Asbestos	107	146	152
Apatite concentrates	100	134	106
Ammonia saltpeter	124	135	153
Synthetic rubber	—	—	100
Tractors*	212	152	144
Trucks	70	53	66
Passenger automobiles*	95	118	114
Bicycles	111	130	127
Television sets	120	147	132
Watches	—	—	99
Cotton fabrics*	305	281	286

Sources: Soviet foreign trade yearbooks for 1958-60.

Note: The table includes all Soviet commodities whose sales to Eastern Europe exceeded $5 million in any year under consideration. Commodities whose sales exceeded $25 million are marked with an asterisk, and those that exceeded $100 million with a dagger.

Data for fourteen lesser Soviet commodities, whose sales to Eastern Europe did not reach $5 million in any year under consideration, have been omitted from the table so as to make it simpler. Average prices of these commodities were as follows in 1960: meat preserves, 125; crab preserves, 98; fodders, 122; newsprint, 120; plywood, 145; hemp, 220; naphthalene, 56; benzol, 99; paraffin, 109; sulfur, 185; potash salts, 105; superphosphate, 259; motorcycles, 70; and cameras, 42.

challenged on several grounds. There is no proof, the critics say, that different prices do not reflect quality differences. Such an assumption can be dismissed, for there is no economic explanation why the relatively poor Eastern part of the Continent should buy grain, cotton, timber, oil products, metals, etc., of a quality the rich free part of the Continent cannot afford. The supposition that there exist superior and inferior qualities of basic Soviet export goods should not be taken seriously, for in fact they are highly standardized.

Another hypothesis is that, although the Soviet Union is over-pricing its East European exports, the prima facie losses of Eastern Europe may be offset by the low prices it pays for Soviet machinery and equipment. Again, it is entirely possible, the critics continue, that the prices the Soviet Union pays for its imports

TABLE 11

NET OVERCHARGING IN SOVIET EXPORTS TO EASTERN EUROPE: 1957-60
(in millions of current dollars)

	1957	1958	1959	1960	1958-60	1957-60
A. Per Country						
Albania	—	1.5	1.5	2.5	5	—
Bulgaria	—	24	18	34	66	—
Czechoslovakia	—	25	68	75	168	—
East Germany	—	69	137	147	352	—
Hungary	—	25	36	28	88	—
Poland	—	10	52	55	117	—
Rumania	—	23	40	34	96	—
TOTAL	104	177.5	352.5	375.5	892	1,098.7
B. Per Groups of Commodities						
Foodstuffs (ten items)	—	16	30	55	101	—
Fuels and derivatives (twelve items)	—	68	116	128	312	—
Ores and metals (nine items)	—	47	130	101	279	—
Raw materials of vegetable origin	—	24	74	67	165	—
Minerals and ferti-lizers (six items)	—	20	9	9	44	—
Industrial goods (eight items)	—			16		—

from Eastern Europe may be inflated in proportion to its export prices. It is difficult to argue for or against the first of these assumptions, for nothing is known about the price structure of the machinery trade between the two areas. On the other hand, an American economist has proved that price discrimination with respect to Eastern Europe prevailed also in Soviet imports from that area in 1955–58. *

It should be conceded that the problem with all its ramifications has not yet been sufficiently examined. In the absence of such an analysis, the weight of evidence supports the thesis that the Soviet Union takes advantage of its monopolistic position and its superior power to impose unfair prices on the dependent bloc countries.

The validity of this thesis has recently been recognized in an important official publication.† This is by no means a trifling issue. It is enough to juxtapose the prima facie losses on East European imports from the Soviet Union and the balance of Soviet-East European trade to understand the importance of this pricing for the economic development of Eastern Europe. During the six years 1955–60, the net Soviet balance in the trade in question reached $1.43 billion, according to Soviet statistics (much less according to national data). In the same period, net overpayments for imports by the seven countries amounted to about $1.32 billion. If the Soviet Union had charged Eastern Europe the same prices as she did for exports to West Germany, the United Kingdom, etc., her net trade balance with Eastern Europe would have

* According to Horst Mendershausen, "The Terms of Soviet-Satellite Trade: A Broadened Analysis," *The Review of Economics and Statistics* (Harvard University) May, 1960, the Soviet Union underpaid its imports from Eastern Europe, of such commodities for which comparison could be made, on average by 13 per cent in 1955, 22 per cent in 1956, 21 per cent in 1957, and 20 per cent in 1958. On a basis of comparison somewhat different from that adopted by the writer, Mendershausen has calculated that the net overpayment by Eastern Europe on imports from the Soviet Union amounted to the equivalent of $149 million in 1955, $132 million in 1956, $145 million in 1957, and $177 million in 1958. If these figures are accepted, East Europe's entire prima facie loss on such imports would total $1.32 billion in 1955–60.

† "Eastern European countries are compelled to pay the Soviet Union higher prices for comparable goods available outside the bloc, and to accept lower prices for goods which they can sell more advantageously in the West " (Samuel Pisar, *A New Look at Trade Policy Toward the Communist Bloc,* Congress of the United States, Joint Economic Committee [Washington, D.C.: Government Printing Office, November, 1961], p. 58.)

been limited to a comparably insignificant total. Things being what they are, Eastern Europe is faced with an enormous effort in settling her accumulated trade deficit through increased exports to the Soviet Union.

Intraregional Trade

Intraregional trade—that is, the seven dependent countries' mutual exports and imports—amounted to about 30 per cent of their entire foreign trade in the early 1950's, declined subsequently to about 25 per cent and, as shown in Table 5, rose to more than 27 per cent in 1960. Its notable increase in absolute figures, from $3.02 billion in 1958 to $4.25 billion in 1960, was primarily due to the constantly growing turnover in finished industrial goods, especially machinery. This in turn was the effect of the division of labor that was gradually being extended over many branches of industrial production. To illustrate this development: Czechoslovakia is gradually curtailing her output of many relatively simple industrial goods, concentrating on producing heavy and precise machinery, and imports such products as freight cars, small electric engines, and heavy chemicals from the less developed members of the bloc—for instance, Bulgaria, a newcomer in the industrial field.

Although intraregional turnover in raw materials is declining, for all countries seek to process them at home, it tends to increase in semimanufactured goods. The sulphur shortage has been alleviated, and that of copper may be alleviated in the future thanks to Czech and East German assistance in opening newly discovered Polish deposits; also, Rumania will soon become a major supplier of cellulose, another material in short supply.

Pricing difficulties do not as a rule arise in intraregional trade, for the bargaining power of the six major countries is about equal and none of them can impose unfair prices upon another. Because of this, and for other local reasons, the further extension of mutual trade lies in the interest of all countries concerned.

Trade with China

The seven countries' trade with Mainland China rose to over 6 per cent of their total trade in 1959, but it has been receding since, mainly because of the Chinese economic depression and the increasing shortage of Chinese export goods. Apart from the ideological ties that until recently linked Eastern Europe with China, the Chinese market, a source of supply of soy beans, industrial oils, and especially tungsten and molybdenum, has been of interest to several of the countries. The Soviet Union is short of these metals so necessary for the production of fine steels, which, because of embargoes, cannot be easily purchased in the West. Almost all items exported to China are industrial goods, mainly industrial equipment. Sales of such equipment in 1955–60 amounted to about $1.15 billion, a large total in comparison to the $2.2 billion worth of Chinese machinery imported from the Soviet Union during those years.

Despite these mutual economic advantages, and the expectation that China will develop into one of the largest importing markets in the world, East European trade with China has been relatively inactive. The main reason for this is China's increasing inability to balance her trade with Eastern Europe. As shown in Table 12, her deficit in this trade amounted to $288 million in 1955–60 (Chinese data; much higher, according to national statistics). This total superimposes itself upon a much larger deficit incurred by China during the first part of the 1950's, so that the joint total may well have exceeded $1 billion. To this estimated figure the cost of transportation of goods from and to China by the area's ships, mainly Polish, should be added. It is fairly clear that, after the loosening of the initial ideological affinity between the two areas, East European countries show little disposition to grant China any more credit.

Trade with the Non-Communist World

Most of East European trade with the non-Communist world is economically motivated. Despite their present efforts to replace the various raw materials by substitutes, the economic development of the six countries requires and will continue to require massive imports of commodities that cannot be produced or are in short supply within the Sino-Soviet bloc. The principal imports are cotton ($150 million in 1960), wool ($97 million), heavy hides ($64 million), natural rubber ($80 million), and copper ($43

million). To satisfy the minimum requirements some foodstuffs
must be imported ($371 million in 1960, including $127 million
worth of grain, $31 million worth of fish, and $42 million of coffee,
cocoa, and spices). East Germany must import much steel from
West Germany. Finally, the area's planned industrial extension
can hardly be implemented without the importation of modern
plant equipment ($313 million). According to the U.S. Depart-
ment of Commerce, all such imports from the West amounted to
$2.18 billion in 1960 and $2.38 billion in 1961—in fact somewhat
more, for these data are not all-inclusive.

These imports must be paid for, even if they are bought on
credit. They were compensated in 1960 by sales of foodstuffs
($468 million, including $266 million worth of meat and dairy and
$58 million worth of sugar), timber (97 million), coal and oil
products ($317 million), fabrics, clothing, and footwear ($165
million), metal manufactures ($164 million), and other goods.
Exports of $300 million worth of machinery practically equaled

TABLE 12

CHINA'S TRADE WITH EASTERN EUROPE: 1955-60
(in millions of current dollars)

	1955	1956	1957	1958	1959	1960	1955-60
Turnover	465	500	534	589	664	601	3,353
Exports	224	235	256	264	293	261	1,533
Imports	241	264	279	325	371	340	1,820
Balance	−18	−29	−23	−61	−78	−79	−288
Per cent of exports	17	15	16	14	14	13	
Per cent of imports	18	19	21	19	16	14	
Per cent of imports from the U.S.S.R.	32	36	51	51	39	32	
Chinese machinery imports from U.S.S.R.	229	304	252	318	597	504	2,204
Estimated machinery imports from Eastern Europe	168	176	192	198	220	196	1,150

Source: Curt Zinnemann, "Rotchina's Wirtschafts- und Finanzlage," Ost-
Probleme (Bonn), No. 22, 1961.
Note: The third part of the table is computed from the above source and
Soviet data on the assumption that machinery constitutes 75 per cent of all
Chinese imports from Eastern Europe.

imports. Total exports amounted to at least $2.12 billion in 1960 and $2.27 billion in 1961.

Two-thirds of this trade was with the sixteen leading industrial countries of the non-Communist world, the rest with the remaining ones, which, for the purpose of this study, will be considered as producers of primary goods. Basically, Eastern Europe imports machinery from the first group and raw materials from the second, directly or indirectly. Conversely, the area sells foodstuffs, fuels, and basic materials to industrial nations, and industrial products to primary producers. North American sales of grain and other farming surplus commodities to Poland (and Yugoslavia), and West German sales of coal and steel to East Germany, as well as increasing Czech sales of industrial products to Western Europe and several countries' sales of coal, sugar, and cement to some primary producers, are the few deviations from the pattern, which has come to resemble West European trade with non-European countries.

Theoretically, the area's imports from the free world are susceptible to very great extension, for its requirements of both primary goods and modern equipment are constantly growing. However, these potentialities are strictly limited by the area's export capacities, which are increasing only gradually. Moreover, the bulk of the area's exports—those to industrial Western Europe— may run into great difficulties in the near future.

Trade with the Common Market

Stimulated by the increasing affluence and the growing import capacity of industrial Western Europe, the area's trade kept developing at a rapid rate between the late 1950's and 1961. West European equipment was often sold on credit, while the area's products were usually paid for in cash. The resulting net balance in foreign currency allowed the area to import many critically needed raw materials, such as rubber, wool, and copper, either directly from Malaya, Australia, and Rhodesia, whose imports from Eastern Europe were insignificant, or indirectly from Great Britain.

This pattern of trade, shown in Table 13, was being imperiled, however, by the gradual implementation of the Rome Treaty. Custom duties were already halved within the European Economic Community in 1962, and were supposed to disappear entirely in 1967. The scope of the Community was extended in 1962 through the admission of Greece and most former French- and Belgian-controlled African states as associate members. Negotiations were held, or expected to be held, with many other European countries with a view to their joining the community. Should this materialize, the self-sufficiency of the enlarged Common Market in foodstuffs and fuels, not to speak of industrial products, would leave little room for the import of duty-paying East European commodities and installations.

Communist regimes have long believed that the Common Market would never come into existence. Stalin assured them in his last work that European "imperialists" would rather fight than unite, and ranking Soviet theoreticians kept prophesying the doom of the West European economy. As late as 1962, the East was confident that France and Germany would never agree on the reduction of agricultural duties. When they did, the Communist press accused the Common Market countries of economic aggression which, the readers were told, would be met by an organized defense of freedom-loving nations, etc. Tito angrily spoke of the duty of neutral countries to resist the imperialist machinations.

These threats and accusations were symptoms of a profound concern. The peril for Eastern Europe was not immediate, but it was drawing nearer. In 1962, East European exports to France and the Benelux countries began to meet with difficulties, especially after the Common Market introduced a new system restrictively regulating the imports of most farm products—the goods the Common Market had been purchasing in large quantities in Eastern Europe. To cite one example, the reduction by one-half of the duty on tobacco, granted Greece in 1962, was expected to result in a gradual elimination from the Common Market of Bulgarian tobacco, the most important Bulgarian export item.

The reduction of Eastern European and Yugoslav exports to the Common Market and, in the near future, probably also to its potential new members, must automatically lead to the reduction of imports not only from Western Europe but also from the rest of the non-Communist world. East European long-term economic planning was based on the assumption, among other factors, that trade with Western Europe would continue to increase. If this premise proves wrong, the ambitious planned rate of economic growth will have to be reduced, and so will the planned rate of increase of living standards. The electrification of Eastern Europe, its planned automobile production, and some branches of the chemical and clothing industry may be particularly affected by the reduced supply of imported machinery and raw materials.

At this writing, however, it is difficult to predict with any precision the future of the trade in question, for the further development of the European Economic Community is still contingent on many unforeseeable political and economic factors. Eastern Europe is not yet in real difficulty so long as the United Kingdom, Austria, and the three Scandinavian countries do not belong to the Common Market. It can, to a certain extent, count upon the pressure, within the Common Market, of West German and other industrial firms that have been manufacturing modern equipment for sale in the Soviet bloc. Such business groups are interested in the continuation of trade with the bloc, and thus in the maintenance of imports from Eastern Europe. Negotiations between the several countries, perhaps even acting as a bloc, and the European Economic Community will have to occur sooner or later, and the issues of common interest will then be discussed. Yet in such negotiations, the Community's bargaining power would greatly exceed that of Eastern Europe, for while the latter's trade with the West is a matter of vital interest, this is not the case with the Community.

None of the recently advanced defensive alternatives open to Eastern Europe seems satisfactory under the circumstances prevailing in 1962. An attempt to organize the neutral states against the Common Market is difficult to conceive of and would not solve the problem. The present plans for further tightening the economic integration of the Soviet bloc in Europe and to create, as it were, an East European counterpart of the Common Market, will for many reasons be hard to achieve. They could, and perhaps will, bring many advantages to the bloc, but again such plans would not solve the problem of required imports of machinery and basic materials. Finally, the presently advocated intention of several countries to replace exports to Western Europe of food-stuffs and semi-manufactures by those of finished industrial products cannot as yet be taken seriously. For even though Eastern Europe will greatly increase its industrial efficiency in the years to come, that of advanced Western Europe will also progress, and the gap between the two is likely to remain for a long time, and Western Europe will have no reason to import Eastern machinery or consumer goods.

Trade with the United States

Table 14 shows that the $96 million worth of American purchases in Eastern Europe (including Yugoslavia) represented only 0.065 per cent of all U.S. imports in 1960. Exports to the same area amounted to $240 million, or 0.135 per cent of the total. They were substantially lower in 1961, because of the reduction of American aid to Yugoslavia and Poland.

TABLE 13

TRADE BETWEEN INDUSTRIAL WESTERN EUROPE
AND EASTERN EUROPE: 1960-61
(in millions of dollars)

Country	Turnover 1960	1961	Exports 1960	1961	Imports 1960	1961	Balance 1960	1961
Belgium-								
Luxembourg	126	118	78	66	49	52	29	14
France	165	194	105	125	60	69	45	56
West								
Germany	995	994	484	489	511	504	−28	−15
Italy	233	286	93	126	140	159	−46	−33
Netherlands	104	123	51	58	53	65	− 2	− 2
Total—Common Market	1,623	1,715	810	865	813	849	− 3	14
Austria	232	241	114	133	118	108	− 4	25
Scandinavia	274	285	140	141	135	144	5	− 3
United Kingdom	302	386	121	187	180	198	−58	−11
GRAND TOTAL	2,545	2,738	1,237	1,382	1,287	1,354	−51	26

Source: U.S. Department of Commerce data. Scandinavia includes Denmark, Norway, and Sweden.

Although insignificant from the American point of view, trade with the United States was extremely important for both these countries. Their ordinary purchases in America were small, for they were short of dollars. But the agricultural surplus goods they obtained from the United States on credit for their own currencies helped offset their chronically adverse trade balances. Between 1954 and 1961, the accumulated Polish trade deficit reached $1.16 billion, and that of Yugoslavia $1.8 billion. Nearly 35 per cent of the Polish deficit and about 60 per cent of that of Yugoslavia were covered by American assistance in grain and other commodities. Without such aid, the economies of the two countries could be exposed to critical stresses, which might eventually lead to a transformation of their status within or attitudes toward the Soviet bloc.

Trade with Primary Producing Countries

Statistical data of East European trade with the primary producing countries cannot be precisely established because of the shortcomings of the "new" countries' statistics and a deliberate suppression by some East European states of information on trade with certain countries. The typical examples of the latter are the

TABLE 14

UNITED STATES TRADE WITH EASTERN EUROPE: 1960-61
(in millions of dollars)

Country	Turnover 1960	Turnover 1961	Exports 1960	Exports 1961	Imports 1960	Imports 1961	Balance 1960	Balance 1961
Albania	0	0	0	0	0	0	0	0
Bulgaria	1	1	0	0	1	1	−1	−1
Czechoslovakia	17	16	5	7	12	9	−8	−2
East Germany	7	5	4	3	3	3	1	0
Hungary	4	3	2	1	2	2	0	1
Poland	182	116	143	77	39	41	104	33
Rumania	2	3	1	1	1	1	0	0
TOTAL	213	144	155	89	58	57	96	31
Yugoslavia	123		86		37		50	
Soviet Union	62	69	39	46	23	23	16	23

Source: U.S. Department of Commerce data.

sales of military equipment, which as a rule are not statistically registered.

Despite these limitations, East European trade with the less developed parts of the world can be estimated at about $1.45 billion in 1960, or about 9 per cent of the area's total trade. The corresponding Yugoslav data for 1960 were $226 million—16 per cent of all Yugoslav trade—the difference between the two sets of figures resulting from Yugoslavia's geographical position at the door of the Near East and her neutralist policy. Over two-thirds of this trade was motivated by nonpolitical needs and considerations. Eastern Europe requires raw materials and is prepared to barter them against industrial goods; primary producers are vitally interested in the sales of their surplus commodities and purchases of equipment and consumer goods. Trade of this character is, or should be, welcomed in the Western world, for it strengthens the economic position of the free countries, especially those depending on exports of only one or few commodities—coffee from Brazil, hides from Uruguay, jute from Pakistan, etc.

East European trade with the several politically sensitive, actually or potentially anti-Western countries may also be economically justified, at least in part, but its present momentum is dictated mainly by the Soviet bloc foreign policy. During the last five years, economic missions from behind the Iron Curtain have been trying to penetrate the former colonial countries by offering them merchandise on easy credit in exchange for all surplus goods, regardless of commercial calculation. Such attempts to dominate the politically promising markets and open them to the Soviet drive have sometimes miscarried (e.g., Burma, and apparently also in Indonesia); sometimes they met with only moderate success (in Egypt, Syria, Iraq). In 1961, they were concentrated mainly upon Ghana, Guinea, Mali, and Cuba.

Czechoslovakia, the area's only country with a net trade balance and expert foreign-trade apparatus, accounted for about one-half of the area's trade with the actively "anti-imperialist" parts of the non-Communist world. Such trade could be estimated at $425–450 million in 1960, one-half of it with the then United Arab Republic ($211 million). It certainly increased in 1961, when great quantities of various products were rushed to Cuba in partial exchange for sugar—i.e., one of the important area imports.

The further extension of this trade depends on several factors. Apart from the fluctuating political situation, it will be circumscribed by the area's (and Yugoslavia's) limited capacity to grant further commercial credits and to absorb the kind of commodities the anti-Western countries possess in surplus. "These countries render great services to us by supplying us with required raw materials," a ranking economic leader in Warsaw stated recently. "We supply them with real goods, and the only thing they offer us in exchange is bananas we do not want," was the opinion of a Czech economic publication. The truth lies halfway between the two evaluations. The fact remains, however, that the area's trade with ostentatiously anti-Western countries is economically unrewarding.

The Case of Yugoslavia

Yugoslav foreign trade has been repeatedly referred to in the preceding pages. Despite her ideological and occasional political contentions with the Soviet Union and its allies, Yugoslavia is a Communist country undergoing basically the same industrial transformation and agricultural stagnation, with similar effects on foreign trade, such as the shrinking of food surpluses and those of other primary commodities. However, the directions of her trade are different. As was the case before 1939, Western Europe is Yugoslavia's main customer and supplier, and accounts for nearly one-half of her foreign trade. Yugoslav exports of finished industrial goods reached 14.3 per cent of all her exports in 1960, a proof of considerable progress in her industrial development; however, in this respect she still lags behind Rumania and Bulgaria.

Trade with the Societ bloc, entirely interrupted in 1948, was re-established six years later, but it has never reached one-quarter of the total and is unlikely to exceed that proportion in the foreseeable future. Though rapidly growing during the last decade, Yugoslav exports have never equaled imports. Only a small fraction of the ensuing trade deficit was balanced by income from tourism and transit through Yugoslav ports, and the bulk of it could only be covered by American aid, totaling more than $1.1

billion between 1950 and 1961. While enjoying this assistance, the
Tito Government was skillful enough to obtain large grants and
commercial credits in Europe on both sides of the Iron Curtain.
Yet the prospect of balancing Yugoslav trade does not seem to be
in sight within the foreseeable future.

Albania—A Special Case

Albania's international trade amounting to 0.03 per cent of its
total in 1960, was insignificant. The principal feature of her trade
is a chronic deficit, the exact dimensions of which are not known.
Until 1960, this deficit was covered by large Soviet and lesser East
European credits and grants, totaling more than $500 million. The
prospects of the repayment of these credits being nil, they had to
be written off periodically.

The future of Albania's trade after her break with the Soviet
Union could not be forecast early in 1962. An ill-defined boycott
of Albania was allegedly proclaimed at the COMECON plenary
meeting in Warsaw in December, 1961, and her trade with the
Soviet Union has apparently ceased. Yet several months later, all
six East European states renewed their trade and quota agreements with Albania, whose imports of machinery and exports of
oil products and chrome ore would thus continue, though on a
reduced scale. In addition, China committed herself to supply
Albania with grain (imported from Australia) and other goods. It
was possible, but by no means certain, that Albania would extend
her trade with Italy and other parts of Western Europe. The shock
of a sudden cessation of the all-embracing Soviet assistance to
Albania was thus somewhat mitigated. The primitive structure of
her economy may help her regime to withstand the consequences
of the Soviet boycott.

The Outlook for the Future

At the end of 1962, it was most probable that, apart from certain exceptions, East European trade within the Soviet bloc in
Europe would develop along the lines determined by COMECON
and attain, perhaps even exceed, the targets planned for 1965 and
the subsequent years. All evidence points to the pursuance of the
area's industrialization on the basis of labor division, resulting in

a year-to-year extension of mutual trade in semimanufactures, industrial equipment, and consumer goods. The already existing interdependence of the area's national economies would thus intensify.

Trade links with the Soviet Union would also tighten, primarily because of the two areas' increasing economic complementarity, but also for political motives, partly as a reaction to the progressive integration of the West European economies and the trend toward the formation of an Atlantic Community. Plans for Soviet trade with several dependent nations called for an increase of 10–12 per cent annually and was to constitute a larger proportion of their entire trade. For the 1960–65 period, the Soviet Union committed itself to the delivery of a substantially greater volume of most raw and basic materials than ever before. There was little doubt that it was capable of exporting to its dependencies the planned quotas of fuels, metallic ores, metals, timber, other basic nonagricultural commodities, and heavy industrial equipment. Whether it would be able to maintain, let alone increase, its deliveries of grain, meat, butter, and cotton was a moot question in view of the evident stagnation of its agriculture since the end of the 1950's.

The area's sales of basic goods to the Soviet Union could hardly be increased, for they were required for home consumption, and difficulties could even be expected to arise in the maintenance of their present level of about $1.1 billion. "Normal" exports to the Soviet Union were planned to reach $3.75 billion in 1965, but they would actually have to be higher, for several countries had to repay the credits the Soviet Union extended to them since 1956. To attain the required levels, exports of finished industrial goods would have to reach almost $3 billion in 1965—i.e., more than 70 per cent more than their 1960 volume. High as it was, this seemed to be a realistic target, for in the preceding five years—1955–60— such exports increased by 115 per cent (from $798 million to $1.7 billion). Among the major planned items of such exports in 1960–65 were the deliveries of an armada of more than 2 million tons of ships and over $1 billion worth of equipment for Soviet chemical industries. An indirect result of the collapse—perhaps temporary—of the area's trade with China (e.g., Czech trade with

China decreased from $203 million worth in 1960 to $76 million worth in 1961) was the growth of its trade with the Soviet Union.

Auspicious as was the outlook for future intrabloc trade, the implementation of the area's economic plans continued to be contingent upon imports of grain, industrial raw materials, and modern factory equipment from non-Soviet countries. So long as the area was able to sell its surplus foodstuffs and fuels to Western Europe and its machinery to overseas countries, it had access to the products it critically required. Its position with respect to this problem improved in 1960–61, when the share of its exports outside the bloc rose to slightly more than 30 per cent of their total, which was regarded as a safe minimum of such exports. (It went to 40 per cent in Hungary and Poland.) The odds were, however, that this favorable situation could not be maintained during the 1960's in view of the extension of the Common Market and the tightening of its external custom duties. If these factors were to result in any substantial reduction of East European exports to the West, a reduction of imports and a slowing-down of the dependent area's and Yugoslavia's rate of planned economic growth would ensue. The 10 per cent decline of intra-German trade in 1961 was one sign of such a development.

A moderate increase of exports of the six countries and Yugoslavia exports to many non-European, especially anti-Western nations, could be anticipated, but these nations do not include those that supply Eastern Europe with such basic materials as wool, copper, and natural rubber, which she could not obtain in barter, nor those supplying grain, which the Soviet Union was delivering somewhat erratically. Imports from the Near East and Africa could not replace those from the United Kingdom or West Germany. In the last analysis, the planned economic development of Eastern Europe, including Yugoslavia, hinges upon the maintenance of the present level of sales for hard currency to Western Europe. In 1962, no easy alternative was in sight. The loss of the West European market or a large part of it was not imminent, but the danger did loom on the horizon.

Contrary to what could be anticipated in 1962, a number of three-year trade agreements were concluded early in 1963 between individual East European and Common Market countries. In these agreements, the average 1960–62 annual quotas of imports from Eastern Europe were as a rule maintained and, in some cases, even extended. Thus, the all-important West German and Italian markets continued to be open to the commodities exported by Eastern Europe. However, the prices commanded by East European foodstuffs and other goods are likely to decrease because of the changing trend in the Common Market's interior and exterior tariffs during 1963–65. Even though maintained at their previous level, exports may well produce less hard currency than East European countries need to meet their growing requirements of raw materials and machinery.

PART THREE

The Politics of Peaceful Coexistence

6. THE INTERNAL POLITICAL ORDER

ANDREW GYORGY

"The important thing about truth is not that it should be naked, but what clothes suit it best."[1] This statement certainly applies to the contemporary East European political scene, where naked truth is often subtly, but more often crudely, camouflaged by ever-changing suits of clothes. Although solidly in the Soviet sphere today, the countries of Eastern and Southeastern Europe, with the perennial exception of Tito's Yugoslavia, still tend to present a challenging "in-between" or "middle-zone" aspect of European political life. The many external pressures, more from the East than the West, still shape, influence, and complicate the internal political evolution of the satellite nations. As the global Communist split widens, several "roads to socialism" appear, predetermined by the geographic and political implications and by the strategic and tactical fluctuations of the current East-West struggle raging around the individual satellite.

Beyond this precarious "shatter-belt" location there are good reasons for making an airtight political classification of various East European countries difficult. Some of the countries have obediently adopted Marxist theories and then proceeded to apply them rigorously (Czechoslovakia, Bulgaria, East Germany), while others have offered variations and deviations on the Leninist-Stalinist-Khrushchevist themes (notably Yugoslavia, Poland, Hungary, and Albania). Some have engaged in frequent waves of semiconcealed terror, while others have shown certain signs of mellowing and progressing far beyond the rigid totalitarianism of the dark days of Stalin. Although the various perspectives of East European postwar development presented by writers in this field stress different ideological aspects endemic to the area,[2] they

159

agree on certain decisive chronological periods, which serve to separate individual phases of domestic evolution. This chapter will trace such trends within a simplified framework built around the sequence of three stages of postwar Communist theory.

Political and Legal Implications of Communist Theory

Characteristic products of the immediate post-World War II period, the "people's democracies" are sovereign in principle, less than half-sovereign in fact, and typically the hybrid creations of the contemporary Soviet empire. Their sudden, and frequently dramatic, emergence was greatly facilitated by the authoritarian traditions inherent in the East European scene. The customary political attributes of Western democracy were seldom accepted by the Danubian and Balkan countries, which never appreciated firm parliamentary institutions and liberal governmental processes. In the prewar political climate, native fascist groups had unusual opportunities for development, and by the outbreak of World War II, a series of military dictatorships had been established. The collapse of German National Socialism and Italian Fascism undermined the authoritarian regimes of Eastern Europe, and the decisive military events of 1944–45 completely destroyed their tenuous framework. The historic upheavals of these years paved the way for the appearance of new ideologies and untried constitutional formulas. As the principal occupying power of Eastern Europe, the Soviet Union exploited popular cravings for a change in political leadership and economic organization. By creating "people's democracies," it left a permanent imprint on the social structure of this region.

Appraising the postwar progress of satellite governments, Communist theorists have viewed their intermediate status between full independence and a Soviet regime in distinctly negative terms: People's democracies were neither bourgeois democracies nor "Soviet democracies." Resorting to a more positive phraseology, the "people's democracy" appeared primarily as a satellite state dependent on the U.S.S.R. and developing in the direction of a more "advanced" Soviet Socialist republic. It was founded on the Stalinist principles of intensified class struggle, a determined fight against nationalist resistance, an iron monopoly of the working class and a complete subordination to Soviet-imposed discipline.

The principal doctrinal aspect of the "people's democracy" was its transitional nature. Based on a revolutionary seizure of power, it was supposed to reflect briefly the total centralization of a dictatorship of the proletariat, only to evolve eventually and inevitably into a full-fledged "socialist" state. In view of the "reactionary" nature of prewar Eastern European society and the multiple remnants of its capitalist wreckage, progress toward the *proletarian* dictatorship was neither natural nor evolutionary. It was distinctly accelerated by the artificial weapons of violence forged by a determined Communist minority. The prescription for a satellite *coup d'état* implied attacks on two related and closely synchronized fronts: one from below, through a class struggle fought by the "working people"; and another from the top brought about by the Red Army and naked Stalinist power.*

The "people's democracy" also serves to establish and strengthen the institutions of Communist rule. Indeed, there seem to be few theoretical or practical differences between the former Stalinist dictatorship in the Soviet Union and the dictatorships of the people's democracies. A monolithic *united* workers' party emerged on the satellite scene, displaying political characteristics fully as rigid and bureaucratic as those of its Soviet counterpart. By means of the tightly organized and highly centralized Communist Party, the remnants of "bourgeois morality" are quickly stamped out and

* *Violence* as an essential ingredient of the entire people's democratic phase is discussed at length in Communist literature, particularly with a view toward forestalling further "counterrevolutionary" incidents on the Hungarian or Polish patterns. *Társadalmi Szemle,* a monthly publication of the Hungarian Workers Party, described both the seizure of power and the dictatorship of the working class over the bourgeoisie as "political (state) forms of violence," in which "the degree and means of violence will depend primarily on the resistance of the bourgeoisie and on those concrete conditions under which the proletarian revolution will triumph." The author dwelt at length on the danger of counterrevolutionary groups which, while preparing their armed revolt, would borrow the "damaging and phony slogan of 'pure democracy,'" as they attack the dictatorship of the proletariat. Thus the legalized use of violence was further justified and buttressed here by the principle of self-defense of a revolutionary society against attacking counterrevolutionaries. (See Béla Vészi, "A szocialista államiság fejlödése a kommunizmus épitésének idöszakában" ["The Evolution of Socialist Statehood in the Period of the Construction of Communism"], *Társadalmi Szemle* [Budapest], December, 1961, pp. 97–109.)

are supposed to yield to the ambiguous phenomenon of "socialist legality." Since most pre-Communist laws are generally considered as undesirable bridges linking Eastern Europe to the West, satellite legislators competed with each other in the changing or elimination of all earlier laws. The most radical legal break occurred in Yugoslavia, where in 1945 all laws that had been valid in 1941, the day of the German occupation, were simply declared null and void. Other countries worked more slowly. In Poland and Czechoslovakia, new laws on marriage, family, inheritance, and property matters were not introduced until the 1946–47 or 1949–51 period, respectively. Above all, the new satellite regimes intended to sever the "legal-missionary vigor" of an earlier, Austrian legal system, which had widely radiated from Central Europe toward Eastern and Southeastern Europe.

The people's-democracy phase of the satellite state was furthermore characterized as a process of highly intensified class struggle. Usually the fight was initiated shortly after the seizure of power. A newly installed Stalinist elite, unwilling to share authority or power with other political and economic factions, began to draw sharp distinctions between class friends and class enemies in the social structure of the people's democracy. Targets of political persecution changed and new tormentors appeared on the scene: The victims of racial prejudice were displaced by the martyrs of class prejudice. The active participants in this class struggle were spearheaded by the working class, the "people's army," and the peasantry, triple foundations of society in a New Democracy. The militant nucleus of the avant-garde was the class of urban industrial workers who were exhorted to act with "proletarian decisiveness." The proletariat, the undeniable focus of power and privilege, forms the bulk of workers' party membership and is the repository of the future aspirations of Stalinist leaders. It includes members of the reorganized "people's armies," which are increasingly diverted to the quelling of internal revolts connected with the class struggle. Soldiers, in Communist reasoning, are workers in uniform: They "radiate workers' party ideology" and often bridge the gap between party and people. They are called upon to intimidate the reluctant nonparty masses, the class enemies of the new East European order.

In terms of the class struggle, the East European peasantry has a distinctly limited choice: It can either follow the revolutionary path marked out by the proletarian elite of the people's democracy, or it can embrace the cause of political reaction leading to annihilation. Surviving peasant leaders are forcefully reminded by the satellite hierarchy that the destinies of the working peasantry are irrevocably tied to the Communist state, and their lives stand or fall with the people's revolution. Peasant resistance to arbitrary collectivization clearly indicates that the class struggle is far from completed in the villages, and the thin dividing line between kulaks and working peasants is hesitantly drawn. In practice, the peasantry is viewed as largely unreliable and politically irresponsible; ever wider sectors of farmers with independent means or inflexible political convictions are labeled "kulaks" and automatically excluded from the privileged social groups of the dictatorship of the proletariat. The politically more pliable working peasantry includes the middle and poor farmers as categories acceptable to Communist leadership. Thus the definition of a peasant's "class origin" is determined largely by his ideological orientation, although the extent of his affluence and prestige position in rural society is also used as a convenient criterion of measurement. "Kulak is a state of mind," Mátyás Rákosi, former Secretary General of the Hungarian Workers' Party, once observed. Omnipotent Communist leaders usually reserve the right to reappraise the past performance, present status, and future promise of the peasant class, invariably emphasizing that the industrial proletariat is the true fountainhead of political power in a people's democracy.

The class struggle is a multidimensional conflict *par excellence*. Beyond its already familiar economic and social components it has a distinct political substance. Basing its actions on a contradictory sequence of events, the Communist Party first attempts to reduce the country's political spectrum by eliminating all non-Communist parties, dissident groups, "deviationists," and other "opportunists." In the meantime, by purging its own ranks, it further restricts the size and scope of the political elite. Then, however, it anxiously sets out to broaden the ideological base by insisting that the presently narrow and rather unrepresentative Party gradually become

the "mass party of the proletariat." How can a party simultaneously appear to be both broad and narrow in its social and political appeal?

There can be no clear-cut and quick reply to this question. Undoubtedly, as one Communist *apparatchik* has suggested, the
Party must skillfully and "correctly" combine legal and illegal
forms of class-struggle in its ultimate goal, which is the winning
over of the masses of non-Party people for its own partisan political purposes. At this point one must stress the all-important role
of mass organizations, these "transmission belts" of a Communist
society. If properly organized and controlled, they would presumably be capable of resolving the "broad-and-narrow" dilemma.

Preoccupation with the continuing class struggle goes hand in
hand with the first emergence of a tightly knit Communist elite.
In this respect, the postwar format of the "people's democracy"
generally echoed a narrow and often inflexible interpretation of
Leninism, particularly as related to the establishment of a monopoly of power by the Communist minority. Lenin's emphasis on an
organized vanguard, on a political elite oriented toward the perpetuation of the social struggle, had been enthusiastically supported by latter-day Communists who were convinced that the
rule of the working class was assured only through the mobilization of special elite groups. These unofficial Party organs were
first called upon to capture the machinery of government with the
assistance of assorted left-wing parties, and then directed to capi-
talize on the presence of the Red Army exploiting the fear of
armed Soviet intervention. Clearly projected to every member of
the revolutionary nucleus, the ultimate objective was to assure the
aggressive minority of a free hand in the establishment of a dictatorship of the proletariat.

Chronologically, the first major and lasting elite groups to appear on the East European political scene were the members of
the politburos and secretariats of the Communist parties' central
committees. These small groups (seldom composed of more than
twenty people) wielded vast policy-making powers during the
Stalinist period; in effect they generally fulfilled the functions of
an invisible (or at best semivisible) cadre guiding Party members
in the struggle against domestic "reaction," as well as continually

alerting them against the dangers of foreign "imperialism." The politburos were invariably small, tightly organized, and highly disciplined. The top Party leaders were thoroughly Kremlin-oriented. Most of them had spent several years in the Soviet Union, particularly during World War II, and many of them went through years of indoctrination in Soviet Party schools. As a result of years of ruthless purging in the 1948–50 period (Rajk, Kostov, Petkov, Pătrăşcanu, etc.) totally reliable Stalinists gradually replaced the native Communists holding home-grown nationalist views and frequently deviation-prone ideas. Interestingly, however, the Stalinist elite itself seldom included professional "ideologists," or experts so well schooled and steeped in Marxism-Leninism that they could apply its theories to their own countries' satellite conditions and even justify or rationalize the rude transition from utopian theory to dismal practice. From Ulbricht through Gottwald, from Rákosi to Gheorghiu-Dej to Chervenkov, the elite-image of this era is almost exclusively that of a team of tough, resourceful, intellectually indifferent, and supremely opportunistic practitioners of the revolution.

Other salient features of this Stalinist "new class" in the satellites suggest that most of them were raised in working-class or lower-middle-class families, that most of them were industrial laborers before joining the Communist Party, that few of them had more than a minimum of formal education, and that a majority of these leaders had had years of experience in illegal underground activities and in subversive Comintern-type operations. In effect, the contemporaries of Ulbricht or Rákosi had served as delegates to the last two or three congresses of the Third Communist International and had invariably spent several years in prison or in concentration camps. These basic conditioning factors ensured—at least in Stalin's lifetime—that thoroughly coordinated joint policies would be pursued in all areas affecting Soviet foreign policy and the dominant power position of the U.S.S.R. in Eastern Europe.* Although local workers' parties were allowed a sem-

* Tito was, of course, the cardinal exception in this respect, but after the open break had occurred in 1948, all of the other Cominform countries angrily "closed in" on Yugoslavia with a typically Stalin-dictated uniformity of purpose and tactics.

blance of *formal* leeway in domestic issues, whenever the new peoples' democracies touched upon essential Soviet interests, complete harmony seemed to reign as if imposed by the invisible conductor of a symphony orchestra. Thus, while minor disagreements among the satellite parties could occasionally have been tolerated under the narrowly interpreted heading of "domesticism," more significant problems or issues—particularly those involving Cominform policies—were invariably and aggressively screened against external indiscretion and promptly resolved by the Stalinist nucleus of the respective Party's politburo.

Since the people's democracy is essentially a transitional state form bridging the wide gulf between capitalism and socialism, its progress and evolution toward the next highest form are both predetermined and theoretically inevitable. At a certain important moment in its history, it will cease being a mere "people's republic" and will describe itself instead as a "socialist republic." When the Czech Constitution of 1960 solemnly referred to the "Czechoslovak Socialist Republic," the implication was clearly drawn that, for this one country at least, the people's-democratic era was over.

For most of the East European satellites, the 1953–60 period was an immensely important *theoretical* building-process based on a two-phase development:

1. On the people's democracy (or the dictatorship of the proletariat), which attempts to translate the revolutionary objectives of Marxism-Leninism into practice. Consequently its historic goal is accomplished when the exploiting classes have disappeared from the home front, when the new economic and social system has triumphed both in the villages and the cities, and when all forms of exploitation have ceased to the point where all (remaining) social groups will be bound by a spirit of friendly cooperation. At this point

2. An "all-popular" (all-inclusive) new political form is expected to emerge with a "novel social content" for the state. The dictatorship phase will then be gradually relegated to the background, governmental forms of violence disappear internally, and

socialism* will be the principal concern, goal, and politico-economic pattern of the day. The new socialist state will be intent on mobilizing all of its citizens so that they will be able to control and direct the affairs of their own society. Conversely, there will be no need for internal organs of repression and the state's entire repressive apparatus will now be aimed at combating foreign espionage and subversive activities from abroad. Thus, as a prelude to eventual withering away and arriving at pure Communism, the governmental organization at this point could be readily described as a "half-state."

The process of socialist state-construction has both domestic implications, affecting each satellite state internally, and external, intrabloc repercussions influencing the whole area regionally. Of the former, the emergence of a full-fledged single-party state is probably the most significant. Other political parties rapidly wither away and even in situations where they do not disappear completely (such as, for example, in Czechoslovakia or in Poland), they are retained only in purely formalistic terms as needless and meaningless appendixes clearly doomed to total extinction at some later date. Undeniably, the fundamental feature of this stage in Communist theory is the single-party state built on a classless society. The original Stalinist vision of this political ideal substituted docile functional organs like youth groups, trade unions, and factory committees for independent-minded opposition parties. There can be only one fully recognized political party in the new states: the Communist Party, revolutionary in all spheres of public life, hastily constructed on the wreckage of previous political groups, and officially devoted to a class alliance of workers and peasants. Advocates of a multiparty system are swiftly and decisively silenced as deviationist subversives who fail to believe in the utopian potentialities of the new social and political order. "What do we need an opposition party for?" recently inquired a Hungarian writer. "We want parliaments of real flesh, where the members make sensible suggestions and formu-

---

* Often confusingly, but significantly, referred to as the "first phase of Communism," as allegedly projected into the future by the Soviet Constitution of 1936.

late criticisms that help in the building of a new state rather than a return to the old system of capitalism, unemployment, and want." Criticism thus becomes the self-critique of an intraparty regime which disregards non-Communist opinions and denounces independent-minded political attitudes. *

In the general area of intrabloc relationships, this period witnessed considerably stepped-up processes of economic integration (CEMA), military cooperation (the Warsaw Pact), and a broad-based, but silent attempt to develop identical legal structures throughout the region from public law to criminal law to election laws, including the introduction of certain institutions known in the Soviet Union but unfamiliar to Eastern Europe proper. The public prosecutor is an example of such Soviet importation. He acts both as an official prosecutor in criminal cases and as the guardian of "socialist legality." He is not responsible to the Ministry of Justice, but rather to the government or parliament.

The ultimate objective is the welding of inseparable ties between ruler and ruled; one of the means of accomplishment is the creation of homogeneous and parallel legal systems between the U.S.S.R. and Eastern Europe. In January, 1953, a few weeks before he died, then Czechoslovak President Klement Gottwald delivered an important speech stressing that the Soviet Union was the true legal-political prototype for all of the people's democracies. It was a "fundamental law of political development" that all

---

* Politically reliable adherents of the Communist Party line are encouraged to indulge in the right to criticism, which is considered a significant factor in balancing the discipline imposed on Party members from above. According to the architects of its flexible doctrine, self-criticism must be "well-intentioned, constructive, and loyal." It must be used to check a "deep-rooted bureaucratism" characteristic of the people's democracies. Each of these clichés is so strictly interpreted that indiscreet critics can be silenced as undesirable deviationists and disloyal *agents provocateurs.* Official criticism asserts itself on the Soviet pattern, as an endless stream of reproachful letters is dispatched to Communist daily papers and periodicals which generally print these "constructively phrased" complaints. Self-criticism is practiced by a handful of militant Stalinists who are encouraged to point out ideological deficiencies and punish reactionaries by publicizing shortcomings of the regime. Instead of reflecting a liberalization of the system, self-criticism is used to strengthen the Party by allegedly improving its theoretical foundations, and aiding it in the struggle against "reaction."

differences, which were of a purely transitional nature anyway, disappear among the European components of the bloc.

Although the politico-legal coordination of the satellites has progressed steadily and inevitably since 1953, Gottwald's sanguine theoretical predictions could not be carried out uniformly in an across-the-border manner. Instead, the legal coordination of the individual Eastern European countries displayed important phase-differences and semantic variations on the Soviet theme. The Soviet prototype is differently approached and implemented in each political system. It is hard to diagnose institutional uniformity at first blush, since in many instances Soviet technical terms are underplayed and old phrases or a locally familiar nomenclature serve to cover up the reform measures of a new political order. The terms "kolkhoz" or "artel" are strenuously avoided and reference is made to the LPG's (*Landes-Produktions Genossenschaft*) in East Germany or the TSZ's (*termelö szövetkezet*) in Hungary.* Instead of local soviets one generally finds national or people's councils. "Popular fronts," "national fronts," and "fatherland fronts" are maintained as formalistic items or semantic and political fiction everywhere (except in Rumania and Albania), although the tightly enforced one-party system does not allow much leeway for other groups beyond the basically meaningless mass organizations. Parliaments are clearly doomed to a fate of legislative degeneracy and paralysis à la Supreme Soviet, and yet the grandiloquent titles of yesteryear persist: Rumania still has a Grand National Assembly, Poland is still proud of the Sejm, and Slovakia maintains its Slovak National Council. Local government also attempts to retain the outer trappings of yesterday while steadily undergoing revolutionary changes. Hungary has retained the historic notion of *megye* (Komitat) for the administrative district, and Poland still uses the term *voivodinate*.

Integration is further complicated by the fact that frequently there is an inevitable time lag in the acceptance of a Soviet in-

* These semantic deviations serve a definite purpose. LPG sounds better to the East German than kolkhoz would. As an East German newspaper phrased it, this gives the LPG members a chance to "glance back into the past for a while longer." The semantics of the situation are clearly transitional, while the socio-economic institutions themselves are there to stay.

stitution or reform measure and its appearance in the public life of the individual satellite. Occasionally deeply ingrained local traditions are superficially observed for a while and the rate of change is slowed down somewhat. In Czechoslovakia, even the 1960 Constitution managed to retain the institution of the individual Chief of State—the Presidency—as a symbol of possible historic deference to the lingering memories of Masaryk and Beneš. On the other hand, the leadership of the German Democratic Republic brooked no delay and introduced the collective, Soviet-Presidium type State Council immediately following the death of the previous incumbent, President Wilhelm Pieck, in September, 1960. Such variations on the time-lag theme imply that some countries act and internally react more rapidly or instinctively than others. National ministries, councils, or cabinets of ministers are normally organized, reorganized, shuffled, and reshuffled according to the current Moscow pattern or practice. Increases and decreases in the number of ministers show a particular degree of satellite flexibility. Yet even here one finds that while Prague followed the exceptionally drastic (50 per cent) Moscow cut in ministries of March, 1953, within a few weeks, Bucharest waited for four years before reducing cabinet posts similarly, from twenty-eight to sixteen.

In summary, the transitional political process of building the "socialist state" has not been carried out simultaneously throughout Eastern Europe. Gaps, lags, and often significant local variations in the over-all pattern have belied the 1953 Gottwald thesis of a simultaneous and totally coordinated political development of these countries toward the "true Soviet prototype." The post-Stalinist era has considerably relativized Communist doctrines, and the manipulators of theory have applied it with increasing flexibility. Instead of "simultaneous progress" toward a higher phase of Communist society, the emphasis now rests on the forward march along a "broad front." The earlier expectation that within a few years the legal and administrative structure of the Soviet Union would be incorporated and applied *in toto* by all European Soviet bloc members has been significantly modified in recent years. The Soviet theoretician F. Konstantinov skillfully reformulated the Gottwald thesis, smacking of officially repulsive

Stalinism, into a "law of the *planned and proportional development* of Socialist countries" in conformity with the general direction taken by Soviet society.

When is the construction process of Socialism terminated? When does the phase of "pure" Communism begin? The dividing line is thin and somewhat confused in Communist theory. Actually the transition point is a negative one, marked by the *total* disappearance of the exploiting classes and related "remnants of capitalism" on the domestic scene. Since, however, the capitalist enemy is very much present and continually alert in the field of international relations, the perfect state of Communism is expected to be postponed until the final victory of "peace-loving socialist forces" everywhere on our globe. As long as this magic moment is still in the dim and unspecified future, the repressive apparatus of the transitional, semi-Communist state has to be kept alive and, to a large extent, externally oriented. The Soviet Union, this glowing theoretical model for Eastern European satellites, thus allegedly maintains its entire power-political and coercive state organization to combat foreign espionage, capitalist attempts at infiltration, and other subversive activities from abroad.

Ultimately, with the fervently hoped for disappearance of the capitalist foe, the practical prototype of the theoretical Communist society image will be established both in the U.S.S.R. and in its adjacent East European satellite empire. This dazzling but truly long-term model reflects the "total political-moral unity" of a then both locally and globally complete Communist society, the "all-people" state that will successfully fuse the Party's activities with the all-inclusive interests of a superbly organized society. This point will mark the disappearance of the last vestiges of the dictatorship of the proletariat, without, however, implying the arrival of a stage of political anarchy, of lack of social discipline, or of the absence of economic organization. On the contrary, the pure and final stages of Communism portray the state as gradually withering away and yielding its place to a political form dedicated to the principle of "total self-administration." Internally this implies a socialist democracy, while in external relations—lacking the customary targets of hostility—it advocates the promotion of fraternal cooperation with other socialist countries in the protection of "universal peace."

Two interesting features emerge from these theoretical analyses. On the one hand, even while the withering away of the state is hopefully anticipated in the professional literature, the role of the Communist Party is not only stressed as part of a historic continuum (without a terminal point!), but its future pre-eminence in the final stage of Communist evolution is asserted with great emphasis. The Party will play a steadily greater role all the time; it will set an example for all; it will always observe the Leninist norms of Party life and the principle of collective leadership. The Czechoslovak Constitution of 1960 proclaims in unequivocal terms that the Communist Party of Czechoslovakia, "the vanguard of the working class," is "the leading force in society and in the State." It refers three times to "the scientific world outlook of Marxism-Leninism," which is supposed to guide all education and all cultural policies. What is even more noteworthy in terms of modern Communist constitution-making, observes Professor Táborský in his excellent *Communism in Czechoslovakia, 1948–1960,* is the recurrent and forceful statement that the "gradual transition to Communism" is the chief goal of state policy in the body of the Constitution itself. "In so doing, the Constitution incorporates, and thus converts into constitutional mandates, the prerequisites that official interpreters of Marxism from Marx to Khrushchev have laid down as a condition *sine qua non* for the advent of the Communist millennium." On the basis of this recent Czech experience, one can confidently expect a re-echoing in the satellite political world of the latest Soviet interpretation of the "withering-away" process, but always in a more-or-less subtle combination with the "primacy of the Communist Party" principle.

A related facet of this doctrinal inquiry injects the element of preventive caution when reaching the crucial, practical point of the time element in the actual transition process from Socialism to Communism. The spectrum of speculation is a broad one indeed. While Czechoslovakia's leaders are convinced that they have already successfully embarked on the highest stage of state development, East German and Hungarian writers foresee certain concrete obstacles and potentially adverse influences as definite roadblocks along the path of ideological progress. In specific terms, a Hungarian writer warns that a great deal will depend on the incidence and intensity of possible "armed counterrevolutionary attempts," which may yet jeopardize the chances of ultimate Communist victory. Such counterrevolutionary groups may actually borrow the "damaging and phony slogan of 'pure democracy'" while attacking the socialist state. East Germans warn (from their perspective with a great deal of justification) that the authors of the Communist classics could not possibly have foreseen the actual, concrete conditions under which the state would eventually wither away, since such conditions would have to be predetermined by the given circumstances of the individual (Communist bloc) nation. Thus while the Hungarian ideologue speculates about the possible recurrence of the October 1956 events, the Ulbricht clique pre-emptively rationalizes and feebly defends the D.D.R.'s exceedingly slow economic and political progress toward the stage of a "people's democracy," let alone toward the subsequent phases of Socialism and Communism. Thus, while there may be a large degree of *theoretical* uniformity on these points among Soviet and satellite political observers, there is enormous *practical* divergence in the political evolution of individual East European countries.

Problems of Political Leadership

Complex problems of political leadership cannot be investigated successfully in a vacuum or within a restrictive short-term time span. An elite analysis must combine a sound institutional approach with a historic perspective that looks at political developments in a chronological sequence. The difficulties of such a survey are obvious. In a study of seven or eight different countries, some nation's political patterns may not fit either the time or institutional framework; it is exceedingly difficult, for example, to fit the political evolution of Yugoslavia into a system of analysis based primarily on the neighboring Soviet satellites. While Yugoslavia had its internal leadership crises and convulsions (witness the dramatic Djilas purge and the related Dedijer story), these show considerably different symptoms and patterns of deviation from the all-East European "norms." This discussion views the peculiar problems of the Yugoslav scene only peripherally.

Proceeding on the general assumption that "purging and blood-letting were indispensable disciplinary measures of the Stalinist system and its major therapeutical methods when something went wrong,"[3] it is clear that a large-scale process of de-Stalinization* had swept through the East European satellites even prior to the dictator's death in 1953. This period of *pre-emptive* or *anticipated* de-Stalinization was conducted by the Soviet leadership and aimed at the immediate removal of those "little Stalins," sub-Stalins, and other Stalinoid personalities who did not fit the specific Soviet Party line of the moment, displayed some form of disloyalty, or in any way aroused the rulers' anger or jealousy. In this manner many potential, aspiring future Stalins were promptly removed from the local or regional scene, among them inveterate Communist leaders who for many years (or even decades) had been closely identified with the Soviet dictator and had obediently carried out his orders, particularly during the stormy takeover period in their respective home countries.

The last few years of Stalin's rule were characterized by the two conflicting processes of rapid ideological unification and reliance on an immense diversity in personnel. Factionalism and intra-Party strife were the dominant features as various elite groups were successfully, but with utter irrationality, exposed to an application of the familiar Stalinist principle of the "sharpening of the class struggle" during the construction of socialist society. The 1948–49 period, for example, signaled the high point of the Tito-Stalin and Gomulka-Stalin conflicts, with lesser, but equally dramatic, campaigns being waged in Budapest around László Rajk and in Sofia over Traicho Kostov. All these purges were aimed at nationalist, home-grown Communists who had strong popular support in their own parties and who had not spent the World War II years in the Soviet Union, but had had only short-term contacts with Moscow. For the confused period of

* This term is used here to denote not the extirpation of Stalin's memory, but the liquidation of people like Stalin, either by Stalin himself before 1953, or by other forces after his death.

approximately four years (1948–51), the pendulum of Stalin's favor actually swung toward the "Muscovites" in most of the satellite parties—that is, toward the group of more-or-less Sovietized leaders who had lived in Russia for many years, had little support at home, and had been reimported to their native countries by the Red Army either in late 1944 or early 1945. The Paukers, Rákosis, Gerös, Slánskýs, Bermans, and Bieruts were the *personae gratae* of this brief, and by definition transitional, era.

The second great wave of de-Stalinization had no definite or precise terminal dates. It operated both prior to Stalin's death (pre-emptively) as well as after March, 1953, in the form of a *retroactive* or *ex post facto* process of de-Stalinization. Its over-all symptom of distinction was the attempt of the satellite parties to get rid of their own Stalins in rhythm with the Soviet search for new, more relaxed, or at least more bearable, forms of leadership. This wave of purges singled out and closed in with great ferocity on the internationally oriented team of the "Muscovite" East European Communists. By 1952–53, many members of this intellectual "cosmopolitan" faction were eliminated from their Party and government positions. The depth of this particular purge varied from country to country. Most of the Slanský group of the Czechoslovak leadership was brutally murdered, while in Rumania the "alien" Ana Pauker group (including Vasile Luca and a few others) was merely dropped from its posts, occasionally placed under house arrest, and only very seldom subjected to formal purge trials or sentences of imprisonment.

In Hungary, the two-wave analogy does not apply too well, nor does the time-phase sequence show up with sufficient clarity. The "Muscovite" team, led by Rákosi and Gerö, engaged in a gigantic and long-drawn-out power struggle with the home-grown group of Communists clustered around Imre Nagy. By July, 1953, Nagy seemed to have won with his appointment as Prime Minister, and yet the years 1955 and 1956 were marked by the desperate contortions of the Rákosi-Gerö clique, which succeeded in recapturing a few positions of political importance. The pendulum then swung again in the course of the October, 1956, revolution briefly and dramatically toward Imre Nagy, finally stabilizing in the wake of the bloody Soviet intervention in the person of the colorless János Kádár, basically a home-grown or national Communist but totally acceptable to the Khrushchev regime.

The dialectics of the leadership process have a certain international logic in Soviet politics. The collective-leadership principle emerged as a more or less expected development and as a fairly intelligible socio-economic pattern. Beyond the obvious, pedestrian reason that the Soviet Union insisted on its acceptance and popularization, it also reflected more profound political trends. The assumption of power by a group of men and their shared participation in the top-level decision-making process was, first of all, a repudiation of Stalinist one-man rule, a useful governmental and Party technique of promising "better things" for the future in the form of a much-desired relaxation along political and economic lines.

Collective leadership also responded elastically to demands for both *external* and *internal* relaxations of tension. As a result of the intriguing Belgrade reconciliation between Tito and Khrushchev, other bloc members began to soften their adamantly belligerent foreign policies toward Yugoslavia, and in the ensuing period of *rapprochement* at least one major area of tension tended to disappear. In internal matters, the adoption of the "Malenkov line" brought gradual relief to the East European consumer, so shabbily treated in the Stalin era. Here the new collective-leadership elite could formally assume the responsibility and get credit for assorted improvements in the standard of living and on the economic home front. Furthermore, at least the first half of this period witnessed a veritable thaw in cultural, artistic, and intellectual life, with a significant lowering of the previously air-tight Iron Curtain barriers toward the West. The voices of writers, poets, and literary figures—so long silent under the black oppression of Stalinism—began to be heard again and were promptly reinforced by the multiple philosophical and political debates carried on by a re-alerted and more relaxed urban white-collar intelligentsia.

Last, but certainly not least, the very human "search for a scapegoat" complex had to be brought into play. The temporary disappearance (or even better—the official removal with censure) of the one-man leader figure successfully pinned the blame for the terrible mistakes of the immediate past on a single, and thus most obvious, culprit. Denunciation of the "cult of personality" from Moscow automatically demanded a chain reaction of similar denunciations on the local scene. De-Stalinization finally reached the political summit in the satellite countries—the Chervenkovs and Rákosis had to go, or at least fade away, for a period of years. The slogan of the day was that somebody would have to pay for the crimes of Stalin. Except for Walter Ulbricht, apparently irreplaceable as the military satrap and omnipotent *Gauleiter* of East Germany, the crises of top personnel affected every East European state. Even Gheorghiu-Dej, ruthless boss of the Rumanian Workers' (Communist) Party, had to relinquish his post of First Secretary in 1954 and join a new Secretariat as one of its four ruling Party members.*

The implementation of collective leadership in the satellites resulted in a job-splitting process on the highest levels: One leader, usually the "boss," retained the position of first secretary (formerly secretary general) of the Party, while another, generally the No. 2 man, became Prime Minister on the government side. Around them clustered a small group of about five to eight colleagues, who were then identified as the "collective" leaders of *both* Party and government. In some satellites the team was incorporated into an all-powerful politburo, while in others it appeared to the outside world as a cabinet of ministers with the inner group of the "collective" holding the more important cabinet portfolios. Thus, while the formal power structure seemed to be of a dual character, fairly evenly split between Party and government, it was essentially monolithic in shielding a strong Party leader behind the relatively thin facade of the new "collective."

It is clear in retrospect that this neither-single-nor-group type of leadership, with its variegated and fluctuating pattern of "now you see me, now you don't," soon became a source of political instability and ideological uncertainty on the satellite scene. The Soviet Union's East European empire was geared to solid and *truly single* leadership, which apparently could not be delegated

---

* It must be noted, however, that Gheorghiu-Dej still retained the position of Prime Minister and eventually switched again, resigning as Premier and taking back the post of First Secretary.

to and diffused among the members of a group enjoying a rather dubious state of co-equality. After a few months of sharing political power and the public spotlight, these elite groups were unable to reach clear-cut, forceful decisions, and the whole governmental process slowed down to a hesitant pace. An atmosphere of watchful waiting pervaded the satellite scene, with all members of the "collective" anxiously eyeing the Kremlin for further instructions either in a liberalizing direction or toward a general retightening.

The eventual *coup de grâce* was delivered by the Polish and Hungarian revolts of 1956. Although the collective-leadership era did not come to a sudden stop, it was significantly complicated by the impact of these two great popular explosions and, by 1958 at the latest, was forced to give way to an already familiar leadership pattern: that of the one-man rule. The tense and fundamentally unsatisfactory conditions in post-revolutionary Poland and Hungary forced the hand of the local elites and of the Soviet Party leadership into reintroducing the political "cult of personality" on the highest levels of government and Party. In the hope that this would be a somewhat different pattern, marked by a distinctly non-Stalinist flavor, the satellite countries fell in step with this round of developments.

After the Soviet signal had been given in March, 1958, the end of leadership duality in Eastern Europe came swiftly. In the final stage of consolidating his power, First Secretary Khrushchev accepted the resignation of Marshal Bulganin as Chairman of the Council of Ministers and assumed the office himself. This event denoted the terminal point of the already moribund collective-leadership principle both at home and abroad.* The dialectic process of twentieth-century Communism again asserted itself with a major qualitative shift toward the more authoritarian and highly centralized form of single leadership.

In its technical aspects, this latest phase did not alter the job-splitting process described above. *Formally,* the duality of power,

---

* Since Yugoslavia and Albania have never accepted the collective leadership idea, this analysis does not apply to their unchangingly monolithic political systems.

in terms of different leaders holding the positions of first secretary and prime minister, has been maintained everywhere except in Hungary.* Invariably, however, true political authority rested with the first secretary, the Party boss. The ceremonially maintained, but substantively near-meaningless position of prime minister, more commonly known as chairman of the council of ministers, remained in the hands of such superannuated permanent figureheads as Otto Grotewohl in East Germany, Jozef Cyrankiewicz in Poland, and Ion Gheorghe Maurer in Rumania.† The first two are ex-Socialists and have never been quite forgiven by their arch-Communist colleagues. Most chairmen of councils have been "kicked upstairs," as it were, and have held their tenuous positions primarily as a reward for past services rendered to the dominant Workers' (Communist) Party. The Bulgarian pattern has presented a slight variation in that the chairmen of councils have been shifted around, appointed, and demoted in fairly rapid succession, while the first secretaryship has for the past several years been firmly anchored in the hands of party chief Todor Zhivkov.‡

While job-splitting has prevailed on the prime minister–first secretary level, the absolute monopoly of one-man rule has been quietly strengthened in another direction. In at least three of the satellite countries, recently introduced constitutional reforms have led to the consolidation of the chief-of-state powers in the hands of the Party boss. Thus Antonin Novotný, the No. 1 Czechoslovak Communist of today, has been able to add the country's Presidency to his office of First Secretary of the Party upon the death

* Since the upheavals of October–November, 1956, Hungary's pattern has vacillated. After the revolution János Kádár emerged as both First Secretary of the Party and Prime Minister. Two years later, he stepped down from the Premiership in favor of a long-time Communist and self-styled "specialist in revolutions," Ferenc Muennich. However, in a major shake-up of his regime, Kádár dropped Muennich in September, 1961, and replaced him as Prime Minister while still retaining the Party leadership. Since that date Kádár's domestic power position has paralleled that of Khrushchev.

† As of the summer of 1963.

‡ This principal line of division continued to prevail in Bulgaria, despite such far-reaching purges and personnel changes as the ones announced at the Bulgarian Party Congress of November, 1962. With the swift political disappearance of the old-line Chervenkov-Yugov group, "unhealthy" remnants of a compromising past, the hand of Party leader Zhivkov was considerably strengthened.

of his predecessor in 1957. Thus Walter Ulbricht and Gheorghe Gheorghiu-Dej also have been "elected" presidents of their respective state councils, merging the highest Party and government offices in their hands and becoming both *real* and *titular* heads of their states.* The designation of the same political figure as head of state as well as head of Party has run counter to the generally Soviet-imposed fashion in the bloc. Observers have noted with interest that the replacement of a Soviet-style presidium by this new state council has made at least the East German and Rumanian governmental structures resemble more closely the system of Yugoslavia than that of the Soviet Union. In the former, Tito has also occupied the Presidency of a seventeen-member State Council on the government side, while presiding as unchallenged boss over the Yugoslav Communist Party.

These reform developments have had a twofold political significance. In each of the four countries, they tended to increase the prestige and status of the top Party *apparatchik* and also accomplished a closer identification of the executive powers of the government apparatus with the politburos and central committees of the respective Communist parties. To this extent there is today an emphatically monolithic aspect to political power in Czechoslovakia, East Germany, Rumania, and—of course—Yugoslavia that is not to be found in the other East and Southeast European countries as yet.

In view of the immense diversity of East European political, social, and economic forces, it is difficult to generalize on the issue of conflicting trends of political liberalization and tightening in a Communist society. One of the few tenable axioms is that Communist Party control is all-pervasive and ubiquitous throughout the Iron Curtain region: It motivates and energizes the political system, dominates both the long-term aspects and day-by-day variations of the decision-making process, and, finally, infuses even the seemingly most nonpolitical areas of human life, such as religion, the arts, and the world of sports, with Communist

---

* The dates of these reform measures were September, 1960, in the D.D.R., and March, 1961, in Rumania. It is quite likely that other East European states will soon imitate these constitutional changes. For a visual presentation of these legal reforms, see charts on p. 181.

ideology. Thus observers of Soviet and satellite societies have frequently noted that under Communism nothing may remain apolitical; few areas, however insignificant, will pass unnoticed by the censor and, as the sum total of myriads of political decisions,

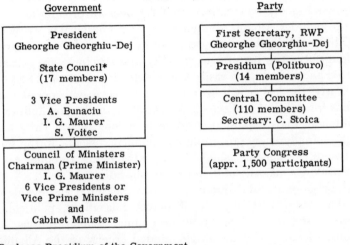

RUMANIAN STATE AND PARTY ORGANIZATION
(as reorganized in March, 1961)

Government

| President Gheorghe Gheorghiu-Dej |
| State Council* (17 members) |
| 3 Vice Presidents A. Bunaciu I. G. Maurer S. Voitec |
| Council of Ministers Chairman (Prime Minister) I. G. Maurer 6 Vice Presidents or Vice Prime Ministers and Cabinet Ministers |

Party

| First Secretary, RWP Gheorghe Gheorghiu-Dej |
| Presidium (Politburo) (14 members) |
| Central Committee (110 members) Secretary: C. Stoica |
| Party Congress (appr. 1,500 participants) |

*Replaces Presidium of the Government

GOVERNMENT REORGANIZATION IN RUMANIA
(March, 1961)

State Council

17 Members

| President G. Gheorghiu-Dej |
| 3 Vice Presidents A. Bunaciu I. G. Maurer S. Voitec |
| 13 Members |

State Council replaces Presidium of Government

Major functions are:
1. Control over Government
2. Supervision of Supreme Court
3. Control over public prosecutors
4. Appoints and recalls Supreme Court members and high command of armed forces
5. Convenes Commissions of Grand National Assembly
6. Controls foreign relations and is represented in person of its President

every aspect of human life will be ideologically saturated and wholly politicized. It is clear, therefore, that regardless of temporarily prevailing atmospheres of liberalization, the Communist Party's control remains both widespread horizontally and profound-in-depth vertically throughout the captive society.

Within the broad framework of this process of politicization, two characteristics of East European totalitarianism emerge with clarity. One suggests that the politically "safest" and more securely established regimes in this area are also the toughest and most narrow-mindedly neo-Stalinist in their over-all orientation. This group includes Albania, Bulgaria, and Czechoslovakia, with the D.D.R. qualifying in toughness if not in safety and a presumption of longevity. The features of stability and strictness are causally related and linked in an easily discernible vicious circle. The safer the Party, the less it will have to be concerned with popular demands for political and economic relaxation or the possibilities of frightening mass explosions leading to revolt. Such a Party elite might actually enjoy governing by "popular dissent," in the face, as it were, of such old-fashioned political values as acceptance and approval by a majority of their own public opinion.

These governmental situations can be measured and evaluated by the conspicuous absence of thaws, relaxations, political or literary stirrings, and naturally of popular demonstrations and revolts. Illustrative of the single-minded cruelty of the Albanian regime is the United Nations Secretariat report stating that between 1945 and 1956, 80,000 political opponents had been arrested, of whom 16,000 were killed in prisons or concentration camps. In view of Albania's small population and the limited scope of a potential political opposition, this is a terrifyingly high figure. The country's savage domestic in-fighting prevented any kind of new course or liberalization on the home front, just as it eliminated a *rapprochement* abroad with such perennial enemies as Yugoslavia, or such a recent and more ominous antagonist as the Soviet Union itself.

A case study of Czechoslovakia stresses the close relation between the absences of popular rebellion (except for a brief flurry of group indignation in Pilsen in 1953) and domestic thaw or political relaxation. The Czech regime's arbitrary and crude handling of a brief literary "spring germination" in 1955–56 is a note-worthy illustration of this point. Several poems and short stories suddenly appeared in literary periodicals in Prague with rather heavy and obviously critical political overtones. One poem described the sun finally breaking through the dark clouds, while a story embroidered on the motif that "even the mountains will bloom."[4] The joyous expectations of an exuberant spring in literature really asserted themselves at a nationwide writers' congress held in April, 1956. Writers and poets kept referring to the "conscience of the nation," while the Communist Party and its leadership were never mentioned. One writer observed that: "Now at last we can truly criticize without regard to the individual person . . . but we may criticize even the ministers themselves. For this, let us thank God!"

Being unfortunately unable to establish rapport with Czech public opinion, "potentially opposition-minded, democratically oriented, but politically already paralyzed,"[5] the Prague writers' circle finally ran into serious trouble with the Party apparatus. Its members were denounced at the Eleventh Party Congress in June, 1958, and shortly thereafter the government permanently suppressed two of the most critical literary magazines. At another nationwide writers' conference in March, 1959, several Party-appointed "conservative" (Stalinist) elder statesmen among Czech literary figures denounced the antigovernment campaign in a series of angry speeches, thus effectively putting an end to Prague's short-lived intellectual flurry of protest, which could never have reached the Budapest or Warsaw stages of revolutionary ferment.

The second characteristic reverses the sequence given above and suggests that satellite Communist parties of uncertain stature and unstable political foundations have been more prone to liberalization and relaxation both at home and in foreign relations. Here again the cyclic mechanism asserts itself with a definite logic: Governmental instability breeds weakness, which in turn creates opportunities for popular resistance, which then enables the public to wring concessions from the ruling elite. Such concessions tend both to liberalize the atmosphere of domestic politics and to inject further elements of vacillation and insecurity into the power position of the governing Party group. This political vicious-circle process must eventually be slowed down either by a change in Party leadership (most frequently induced from external sources—by the Soviet Union as the dominant colonial power), or by a reversal of gears in the liberalizing trend and by a consequent introduction of ideological re-Stalinization on the home front. At the present time, the most salient East European variant of "the more instability, the less toughness" pattern is offered by Poland.

The case study of Gomulka's Poland, stretching all the way from October, 1956, into the 1960's, is particularly challenging to the interested observer. It introduces an additional theme in emphasizing the immense importance of the personal whims, prejudices, or political predilections of the leadership in setting a national course of navigation between the Scylla of Communist Party weakness and the Charybdis of popular discontent and demand for concessions. In surveying the accomplishments of the Polish October (the bloodless revolt of 1956, which returned Wladyslaw Gomulka to power), William Griffith draws the line sharply between the two categories of decisive and peripheral gains. The former group includes those four in which Party boss Gomulka "from the beginning genuinely believed in, as distinguished from those he was forced to accept."[6] The first or top-priority category lists, under the heading of "decisive gains," the collapse of police terror combined with the restoration of personal security and freedom of private conversation; the partial internal autonomy of the Polish Communist Party as against Moscow; a temporary understanding with the Roman Catholic Church; and a retreat from previous drives toward agricultural collectivization. The conclusion reached in connection with these important political and economic features is that they have been essentially retained throughout the subsequent five- or six-year period, even if occasionally modified or attenuated in some sectors.

The areas considered peripheral by the Gomulka regime involved the broad fields of economics and culture. Here the interesting correlation of two factors—the fundamental indifference of the Party elite coupled with its apparent belief that liberalization in police, intra-Party, or even church matters would be far more relevant to its own stability and survival than economic relaxation or cultural freedom—have produced a gradual tightening process. More specifically, industrial decentralization and workers' self-government through workers' councils have been strangled by Gomulka despite the hopeful expectations voiced by leading Polish economists in the 1956–57 era. Capital investments in heavy industry have continued to rise slowly, workers' norms have been steadily raised, and the drift and lack of any real improvement in the economic sector has largely accounted for the atmosphere of apathy and hopelessness so characteristic of the country.

In the cultural area, the signal accomplishments of the "Polish October" have tended gradually to evaporate. The enormously liberalized cultural freedoms of publication and performance have been eroded by Party censorship and a series of flagrant retaliatory actions to the point where—especially in the fields of press, radio, theater, and printed academic research—a pre-1956-style sterility, dullness, and sense of oppression have been slowly creeping back. This checkerboard pattern of uncertainty—surprising relaxation balanced by unreasonable strictness—has been the source of both popular anguish and governmental embarrassment. Criticism and discontent have been openly voiced against the Gomulka regime and the "revolutionary" luster of the once-revered leader has dimmed significantly in the late 1950's and early 1960's.

In the complex process of the sovietization of Eastern Europe, problems of political leadership are only one, although crucial, facet of the many institutional changes that have taken place since 1945. Among the more relevant institutional developments that have characterized the status of this turbulent area under Soviet domination, three instruments of control have emerged as being the most significant in the long run. These are the various mass organizations, the police, and the army.

It is a fair generalization to assert that the Communist parties of Eastern Europe have both direct and indirect instruments of control at their disposal. While the direct means consist of a firm and tightly organized Party apparatus (the cadre of the Party), as well as of a more complex state apparatus consisting of the organs of justice and public administration, the most interesting indigenous forms of political sovietization have been the rapidly mushrooming mass organizations. These can be described as social, political, and economic groups created by the regime for the non-Party masses. Thus they serve the useful functions of political control mechanisms for the ruling Communist Party as well as of transmission belts for the endless outpouring of official propaganda. Consequently, there has been a not unexpected proliferation of satellite mass organizations, almost as if a Marxist Parkinson's Law dictated their numerical inflation. In effect, a challenging inverse relationship has asserted itself in this respect: The more unstable the regime, the more extensive the proliferation of these organizations; the smaller the "core" or "cadre" of the Party, the larger their size and the broader their professional base. Thus in Albania, Bulgaria, and Czechoslovakia, mass organizations have been underplayed in recent years by the regimes; in Hungary and Rumania, they have been increasingly exploited by fundamentally weak or insecure leaderships; while in Walter Ulbricht's so-called German Democratic Republic, they have displayed a truly phenomenal range and variety in their scope and activities.

Indeed, the mass-organizations of the D.D.R. have been constructed with such Prussian thoroughness and Communist fanaticism that a brief description might be in order. Described with Teutonic heavy-handedness as "community of interest" organizations (*Genossenschaftsorganisationen*), they include among their membership well over half of the country's total population, and their twenty-five major types range from the Democratic Housewives' Association (DFD) to the Cultural League (KB) to the Free German Youth Movement (FDJ—with 3 million members) to the Democratic Peasants' Organization (DBD) to the League of Nazi Victims (VVN) to the well-regimented artisans and skilled workers of the Free German Trade Union Federation (FDGB—with more than 5 million members). It is interesting to note that most of these organizations have their own schools and instructional systems based on the typically Marxist-Leninist principle of mass education (*Massenschulung*), which in the D.D.R. extends both to resident and nonresident students. As an East German refugee writer observed: for "fledgling professionals in the

D.D.R. it is most difficult to avoid being caught in this educational network."

In East Germany, as in several of the other satellites, the mass organizations have been called upon to perform two main functions. One has been to offer an illusion of political choice and of social or economic alternatives to the non-Communist middle class, particularly the urban elements of the population. Through the *indirect* operation of these control groups, the starkness of the Party line can be somewhat blurred, the elite's (in this case the ruling SED) ruthless economic and political objectives camouflaged or diluted without modifying either the ultimate goals or even the timetable of accomplishment. Thus the mass, or more properly *front*, organizations of the D.D.R. materially assisted in such long-term and essential SED policies as the nationalization of small business and the agricultural-collectivization drive, both of which were carried to completion in the 1958–60 period. The success of these frantic attempts to create a sense of ideological satisfaction or of political competition was limited indeed. "Yes," observed Professor Arnold J. Heidenheimer in his *Governments of Germany*, "there is competition among political groups in East Germany, but only in the sense that there is competition among different Community Fund solicitation teams."

A related function has been the *tactical* mobilization of mass organizations for short-term regime objectives of an *ad hoc*, temporary nature, but nevertheless of a distinct political significance. While the mass organs are often reluctantly drawn into such sharp battles, their actions are of immense usefulness to the regime in view of their allegedly nonpolitical orientation and seeming neutrality in public affairs. Often the most sensitive or unpopular campaigns can be entrusted to these organs, which will then act as tools or weapons of a semicamouflaged and officially "disinterested" Party or government. Again the D.D.R. offers the most dramatic illustration of this point. In 1957 and 1958, several mass organizations were mobilized to spearhead the East German regime's fight against the Protestant Church and in particular against its courageous Bishop Dibelius. The issue of conflict was a most painful one: the substitution for the religious confirmation of youth of a Communist state initiation or dedication (*Jugend-*

weihe), the acceptance of which had to be secured despite the frantic opposition of angry parents and irate church authorities. As a result of tremendous political pressures this resistance was broken, the Church temporarily retreated, and as a gloating official bulletin phrased it, "the mass basis of *Jugendweihe* was guaranteed and enlarged" among the youth of East Germany. Such incidents have not been confined to a single satellite, but they have been rather symptomatic of the scope and activities of mass organizations in the broader panorama of East European politics.

It has often been suggested that the Soviet concept of government for the era of the 1960's is rule by a decentralized system of terror. This seemingly contradictory phrase certainly applies to the current methods of police operation in the satellites. Violence has greatly abated since the grim days of Stalin, police corps have repeatedly been purged, their leaders removed and silenced—and yet police control is still all-pervasive. It lurks around the edges of society in a semivisible manner and operates in a truly decentralized pattern of administration. After so many years of silence and subjection, the individual satellite government works on the assumption that in view of the absence of overt resistance there is no need for violent measures. Thus police readiness is of a *potential,* rather than actual character: It is indeed a prophylactic for the purpose of preventing social or economic disturbances, a policy preferable to engaging in Stalin-type open battles against the population.

Although this potential or prophylactic pattern of behavior has characterized Hungary's or Poland's police systems in recent years, the generalization formulated above must be sharply qualified for three of the other satellites. Hoxha's police keeps Albania under constant tight and terrifying surveillance, ruthlessly eliminating even the mildest forms of dissidence or opposition. Ulbricht's *Volkspolizei* has become much more obvious and—despite numerous defections from its own ranks—insanely violent ever since the August 13, 1961, erection of the wall in divided Berlin. Finally, Czechoslovakia's police and the related system of judicial administration should be cited as arbitrary, neo-Stalinist, and frequently

irrational in the severity of its actions against its own citizenry.*
Clearly, even in the more relaxed political situations, the police
is always an arm of Party and government, never too far or too
weak and always ready to jump into instantaneous action to fight
real or alleged "enemies of the state." If the political police were
too widely decentralized, the insecurity and fear of the ruling
elites would almost immediately create intolerable domestic tensions leading inevitably to new waves of police rule, violence, and
repression. This political vicious circle then sets tangible limits
to the mellowing or minimizing of the police as an institution of
satellite government.

The role of the army is a sensitive issue involving a double-
edged problem: on the one hand, control of the East European
states by the forces of the Red Army, and, on the other, the
function of an indigenous armed force as a method of Communist
rule. The impact of the Red Army during the 1960's should be
visualized more in terms of remote control—of a *psychological
deterrent* that can be mobilized and brought into the troublesome
satellite—rather than in terms of a massive force sitting forever
as an occupation army. Here again the complex mosaic of East
European politics forces us to mention two exceptions. Hungary
now has, and will continue to have, Soviet troops, both armored
infantry and a sizable airforce, which controls key Hungarian air-
fields and airlanes. The other area of high vulnerability for the
Soviets is Ulbricht's beleaguered East Germany, whose government undoubtedly could not survive without the tangible and
permanent presence of large Russian troop concentrations, re-
liably estimated as 22 divisions, or 420,000 men. Kept in the
D.D.R. under the official auspices of the Warsaw Pact, these occupation troops are also held in a state of readiness should trouble
in any one of the satellites (similar to the Hungarian revolution
of 1956) directly involve the dominant colonial power itself.

* Witness, for example, the absolute ruthlessness with which a Moravian
resistance group was punished in Moravska Ostrava in November, 1962. "Sab-
oteurs," who received long-term prison sentences, apparently penetrated
deeply into the provincial police administration.

In recent years, the native armies have been organized and reorganized, purged and "purified," and deprived of their leaders, until their long-term military value and strategic significance has shrunk to a merely *defensive* level. Useful at most for the internal security-policing of their own countries, they could not play the role of a major offensive army in any future war-planning of the Soviet Union. It is not implied here that the Warsaw Pact is a mere paper organization. On the contrary, since its inception in May, 1955, it has played an increasingly greater role. Yet, in estimates by the Soviet Union of satellite political and military reliability, the Hungarian and Polish revolutionary activities must loom large. The strategic conclusion to be reached is that while a native East European satellite army may be immensely useful as a weapon of *domestic sovietization* and of effective support of the local Communist regime, it cannot be trusted to do more than defend its homeland against the West. Clearly, the armies of Czechoslovakia or Poland would fight valiantly against a (hypothetical) West German invader, but would show no enthusiasm at all in attacking West Germany on Soviet initiative. This important political factor thus places a severe limitation on the military network so assiduously developed and cultivated by the U.S.S.R. in its East European domain.

A Balance Sheet for the 1960's

Undeniably, the years since 1956 have been *postheroic* times for the countries wracked by the feverish convolutions and crises of East Berlin, Poznan, and Budapest. It has been painfully clear that the magic moment for popular uprisings had passed long ago and that the last of the freedom fighters have fled or are languishing in jail. Both leaders and followers have had time to simmer down and have been forced to view the cataclysmic events of 1956 with historical detachment, if not with objectivity.* Since elaborate police precautions have been taken in the critical urban

---

* A journalist recently visiting Budapest was asked by a Hungarian acquaintance whether he could answer a politically loaded question: "If a successful revolt is named a revolution, and an abortive revolution is called a revolt, what would be the proper name for a revolution that subsequently is downgraded to a revolt?" Another of his Hungarian friends then supplied the proper reply: "We won, but later we were disqualified!"

areas of the most suspiciously restive satellites, there seems to be plenty of time for an agonizing reappraisal of the violent past and for a hopeful formulation of new popular waves—whether above ground or of the underground variety.

In retrospect, the most intriguing single feature of the East European rebellions has been the clear-cut causal connection between the explosion itself and a genuine, nationwide political and economic spirit of relaxation. These revolutions were not born in the midst of the deepest misery of a concentration-camp atmosphere;* on the contrary, they seem to have alternated with and were closely linked to periods of psychological and physical improvement. The complaints they have proffered appeared more as retroactive recriminations or demands aimed at future improvements than as concerns related to the immediate moment of the uprising. The East Berlin revolt occurred three months after Stalin's death, in the midst of a visible relaxation of secret police and political tensions, while the Polish and Hungarian revolutions came in the wake of a new-course reform period introducing economic and political measures of progress and a betterment of living standards in both countries. The revolts have thus been a curious reaction to a certain degree of improvement coupled with short-term irritants, incidents which proved immediately explosive and beyond party—or government—control in a generally volatile and inflammable situation. These revolutions were not primarily the result of physical hardship and momentary suffering, but were prototypes of what Professor Alexander Rüstow of the University of Heidelberg has picturesquely described as the *"freiheitliche Revolution,"* or "freedom-aspiring revolt." Thus they have been primarily motivated by the objective to sweep aside, or at least minimize, the impact of their highly oppressive regimes. As more accurate guiding slogans they should have carried "Freedom and Bread" on their banners—in that order of priority—instead of the economic demands placed ahead of the more fundamental yearning for political liberty.

* "Amidst terror ideas are silent. But the veil of silence conceals a dormant life. When terror relents, or when circumstances prevent its full use, those ideas may spring into insurgent action." See Erich Goldhagen's excellent article on "The Glorious Future—Realities and Chimeras," *Problems of Communism,* November–December, 1960, pp. 10–18.

Such revolutions "from below" are seldom successful. The achievement of their sweeping popular objectives is clearly dependent on a series of miracles: So many conditioning factors have to materialize simultaneously and assert themselves serially, in the form of instantaneous chain reactions, that the ultimate chances of such a complex process of political catalysis are indeed remote. Two types of forces are required to produce this revolutionary explosion:

a. Certain *long-term* preconditions, basic and environmental, will play an essential role. These are a deep-seated intellectual ferment among the population; the ever-present physical and psychological threat of police terror; an obvious economic dissatisfaction on a continuing basis despite the short-term improvements of certain new-course policies; and a truly unpopular government ruling by arbitrary and irrational means, including a flagrantly inconsistent application of the laws.

b. Superimposed on this stark background picture, certain *short-term* forces must be expected to crystallize in order to set in motion the revolutionary sequence of events. A primary motivating factor is the palpable presence of widespread hope among the population that the country's condition can drastically improve in the near future. Such a streak of sudden hope, the optical illusion of a silver lining against the towering clouds of dark totalitarianism, is an essential precursor to the revolution itself. Utter discouragement and cynical despair have seldom generated momentous political forces—only the hope in peoples' hearts that a miracle can be performed, that a match can be set to the keg of dynamite, can produce the spirit of abandon and recklessness that leads to revolt. But at this point, popular excitement and hopeful anticipation must be buttressed by an equally important catalytic factor: the suddenly materialized miracle of charismatic revolutionary leadership. The absolute imperative of the "right hero at the right place" is implied here, the sudden emergence of a dynamic and shrewd politcial leader, a persuasive speaker, a responsible Party man, and withal a *popular* personality of exceptional courage and a good sense of timing.

This aspect of the revolutionary catalysis clearly demands the impossible. Few magic moments in history can produce the superman of such unlimited and strategically exceptional virtues. Even if other preconditions have been met, the absence of such charismatic leadership may yet defeat the national revolution. Often the revolt seems to be propelled by the imaginary virtues or semi-fictitious popularity of the leader, as in Gomulka's case. When the true picture materializes in such instances, the illusion fades—and the hero has feet of clay. Thus Gomulka's momentum was dissipated after seven or eight months at most. In Budapest there was no leadership miracle at all, for Imre Nagy could not live up to the heroic demands of October, 1956. The East German revolt of June, 1953, seemed to be utterly leaderless and collapsed after little more than forty-eight hours.

The unmistakable conclusion to be drawn from this analysis is that the *successful* revolution must be the product of a magic confluence of at least six historical factors, some of short-term, others of long-term significance. In view of the miraculous synchronization necessary to bring all these forces to bear at the split-second moment for the ideological and political catalysis, the prognosis for revolutionary successes from below, occurring within the given satellite social system, must be gloomy indeed.

Of all cohesive factors on the East European scene, Soviet military domination and the Russians' resultant political control are the most basic and unshakable. The goals of the U.S.S.R. have an aspect of permanence and constancy for the satellites: Security and the maintenance of a broad and exclusive sphere of influence are the primary long-term motives, while operational techniques and concrete policies may change and fluctuate considerably.

The effectiveness of Soviet political control is further enhanced by the seeming pervasiveness, or at least aggressiveness, of Communist ideology. It is clear to the outside world that the longer the Soviet Union remains capable of maintaining itself in power, the larger will be the sectors of satellite populations that will have acquired vested interests in the perpetuation of the *status quo*. Communism will not need dynamic ideological vigor; it can yet score its long-term victories through popular indifference or the silent acquiescence of the masses. The ruling regimes, from Poland to Bulgaria, have been significantly aided in their search for internal stability (and even acceptance) by a profound moral vacuum composed of public apathy, the inner emptiness of the younger generation, a mass aversion to political ideas, philosophic beliefs or convictions, and an increased sense of isolated provincialism. This moral weakness is then compounded by an increasingly obvious, and even frantic, search for materialistic satisfactions, a struggle for personal comfort, for economic rewards and concessions given in lieu of personal or cultural freedom. Moral weakness thus leads to economic corruption and ultimately to a gradual disintegration of the ethical foundations of society. While Party leaders of East European countries have loudly and hypocritically bemoaned the widespread "economism" (materialism) of the public, Communism has shrewdly and persistently exploited the weaknesses inherent in such a social atmosphere. In a recent book, Barbara Ward rightly diagnosed this exaggerated drive toward materialism and "this-worldliness" as one of the four principal revolutions currently sweeping our political world.[7]

Soviet-controlled Communism is bound to be exposed to many divergent pressures during the decade of the 1960's; some will assert themselves in a divisive or centrifugal direction, while others may tend to enhance cohesion, unity, and the centripetal orientation of a structurally totalitarian society. On the whole, the internal politics of the area will be characterized by the dialectical contradictions of processes of obvious *tactical* change generally operating along the lines of a great *strategic* continuity. In the short run, Communist regimes will be forced to adopt certain more or less revisionist policies of rational political freedoms balanced with economic concessions. Such short-term policies of "humanization" and "liberalization" will then be widely heralded as harbingers of the triumphant (and inevitable) transition leading from Socialism to Communism.

Yet the axiom *"plus ça change, plus c'est la même chose"* startlingly applies to the long-run perspective of East European politics. The contemporary revision of Communism does not and cannot imply—over a longer period of time—the liberalization and relaxation of the power apparatus, the democratization of a monolithic Party dictatorship, or, especially, the personal mellowing and intellectual emancipation of its theorists and practitioners.

7. EASTERN EUROPE AND WORLD COMMUNISM

William E. Griffith

"Coming events," the old saying goes, "cast their shadows before." Yet had this essay been written in 1960 instead of 1963, it would certainly not have paid sufficient attention to the implications of the already visible Sino-Soviet dispute for the East European satellites. Today, when the dispute has become a public and probably irreversible split, the East European Communist parties, like those elsewhere in the world, can only be understood in its context.

Yet Khrushchev's Eastern Europe, with the single exception of small, isolated Albania, has not, at least as yet, changed in his disfavor. On the contrary, he probably still looks upon his work in Eastern Europe and finds it good. It was after all primarily he who, in 1955, initiated the *rapprochement* with Yugoslavia and who, in 1956, came to terms with Gomulka's autonomy and smashed Nagy's secession. Since November 4, 1956, when Red Army tanks crushed Hungarian independence and neutrality, Soviet policy toward Eastern Europe has been primarily aimed at convalescence and consolidation. Even if one takes into account the Albanian revolt and the already existing signs of some renewed unrest in some of the East European countries, one can still only feel that Khrushchev's policies toward this area must still be considered successful on balance.

In 1953, when Stalin died, Khrushchev (and, quite likely, Malenkov as well) realized that controlled relaxation of tension was necessary in Soviet internal affairs, on the international scene, and in the relations between Moscow and China on the one hand and its East European satellites on the other. Only thus, Khrushchev correctly believed, could East European mass discontent, arising from nationalistic and economic causes, be contained; could he afford, as he both needed and wished, to withdraw from the day-to-day supervision of East European affairs at all levels; could the satellite leaderships acquire more stability, popularity, and authority; and, as in the Soviet Union, could there occur some revitalization of the moribund Communist ideology. On both the international scene in general and the East European scene in particular, such a policy of relaxation required a *rapprochement* with Tito. Stalin's break with Belgrade had resulted in purge, terror, and oppression throughout the Soviet bloc; its reversal was a necessary part of any effective general de-Stalinization program. Such a *rapprochement,* like relaxation in general, was for Khrushchev a calculated risk, but he hoped through it to win Tito back to the bloc and thus gain Yugoslav aid in making political and ideological conquests in the underdeveloped countries with which the Yugoslav dictator had developed such close relations.

In internal Soviet affairs, Khrushchev's calculations have in general been successful. In the international arena, his failure to check the surging flood of West European prosperity and unity has been at least in part counterbalanced by the losses of the West and to a lesser extent the gains of the Communists in the underdeveloped areas and, most recently, by renewed West European disunity. In the East European satellites, however, at the end of 1956, Khrushchev's policy of controlled *détente* seemed to lie in ruins. After 1955, splits in the Moscow and East European Communist leaderships had allowed intellectual ferment among Party and literary elites to link up with furious mass hatred of the Russians and of Communism. In Poland, Khrushchev succeeded in preventing the dam from breaking only by making concessions to Gomulka that gravely reduced effective Soviet influence over the country and established a dangerous precedent for the rest of Eastern Europe: the ending of agricultural collectivization, the collapse of police terror, and the *modus vivendi* with the Roman Catholic Church. In Hungary it seemed that Soviet military rule would be the only safe course perhaps for years to come, while the damage throughout the world that the Soviet image had suffered from the Budapest massacre detracted from past Soviet successes. The Yugoslav involvement in the Hungarian affair was one of the major reasons (along with the Chinese policy shift to the left) why at the end of 1957 the continued efforts of both Khrushchev and Tito toward a complete reconciliation ended in renewed polemics and break.

Yet, in one of those remarkable demonstrations of personal and political resilience that have so often characterized his rise to supreme power and subsequent career, Khrushchev overcame and crushed his challengers at home in the summer of 1957, poured Soviet economic aid into Poland, Hungary, and East Germany, skillfully exploited Western inaction in 1956 to demonstrate to the East European peoples that they had nothing to hope for from that quarter, and stubbornly continued his policy of controlled relaxation in East Europe and in the Soviet Union itself. By the end of 1959, he had scored remarkable successes. The renewed rift with Yugoslavia, although regrettable from his viewpoint, served as an ideological peg on which to hang his new, harder line against revisionism. Gomulka, aided by the Polish people's realization that another Budapest was the only alternative to his rule, that the Russian alliance was the necessary guarantee of Poland's western frontiers, and (an important but often neglected point) by his lack of ambition to play any role on the international Communist scene, successfully reconsolidated his own position.

In Rumania, Bulgaria, and Albania, the Balkan satellite leaders had only too readily responded to their post-Hungarian revolution opportunity to crush their revisionist dissidents even more strongly. This had been possible in Bucharest and Sofia without any significant changes in the Party leaderships, and it had been easy because of the lack of any tradition of intellectual ferment and successful popular opposition. In Tirana and East Berlin, the Hungarian events had probably saved the Stalinist dictators Hoxha and Ulbricht from Khrushchev's intention to remove them, in the former case primarily because of Yugoslav pressure, in the latter, as a belated purge of a prominent Stalinist comparable to Rákosi or Chervenkov. Thereafter, Hoxha and Ulbricht immediately crushed their parties as they had their intellectual opponents. It seems unlikely that Khrushchev had contemplated removing the Stalinist (but secure and safe) Czech leadership, which in the spring of 1956 had so efficiently crushed the momentarily menacing literary and student opposition.

Most Western observers at the time thought that Khrushchev's problem in Budapest was by far the most difficult. Could he ever hope, even partially, to stabilize the Hungarian situation with a motley crew of quislings headed by the notorious Kádár? Yet Hungary today is remarkably stable, primarily because it is resigned to its Communist fate, but also, more unexpectedly, because Kádár, at least among many of the intellectuals, enjoys a certain grudging respect as a man who is far preferable to Rákosi, seems increasingly willing to let them alone, and recently has gone rapidly and far toward renewed liberalization. One can best study Khrushchev's failure in his policies toward China and Albania; in his policies toward Hungary and Poland one can best study his successes.

The recent course of the Sino-Soviet dispute has made clear what many earlier signs had pointed to: Gomulka and Kádár are the two East European leaders closest to Khrushchev personally, ideologically, and politically. Their line—centrist and domesticist—is just what he wants in Eastern Europe. They share neither the Stalinism of Molotov, Rákosi, and Ulbricht, the revisionism of Nagy, nor the international ambitions of Tito. They support Khrushchev's policies against those of China and Albania out of conviction as well as out of expediency or fear. They have neither forced total conformity upon nor allowed their rebellious intellectuals total freedom. They are themselves neither intellectuals nor Westernized nor totally unpopular. They have not recently caused Khrushchev any serious trouble.

One may also look at the 1957–59 reconsolidation of Soviet power in Eastern Europe, the fruition of Khrushchev's stubbornly held and (it seemed at the end of 1959) remarkably effective policies, from another viewpoint. The Soviet Union by 1959 was well on the way to becoming an economically developed society. In many important sectors—industry, science and technology, military power—it was one of the most developed countries on earth. Although this was true of East Germany and of the Czech lands as well, and to some extent of Hungary, Eastern Europe in general was still largely agrarian. Economic development continued at a forced pace, although not so rapidly and not at such a cost in human lives and suffering as in the Stalinist period. Nevertheless, by 1959, East European industrialization had reached a creditable level, and East Germany and Czechoslovakia were already important factors in the economic-aid activities of the Soviet bloc in underdeveloped countries. This economic development of the East European satellites had major albeit paradoxical significance for Soviet policy in the area.

The newly acquired East European heavy industrial base made possible, and Khrushchev's policy encouraged, expansion of consumer-goods production. Simultaneously, the pre-1956 Stalinist-type Soviet economic exploitation of the East European satellites had been replaced, particularly in Hungary but to a considerable extent in the other countries as well, by significant Soviet economic aid. The confluence of these two processes had substantially increased the living standard throughout the area, thus lowering the level of mass discontent and significantly easing the Soviet problem of control.

In addition, the remarkable Soviet economic, technological, scientific, and military successes that began with the 1957 Sputnik, plus Khrushchev's 1956 demonstration that if necessary he was ready and able to use military force to preserve Soviet control over Eastern Europe, had further increased popular submissiveness. At the same time, it increased the numbers and raised the loyalty and morale of the managerial new class, which was increasingly replacing the original conspiratorial Stalinist revolutionaries in the top and middle levels of the East European regimes. Another normal phenomenon in a rapidly developing backward country, particularly where tradition was not totally anti-Russian, was beginning to take effect: The intelligentsia, itself a preindustrial phenomenon, was becoming increasingly differentiated and therefore less effectively hostile to Soviet policy and control. In Poland, however, anti-Russian feeling and the continued consciousness of the German threat appeared to be maintaining traditional intelligentsia behavior patterns.

The 1956 Polish and Hungarian events had dealt major if not fatal blows to ideological belief and commitment among the East

European elites, far more so than in the Soviet Union itself. Nevertheless, the remarkable post-1956 Soviet successes, plus the inaction of the West in respect to East European affairs, have enabled Khrushchev to substitute to a remarkably successful degree an ideology of power and success for the previous ideology of sacrifice and messianic hope.

Finally, it became clear in the 1957–59 period that Khrushchev meant what he said when he proclaimed that the East European leaderships would no longer, as Stalin had demanded, have to enforce slavish conformity to Soviet models, but rather would be permitted considerable concessions for "national peculiarities," always with the provision that they followed the general lines of Soviet ideology and policy and totally conformed with Soviet foreign and military policy. Contrary to many Western fears and undoubtedly to the wishes of such Stalinists as Ulbricht and Novotný, Khrushchev did not force Gomulka to resume forced agricultural collectivization. On the contrary, he allowed him to pay lip service to it as an ultimate aim but to maintain a practice little different from that in Yugoslav agriculture. Kádár pushed through full collectivization in 1959, apparently not in response to an order from Moscow but rather because of his own desire to reestablish full control over the Hungarian peasantry. Rumania and Bulgaria remained Stalinist in their backwardness; Czechoslovakia neo-Stalinist in its prosperity. All in all, in late 1959 and early 1960 it seemed that Khrushchev's experiment in differentiated, controlled, partial decolonization held out a promise of success similar to that of the 1867 British North America Act in Canada, although not at all for the same reasons.

But as we now know, Khrushchev's reconsolidation of his control over Eastern Europe appeared more successful from the outside, and probably even from Moscow, than it was in fact. While Khrushchev was disposing of his opponents at home, forging ahead against the West and in the underdeveloped areas, and increasingly less concerned about a revival of domestic unrest in Eastern Europe, a greater danger than the 1956 East European events was threatening him from the East, one which in 1963 seemed potentially to menace his successes in Eastern Europe and perhaps to bring to that area another period of uncertainty and unreliability for Moscow.

This is not the place, nor is there by now any need, to retrace the course of the Sino-Soviet dispute. Several penetrating studies of it have already been published, and more will undoubtedly follow. Nevertheless, some preliminary remarks concerning it are necessary before attempting to give some clearer indication of its past, present, and probable future implications for the East European area.

Stalin feared Chinese Communist control over all of China. He foresaw that such an enormous, indigenously based Communist power would not long be subject to Moscow's control, all the more so because it had successfully survived his blunders and come to power not only without major Soviet help, and certainly without Red Army direct assistance, but in fact in contravention of his advice and guidance. During the early 1950's, Mao was far too busy consolidating his control over mainland China, and during the Korean War successfully preventing the United States from pushing to the Yalu River, to challenge Soviet influence in an area so distant and so completely under Stalin's terroristic dictatorship as Eastern Europe.

But after Stalin's death, Khrushchev's policy of cutting down direct Soviet control and giving more domestic autonomy to East European Communist rulers was not limited to that area. The very fact that he and Bulganin went to China in 1954, before their pilgrimage to Belgrade, was the best indication that this new Soviet policy involved major readjustments in Sino-Soviet relations as well. Realizing that Khrushchev, unlike Stalin, was amenable to granting concessions and having acquired a modernized army and air force as a result of the Korean War, Mao was able and eager to take advantage of Soviet disarray at the time of the 1956 Polish and Hungarian developments.

In the summer and autumn of that year (in so far as one can form a fairly accurate estimate of what then went on in the murky area of Sino-Soviet relations), Mao began to intervene in East European affairs, first by urging the Soviet Union to make some concessions to Gomulka and the Poles rather than pressure them, and then, the Chinese have since claimed, by pressing the Soviets

to crush the Hungarian revolution when Khrushchev was waver-
ing. In early 1957, Chou En-lai's trip through the East European
satellites was public evidence, at least to the Eastern European
elites, that China was no longer willing to be merely an object,
but insisted upon being a subject of the politics of the international Communist movement in general and in Eastern Europe in
particular.

But this was only a prelude. At least to the public eye, China
had still done nothing that indicated a desire to challenge directly
the primacy of Soviet influence in the East European area. But in
late 1957, at the time of the renewed Soviet break with Yugoslavia, such a challenge for the first time appeared in the form of
a new and much more extreme Chinese ideological general line
on revisionism in general and Yugoslav revisionism in particular
than that of the Soviet Union or of any East European satellites
except Albania. In retrospect it is apparent that the Peking-Tirana
axis was already beginning to form.

The Hungarian revolution did not immediately produce a new
break between Khrushchev and Tito. On the contrary, 1957 had
seen Tito's recognition of East Germany, a step probably intended
by Khrushchev, and perhaps also by Tito, as the next to the last
one before Yugoslavia rejoined a more loosely organized "camp of
socialism." But the course of events and the ambitions of Mao and
of Tito ran counter to these plans. Tito's international ambitions,
evidenced ideologically by the 1957 Yugoslav draft program and
politically by his insistence on maintaining an independent, "non-
aligned" foreign policy, made it most difficult for Khrushchev to
bring about a total Moscow-Belgrade reconciliation. Mao, driven
to a left-extremist policy by the disastrous failure of the "hundred
flowers" attempt at liberalization domestically, and emboldened
on the international scene by a far higher estimate than Khrushchev's of the significance of the 1957 Soviet successes in intercontinental guided missiles and sputniks, had sometime that
autumn determined to shift sharply to the left. The Chinese had
also been genuinely frightened by the Hungarian revolution,
which, they felt, threatened the power and cohesion of the bloc
and therefore their own security. Initially they did not seem to
have wished drastically to decrease Soviet influence within the

bloc in favor of greater autonomy for themselves and any potential allies they might wish or be able to acquire. All reports indicate that it was the Chinese and not the Soviets who, at the November, 1957, Moscow meetings, insisted that the phrase "the camp of socialism headed by the Soviet Union" be included in the declaration, thus making it impossible for the Yugoslavs to sign it and leading directly to the Moscow-Belgrade break. Yet in retrospect may this not also have been a Chinese move against Khrushchev's policy of reconciliation with Yugoslavia, a successful attempt to force him to take a more radical, antirevisionist course?

Be that as it may, in late 1957 and early 1958, Chinese (and Albanian) ideological pronouncements made clear their differences on many issues with Soviet foreign policy and clearly indicated Chinese pressure for a more radical line in foreign policy, particularly toward the United States. In 1958, the Chinese also introduced the people's communes, not only a leftist extremist measure internally but also an implicit but nevertheless clear bid for ideological primacy in the method and speed of the transition to Communism. During these years the remarkable similarity of the Albanian ideological line and that of China continued. This might have been ascribed only to the furious Albanian hatred of the Yugoslavs, whom the Chinese had selected as the most convenient symbolic whipping boy for all the revisionist tendencies they now detested. But there were also signs of sympathy for Chinese policies in those East European leaderships that themselves followed left-extremist policies (East Germany, Czechoslovakia, and Bulgaria) and in other countries (e.g., Poland) among the surviving Stalinist minorities.

In view of the still major degree of Soviet control, particularly over the otherwise weak Stalinist regimes in East Germany, Rumania, and Bulgaria, dependent for their power and survival upon the presence or threat of the Red Army, the fact that in 1958–59 this sympathy for the Chinese was allowed to be expressed indicated that the contest between Moscow and Peking was still one in which both sides hoped and expected that there would be no open outbreak of ideological polemics. The ideological challenges of the Chinese people's communes seemed by 1959 to have been averted by the Soviets when, at the 1959 Twenty-first Soviet Party

Congress, the equivocal formula was adopted that all socialist countries would make the transition to Communism "more or less simultaneously."

But the spring of 1960 saw the open outbreak of the Sino-Soviet dispute: first, in April, in the form of Chinese ideological articles challenging all aspects of Soviet policy and ideology; and then, in June, in international Communist meetings—at the World Federation of Trade Unions in Peking, and later that month in Bucharest, at an international Communist meeting on the occasion of the Rumanian Party congress. In both of these meetings the full nature and extent of the Chinese challenge, as well as its immediate implications for Eastern Europe and specifically for Albania, became clear. Later in the summer the Soviets tried, and failed, to overthrow Hoxha and Shehu through cuts in economic aid and conspiracy with their Albanian opponents.

The November, 1960, Moscow meetings worsened rather than contained (as it first seemed) the dispute. Soviet economic pressure on Albania accentuated rapidly immediately thereafter. By late spring, 1961, Soviet-Albanian relations were at the breaking point. Sino-Soviet relations, although on the surface somewhat improved, probably continued to worsen.

The October, 1961, public attack by Khrushchev upon Albania at the Twenty-second Congress, and the resultant diplomatic rupture between Moscow and Tirana and further worsening of Sino-Soviet relations, although undoubtedly a qualitative change, still represented tendencies at work long before they became so publicly apparent. By early 1963, it seemed that a genuine reconciliation between Moscow and Peking was highly improbable, and a Sino-Soviet split already existed in fact, and that a total, public split was sooner or later probable.

What is not yet clearly realized is a point that has quite as much if not more potential reverberations for Eastern Europe. The impact of the Sino-Soviet dispute within the Communist camp cannot be properly understood if it is primarily regarded as a struggle between, say, the "rightist" Soviets and the "leftist" Chinese and Albanians. It can best be grasped as a far more complex, polycentric situation.

Khrushchev is following, as he has done since he first achieved power, a quite genuinely "centrist" policy, which in terms of bloc relations has consistently sought to increase domestic autonomy while retaining international solidarity and decisive control, particularly in foreign affairs and ideology, by the Soviet Union. Since the Sino-Soviet conflict became acute in early 1960, Khrushchev has successfully enforced public loyalty to his position from the East European satellites, with the one exception of successfully rebellious Albania.

The left wing is represented by China and Albania, plus the support China has in, for example, the North Korean Party, the Bengali section of the Indian Communist Party, the Burmese and Malayan parties, and in most sections of the Indonesian and Japanese parties. Then there is in Asia one "Communist neutralist," the North Vietnamese Party. Ho Chi-minh seeks to profit from the Sino-Soviet rift by leaning toward the Chinese ideologically but also retaining his formal good relations with the Soviet Union and profiting from them; in brief, by maneuvering between the two in order to gain for himself more autonomy and freedom of action. Of late, however, he has moved farther toward Peking.

One final point must be made. Some of the smaller parties, like those of Poland and Italy, which genuinely support Khrushchev's policy position against Peking's, do not share his organizational insistence on the primacy of position due to the "vanguard" Soviet Party. On the contrary, on the organizational issue they, like the Albanian and Indonesian parties, do not desire total domination by anyone—Khrushchev or Mao.

To return to Europe. There the Yugoslavs continue to represent rightist tendencies, but their recent large-scale *rapprochement* with Moscow renders these less effective. The Italian Communist Party is more rightist; actually, if opportunistically, revisionist. Within the East European states, the only Party in substantial although far from complete sympathy with the Italian viewpoint is the Polish Party. Gomulka, however, as well as the Polish Party generally, is much less venturesome than the Italians; he can much less afford to be. Polish international conformity to Soviet policy is much clearer than that of the Italians, while Gomulka profits from his total foreign policy and less total organizational support of Khrushchev's position to consolidate his domestic divergences from the general line of bloc policy, particularly in agriculture. Not surprisingly, neither Gomulka, Kádár, nor Togliatti wants an open, total Sino-Soviet break; it might decrease their freedom of maneuver.

Kádár and the majority of the Hungarian leadership, not Stalinists but (as they have been since 1945) centrists, now also represent a rightist trend, less so than the Italians and, in part, the Poles, but still one of considerable significance. Like Gomulka, Kádár, by his enthusiastic support of Khrushchev's international policy positions, has also gained more domestic freedom of maneuver than Moscow might otherwise be willing to grant; now that he has successfully consolidated his power, he has used it to liberalize many aspects of Hungarian life.

The other East European parties—the East German, the Czech, the Rumanian, and the Bulgarian—represent what may best be called "frustrated Stalinists" forced by Khrushchev into allegiance to his centrist position. East Germany, Czechoslovakia, and Bulgaria demonstrated this in 1958–59 by their interest and support for Chinese developments, manifestations that ceased abruptly in June, 1960, after the Peking and Bucharest meetings, when Khrushchev enforced total conformity with his anti-Chinese views.

The Albanian Party, having broken with Moscow and aligned itself with Peking, has also gained increased autonomy. Peking is far away, weaker than the Soviet Union, and needs Albania, its only other total supporter among parties in power, much more than the Soviet Union needs this isolated, poverty-stricken satellite. Tirana has utilized its increased autonomy to increase its economic relations with the West, notably with Italy, thus somewhat decreasing its total dependence on Peking.

The primary reason that the Albanians exchanged Soviet for Chinese protection was that Hoxha and most of the Albanian leaders feared that Khrushchev would again turn them over to Tito, who had almost deposed them in 1948 and again in 1956. In 1956, they had had no potential ally other than Moscow; by 1960, the Chinese were willing and ready to support Albania's permanently deficit economy and grant Albania political and ideological protection against Moscow. From the Albanian point of view, the defection from Moscow to Peking serves to safeguard them against Belgrade, allows them to continue their domestic Stalinism (their own only chance of internal survival), helps to increase their nationalistic support among the anti-Serb and anti-Greek Albanians, and, since Peking is both a powerful and above all a distant protector, gives them more domestic autonomy. The Albanian leaders, like Tito and his associates, came to power primarily through their own efforts, although under Yugoslav direction. (Most of the current Polish leaders, including Gomulka and his closest associates, were in Warsaw, not in Moscow, during the war, fought there in the Communist underground, were persecuted under Stalinism, and thus share some of the feelings of the Yugoslavs and the Albanians.)

At least some of the "frustrated Stalinist" parties in Eastern Europe also seem to have acquired some increased freedom of maneuver in domestic affairs. The arrest in 1962 of former secret police chief Barák of Czechoslovakia for anti-Party activities is the most significant leadership change to have occurred there since 1952. Except for the purging of Belishova and Tashko of Albania in the summer of 1960, it is also the most significant change in the entire Communist camp since the onset of the Sino-Soviet polemics in early 1960. Barák may have been ousted because he, like Schirdewan and Wollweber in East Germany in 1956, hoped to outmaneuver Novotný by following a more anti-Stalinist course, thus gaining Khrushchev's support in taking over the leadership in Prague. Certainly Novotný feared this. Barák lost, quite possibly in large part because Khrushchev was willing to tolerate continued domestic Czechoslovak Stalinism rather than risk the unfavorable international reverberations of so obviously changing the leadership of another Communist Party. But Barák is not dead; he was merely given a prison sentence, and he remains a dangerous alternative to Novotný's continued rule.

The purge in the late spring of 1963 of Slovak First Secretary Bacilek and Czech Politburo member Kohler plus the weakening of the position of Prime Minister Široký, on the other hand, were sacrifices by Novotný of his former Stalinist associates under pressure from the literary ferment in Slovakia and from general popular discontent arising from the economic crisis. Thus the Czechoslovak crisis continues, with Novotný's position as of this writing (June, 1963) increasingly shaky.

Rumania has also shown increasing signs of successful resistance to the Soviet-sponsored intensified coordination through CMEA of the East European economies. Such coordination would automatically favor the already existing industries in more developed countries (East Germany and Czechoslovakia) and thus discriminate against countries like Rumania that do not yet have a complete industrial base. As of this writing, the Rumanians have refused to accept the Soviet view. Furthermore, they are apparently using the Sino-Soviet dispute to maintain their objections—they have made favorable (and reciprocated) gestures toward China and Albania. Like Poland, Rumania can, without deserting the Soviet Union (as did Albania), utilize the dispute to resist Soviet pressure more effectively.

How will the Sino-Soviet dispute influence the actual policies of the East European regimes and the existence of their peoples? We do not yet know when, whether, or if it will lead to a total break between Moscow and Peking, but an actual split has occurred and an open break seems eventually likely. Were a break to occur, the Soviet Union, no longer having to take account of China and determined to stamp out any pro-Chinese feeling, might return to a policy of greater control over Eastern Europe. This, however, seems unlikely. Competition between the Soviet Union and China would still continue in parties outside the Communist camp, whose leadership would certainly be affected by what the Soviet Union and China did in areas within the camp. This in turn would continue to inhibit any sharp increase in Soviet control in Eastern Europe.

Polycentrism, now increasing, will probably continue to grow. As is clear from the present major *rapprochement* between Moscow and Belgrade, Warsaw and Belgrade, and particularly the Italian Communist Party and Belgrade, this polycentric development has resulted in a partial re-entry of Yugoslavia as an active factor in East European affairs. It seems unlikely, on balance, that the Sino-Soviet dispute will result in anything nearly like the drastic 1956 East European events. Such developments would require a key permissive factor now absent: a succession struggle in Moscow.

With the exception of the increased challenge to Novotný described above, the positions of the East European Party chiefs do not appear threatened at present. Gomulka is completely in control in Warsaw; so, by now, is Kádár in Budapest. The more rigid of the East European leaders, Gheorghiu-Dej, Zhivkov, and Ulbricht, seem still able to retain their positions.

Of all these three, Zhivkov is most likely to have trouble. Bulgaria is the country in which the ethnic and territorial factors involved in the Albanian and Yugoslav situations, particularly the question of Macedonia and in the Soviet-Yugoslav *rapprochement*, are likely first to have reverberations. As of this writing, however, Zhivkov's control was confirmed at the Bulgarian Party Congress in December, 1962. Gheorghiu-Dej's defiance of CMEA coordination probably strengthens his position.

There has recently been some speculation that Ulbricht may be in trouble in East Berlin. On balance, this seems unlikely. He, much more than any other East European leader except Hoxha, remains an unreconstructed Stalinist. The halfhearted experiments Moscow seemed ready to initiate in East Germany in 1953 and 1956 initially may well have included at least serious consideration of Ulbricht's removal; both ended disastrously. Khrushchev now probably (and correctly) realizes that East Germany can never have a Gomulka: It is neither a state nor a nation, neither German, nor democratic nor a republic. Moscow will therefore probably maintain Ulbricht in power for the present. But Ulbricht is sixty-nine; he cannot go on forever, and a change in the SED leadership will in a few years become inevitable. It will, however, much more than any of the others, reflect the East-West relationship, particularly over Berlin; it is therefore not likely to be anywhere nearly as significantly influenced by the Sino-Soviet rift.

Hoxha is using his own increased autonomy not only to maintain his domestic Stalinism, but also to increase his commercial and diplomatic ties with the West. It may well be that the same will eventually happen with other Communist countries in Eastern Europe. It does not, however, appear immediately likely, particularly as long as tension over the Berlin situation continues. Another international crisis that might change relations in the Communist camp and, therefore, the East European situation, is the one in Southeast Asia. There, Ho Chi-minh's balancing act between Moscow and Peking makes more difficult than before the prediction of Communist moves. One may venture to guess, however, that a continuation of the present guerilla-type warfare is more likely than major escalation. The latter would almost inevitably throw Ho Chi-minh into the hands of the Chinese; their army, as in Korea, would have to flood in to redress the balance against American military power. Should the Southeast Asian situation escalate greatly, it might bring the Russians and the Chinese together again, with a resultant slowing down of centrifugal tendencies in Eastern Europe—but such escalation seems quite unlikely.

Events such as those in 1956 in Poland and Hungary seldom recur in the same generation. Changes in Eastern Europe are certainly again under way, in large part because of increasing polycentrism within the Communist camp. They will probably not have the same economic and nationalistic mass momentum; they will not, at least initially, be pushed forward by power struggles in Moscow or in many of the satellites. Intellectual revisionism in Eastern Europe is likely to be a lesser force than it was in 1956; there are by now fewer ideologically committed East European Communist intellectuals in whom revisionism could be engendered by the dynamic of loss of faith. Yet the recent intellectual ferment in Slovakia shows that revisionism is always potentially alive. Slow, gradual differentiation and decline of regime pressures (particularly in Poland and Hungary), greater emphasis on "national peculiarities," improved relations with Yugoslavia (especially by such rightist parties as the Polish and Hungarian), are more likely to be the order of the day. The Sino-Soviet dispute in the long run is likely to erode ideological commitment, but 1956 dealt such commitment a near death blow in Eastern Europe anyway. The Communist parties in the East European countries today are far more influenced by opportunism and by the feeling that the Soviet Union is scientifically, technologically, and militarily becoming more powerful than the West. This source of Communist strength, however, is potentially threatened by the onrushing prosperity and consolidation of Western Europe.

If the Sino-Soviet split does result in a complete break, if West European unification and prosperity continue, and if the Berlin and Southeast Asian crises can be contained, there is a greater prospect for a gradual, differentiated improvement in the lot of the East European peoples and for a higher degree of domestic autonomy from Moscow on the part of their regimes.

8. EASTERN EUROPE AND THE NON-COMMUNIST WORLD

Hans E. Tütsch

The relations between the Communist states of East Central and Southeastern Europe and the non-Communist world cannot be considered separately from their connections with the Soviet Union; while the links to the West are tenuous, like the web of a spider, the Communist countries are bound to Moscow by iron chains. Stalin, with the tacit or open consent of his wartime allies, built up his own "Continental system" by absorbing the Baltic states, together with territories torn off from Finland, Poland, Czechoslovakia, and Rumania, into the Soviet Union, and by creating further a ring of satellites on its western borders reaching far into the center and south of Europe. He thus formed a hard core from which revolutionary Communism could spread all over the world.

Khrushchev is expanding this plan by attempting to shield the Soviet empire with a large zone of neutralist states in Europe, Asia, and Africa, over which the Russian hegemony can be established and which in time may be taken over by Communism. While Moscow is not yet in a position to dictate to the neutralist countries, their leaders are following the Kremlin's line more and more, whereas ten years ago, in the pre-Bandung era, Burma, Ceylon, India, Naguib's Egypt, and even Yugoslavia, which signed the Balkan Pact, leaned more toward the West. In its relationship to the neutralists, the Soviet Union uses the East European Communist states as an instrument for their political infiltration. The relations between the Soviet Union and the Communist states, between Moscow and the West, remain outside the scope of this article; therefore, the centripetal and centrifugal forces in the

212

Communist bloc are considered only in so far as they affect the contacts between Eastern Europe and the non-Communist world.

Soviet Supremacy and Ideological Unity

Of the European Communist countries only Yugoslavia—and later Albania—have acquired a measure of independence from Moscow. Poland, the German Democratic Republic, Czechoslovakia, Hungary, Rumania, Bulgaria—the members of the Soviet bloc—enjoy only an insignificant margin of free movement in foreign policy. A clear distinction, thus, is to be made between the members of the Soviet bloc, justifiably called satellites, and European Communist countries like Yugoslavia and Albania that have strayed from the fold.

The Soviet Union's supremacy was established by conquest, not by conviction. Only in Yugoslavia and Albania was the Communist regime not established by the Red Army. In all the other countries the Communist parties, a minority, needed the indirect or direct support of the Soviet Union and its armed forces to maintain themselves in power; the Soviet armed interventions in East Germany in 1953 and Hungary in 1956 served as drastic examples to all other satellite countries. Most of the powers of the Communist regimes, therefore, derive directly from Moscow; the powers inherent in a sovereign state are limited in the case of the satellites. In examining every action of a Communist state it must be ascertained whether or to what degree an original or a derived function is involved, whether the state acts for itself or in the name and sense of the Soviet bloc.

All Communist parties are bound together by a set of common convictions based on Marxist-Leninist ideology. They share the belief that capitalism is inevitably doomed and the victory of Communism historically preordained. This historical development cannot or shall not be frustrated by the West, and it must be helped by the East. Formulas like "peaceful coexistence" or "*status quo*" therefore have to be understood in a historical context in which they assume a Janus face, turning a static aspect to the West and a dynamic one to the East; for the West they mean noninterference, but for the East they mean support for "just wars of liberation" and progress to final victory. These basic tenets are accepted by all Communist parties in Europe, including the Yugoslav Party, whose leader, Marshal Tito, proclaims that the goals are the same, that only the methods adopted by Yugoslavia differ from those advocated by the CPSU.

Not content with the ideological unity of the Communist parties, Moscow formalized the relations between the different organizations and set up a system to coordinate their activities. This system underwent repeated changes; the dissolved Comintern was revived in the shape of the Cominform in the fall of 1947, but dropped again after eight and a half years. A further attempt at ideological coordination through the publication of an ideological newspaper for the Communist parties, *Problems of Peace and Socialism,* met with little success. The rigid central organization of the Communist parties has disappeared since 1956; more frequent meetings of the several Party leaders have taken place since. Although the hierarchic order is still evident at these international gatherings, it is no longer institutionalized in a permanent centralized organization. The conclaves of Party leaders are completed frequently by bilateral exchanges of visits of Party delegations—usually connected with visits of state leaders—which unroll according to an elaborate "Mandarin" protocol and invariably end in a declamation of mutual friendship. The real objects of the talks are kept secret, but under the cover of diplomatic ritual and within the limits of Soviet assignments, differences may be ironed out by technicians and some pressure exerted on parties in danger of deviating from the right line.

Like the exchanges of thought and information between the different Party organizations, the mutual visits of cabinet ministers, prime ministers, and heads of states may bear on the politics pursued by the Communist countries toward the West. They are, certainly, one of the means of keeping the Communist states in step. Taken separately, these countless visits may have little significance, but they lend a little status to the countries in the Soviet hegemonial sphere resulting from the network of bilateral treaties on cultural, economic, or political affairs.

Multilateral pacts have never been welcome to Moscow unless the Soviet Union is the center from which all activity can be controlled or directed, as in the Warsaw Pact for political and military cooperation and in the Council for Mutual Economic Assistance for economic coordination, or as was the case in the defunct Cominform. The attempts at multilateral cooperation, like the economic agreement between Poland, Czechoslovakia, and Hungary, or Tito's and Dimitrov's plans for a Balkan federation, were thoroughly frustrated by the Soviet Union. Even the attempts to institutionalize the contacts between neutralist countries, spearheaded by Tito, Nasser, and Nehru in the Asian-African Solidarity Conference and its permanent secretariat, or in the neutralist summit conferences, met with Moscow's criticism or active opposition. The Kremlin will not willingly allow new centers of gravity outside its direct and permanent sphere of influence.

The fundamental opposition against all multilateral pacts in which the Soviet Union does not participate as dominating member extends naturally to the regional politico-military organizations set up by the West. They are branded as aggressive according to the Communist doctrine, proof of the war-proneness of the capitalist world. The destruction of the North Atlantic alliance (NATO), the Central Treaty Organization (CENTO, formerly the Baghdad Pact), the South East Asia Treaty Organization (SEATO), and the economic agreements that led to the rehabilitation of Western Europe—e.g., the OEEC and OECD, the Common Market, or even the Council of Europe in Strasbourg—seems to be one of the major aims of the U.S.S.R. and the other Communist countries. These states act together to isolate the different "capitalist" countries and to demolish their military potential, as in the demand for an evacuation of all military bases on foreign territory, or for a withdrawal of American troops from the European Continent, or for uncontrolled disarmament. They act together to disrupt the economic cooperation of the West. These general aims are pursued in the political field through international conferences on different levels and with different participants, in the United Nations where the neutralist myrmidons are set in motion for Russian goals, by blackmail in Berlin, or with threats of nuclear weapons carried by intercontinental missiles.

Since Stalin's death, direct aggression, or aggression by proxy, has given way not to subtler but to less provocative methods. The three doors of the Slav world to the Mediterranean—the Turkish Straits, the Vardar Valley, and Trieste—all of which the Soviet empire tried to force open in the postwar period, have remained closed and are now in a zone of temporary calm. With Turkey, the open antagonism was allowed a respite after the revolution of May 27, 1960; the Vardar Valley access road to Salonica, coveted by the Slavs, ceased to be an object of dispute after the Communist defeat in 1949. (Tito claimed special rights for the Slav minority in Greece in December, 1961; however, he denied later that this claim had any territorial implication.) Yugoslavia's push to open the way from the Lubljana Gap to Trieste has not been renewed. Military aggression has been restricted to Asia, where Communism's Chinese mutation follows its own policy. But the Berlin Wall stands as a symbol of Moscow's "peacefulness."

Economic Strategy and Tactics

The Soviet Union, aided by its satellites, has fought Western Europe's economic rehabilitation and unification step by step. The list of critical articles in official newspapers and of protest notes to West European governments cautioning them not to join the Common Market is interminable. Economic policy in the Communist states is subordinated to general political considerations; the state-run economy has to further Communist political expansion. The general lines of trade and production in the Soviet bloc are determined by bilateral agreements with the Soviet Union and the other Communist countries, and by the multilateral coordination in the framework of the Council for Mutual Economic Assistance. COMECON determines the economic "strategy" of the Communist countries, but it leaves them a certain freedom in the "tactical" field of their relations with the West in which they march separately toward the common goal. Commercial policy is hardly more than an instrument of foreign policy. When the Soviet Union deemed it expedient to show its disapproval of Israel, the contract for delivery of Russian oil was broken. Before the Greek elections of 1961, Moscow, exerting political pressure, interrupted oil exports to Greece; Rumania quickly followed suit. At the same time the Russian oil-dumping on the world markets continued, disrupting the price structure established by Western private companies. Trade agreements with neutralist or noncommitted nations have obvious political overtones. Extensive Western trade commitments, embodied in attractive long-term agreements with the Soviet bloc, have also furthered Communist aims. The effects of long-range agreements that alter the original economic structure of a country may be seen in Finland. They are also strongly felt in Greece and Turkey, which already export one-quarter or more of their products to the bloc and are thus suspectible to eventual commercial blackmail. A standard argument used by Western exporters and importers lured by Communist offers is that the same products would be available elsewhere; therefore, why not make a profit? The limitations imposed on Western trade relations with the Soviet bloc after the outbreak of the Korean War had very little effect and were abolished step by step or in many cases fell into disuse. Fear that a boycott of the U.S.S.R. and the satellites would be taken by the subject populations as a trade war against themselves (as happened in Spain after 1945) rather than their governments, toward which they feel hardly any solidarity, precludes such action by the West.

Instruments of Amplification

The Communist states in Europe, being held together by a common ideology and—except Yugoslavia and Albania—by multilateral organizations, bilateral treaties, and a permanent exchange of ideas, are assigned or, based on their common convictions, have assumed a political division of labor; its most important function appears to be amplification of the Marxist-Leninist word enunciated by the Kremlin. The main instruments used for this amplification are, of course, the Communist parties in power as well as *in partibus infidelium.* Communist parties in Europe indeed play the role of godfathers for their counterparts in "underdeveloped" regions of the world, as exemplified by the relation of the Partito Comunista Italiano to the Egyptian Communists.

Asian and African Communists and sympathizers are invited not only to Moscow, but also to Budapest and Prague; they are showered with gifts and propaganda tracts in their own languages and in turn proclaim their admiration for the wonderful cities built centuries before Karl Marx published his Communist Manifesto.

The trade unions of the satellite countries and the World Federation of Trade Unions impress the workers from countries where trade unionism has not yet reached the *status nascendi* and where no Communist parties have yet been organized, as in the whole of Black Africa. Women's organizations, youth groups, professional associations (lawyers, physicians, journalists, etc.), sports contests, and the various friendship societies promote the interests of the Communist states. Cascades of propaganda from Moscow and the East European capitals descend on the West and the rest of the non-Communist world.

The variegated organizations, all serving one and the same purpose, achieve a deep penetration on levels where the West, due to the freedom of its associations, which need not follow governmental orders, can only muster uncoordinated forces that are neither directly nor indirectly prepared to spread or counteract any sort of propaganda. The Communists, thanks to their subtle instrumentation, may even lend support to opposing factions or interest groups without losing sight of their fundamental aim; in any case, they try to be on the winner's side. The Communist propaganda instruments reach out like the tentacles of an octopus, or rather of two big and several smaller octopuses. Their function of amplifying Soviet slogans is evidenced in the United Nations, which the Communists attempt to turn into an enormous sounding board.

The problems of coordinating the different forces are enormously difficult. Khrushchev has found Tito, Hoxha, and Mao too difficult to handle, and one-time camp followers like the late Kassem, Abdel Nasser, and Sékou Touré have shown disheartening willfulness. The coordination of policy in the North Atlantic alliance may sometimes appear a heavy chore to Western statesmen, but what greater, appalling difficulties to keep the Communist countries in step! Collaboration between them has often been overestimated; it is aspired to and ordered yet often not achieved, due mainly to national contrasts, but more often simply to *Svejkism* and *Oblomovshchina*. Historical differences between the Communist nations are not as easily overcome as assumed by Marxist-Leninist doctrines; as soon as territorial disputes are "arbitrated," the hydra of nationalism lifts a new head in the form of economic jealousies and divergent interests. The inability of Communism to adapt itself to national conditions leaves loopholes for Western ideas; nationalism proves the most disruptive force encountered by the Marxian aspiration for unity.

Communist doctrine proclaims its ability to overcome national divergences. "But power which is cultivated for the execution of tasks determined by ideological perspectives raises issues which inevitably produce conflicts. Matters pertaining to the domestic development of any one state become critically relevant for purposes of international association of such states and generate polemic issues of doctrinal purity," states Zbigniew K. Brzezinski in *The Soviet Bloc: Unity and Conflict*. Obviously the centrifugal forces in the Soviet bloc stem from two different sources. They develop inside the Communist parties where national traditions are never altogether eliminated by the countless purges. National interests are seldom expressed in matters of foreign policy and defense, but in economic discussions, e.g., during the meetings of the Council for Mutual Economic Assistance, they come to the fore time and time again. Even during Stalin's despotic rule, the Council representatives of the different Communist states defended the interests of their governments with utmost hardheadedness. That economic problems played a certain role in the break between the Cominform and Tito is well known.

National self-interest, of course, can also make for closer collaboration with the Soviet Union. Common fear and antagonism against the successors of the former Germanic empires—the Habsburg, the Hohenzollern, and Hitler empires with their perpetual *Drang nach Osten*—act as a definite centripetal force in the Communist world. The antagonism against everything German remains stronger in the Slavic states than in Hungary and Rumania—with the exception of Slovakia, which enjoyed its only period of relative independence under Germany's protection. Poland, because of the transfer of its border and part of its population to the West, and Czechoslovakia, which expelled the Sudeten Germans, are politically dominated by a nearly unbridgeable opposition to Germany. Their distrust of the German Democratic Republic reveals itself hardly less virulently, although less openly, than their distrust of the Federal Republic—especially each time they are asked by Moscow to subscribe to new measures for the rearmament of the Pankow regime. Prague and Warsaw live under the threat of an unscrupulous Soviet attempt to win over West Germany—the highest prize in Europe—for which they would have to foot the bill. "The only alternative for the Poles and Czechs to being made the object of cynical bargains by the Soviet Union is that they should themselves obtain a direct settlement with Germany," proclaims Hugh Seton-Watson in his *East European Revolution.*

The Communist leaders may be fairly free from illusions concerning their Soviet overlords, but they are also fully aware of the harsh punishments meted out by Moscow. The path for an eventual *rapprochement* between West Germany and Poland and Czechoslovakia would have to cross the terrifying barrier imposed by German separation and the problem of reunification. Bonn refuses to recognize any regime that entertains diplomatic relations with the Democratic Republic, and while this policy, formulated in the Hallstein Doctrine, has kept neutralist countries from recognizing the Communist part of Germany, it has not facilitated normalization of West Germany's contacts with its Slav neighbors who do recognize East Germany.

Nationalism—A Centrifugal Force

Strong repugnance against any sort of Sovietization and *Gleichschaltung* is doubtlessly felt by the peoples subject to Communist rule. Since these peoples have no possibility of expressing openly any opinions that do not conform with those of their dictatorial governments, they manifest their feeling in hidden corners of their lives in which the police are not permanently effective. The dedication to Western fashions, American jazz, and nonrealistic Western art has never been completely suppressed. The enormous pressure exerted by the Communist regimes on the non-Communist majority of the peoples leads to an exacerbation of nationalism in the conscious or unconscious parts of the soul, but it may break to the surface with extreme explosive violence, as witnessed during the Hungarian revolution of 1956. Nationalism, strengthened since the nineteenth century and reinforced by decades of chauvinist education, still burns on in the masses and makes itself felt inside the Communist parties, which can never be completely denationalized. In the conflicts that led to the breaking away of Yugoslavia, China, and Albania from the Soviet order of command and to the advocation of disruptive "polycentrism" by Palmiro Togliatti, the leader of the Italian Communist Party, nationalism reveals itself as a force that is a match for Communism. No church or empire has ever survived for long with two capitals. The Communist leaders are well aware of this historical fact—and so is the West.

Nationalism creates points of contact with the West, which has never disclaimed nationalism and in many instances—but not always—has stood in the forefront of fights for national self-determination. However, it must be borne in mind that one cannot promote a heresy within a church to which one does not belong; therefore, the possible initiative by the West appears rather limited. Like the West, the Soviet Union and Communist China have proclaimed their adherence to the principle of self-determination (for instance in the five principles of Bandung), but when Imre Nagy tried to apply these principles to Hungary he was cruelly taught better. According to the Soviet doctrine, the Communist countries have already decided about their future—forever. Not even neutralism will be permitted to them.

The initiative of Communist countries stems from the common aims established by the various command posts and transmitted through the different channels described above; in certain cases, it may also stem from original decisions by a single government. To distinguish between derived and original initiatives is not always an easy undertaking. But in the states that still belong fully to the Soviet bloc one could not conceive of a major move in foreign policy without previous agreement from Moscow; otherwise power conflicts covered up by ideological discussions would immediately break out. The only members of the Communist bloc that have come forth with noteworthy foreign-policy initiatives are Poland and Rumania; the most important projects are the Rapacki Plan and the Stoica Plan.

The Rapacki Plan and the Stoica Plan aim at the creation of a "peace zone" in which armaments should be curtailed, especially by the renunciation of nuclear arms. The Polish Foreign Minister, Rapacki, submitted his plan on October 2, 1957, to the Twelfth Session of the United Nations General Assembly; the main part reads as follows:

> In the interest of Poland's security and of a *détente* in Europe, having agreed on this initiative with the other members of the Warsaw Pact, the Government of the Polish People's Republic declares that should the two German states express their consent to impose a ban on the production and stockpiling of atomic and thermonuclear weapons in their territories, the Polish People's Republic is prepared simultaneously to impose a similar ban on her territory.

The Polish delegate was careful to point out that the other members of the Warsaw Pact had previously agreed to this initiative. This placet shows the plan as well within the scope of Soviet foreign policy. In separate declarations, the delegates of Czechoslovakia and the Government of the German Democratic Republic adhered formally to the Rapacki Plan. That the Polish Government pursues a serious aim with the plan cannot be doubted; it fears—like other satellite governments—becoming a combat area in a nuclear war and destruction between the millstones of the superpowers. That this fear is shared by the population of all the Communist countries was evidenced by the panic-buying after August 13, 1961, when an international conflict seemed to be near with the erection of the dividing wall in Berlin.

Poland stretches out its hands in the Rapacki Plan, hoping to find a way of linking itself with the disengagement projects developed in the West, especially the Eden Plan and the Gaitskell Plan. Regional disarmament in the West appears as a first step towards neutralization. A disarmed, neutral glacis in the center of Europe would lie defenseless between the anvil of Communist subversion and the hammer of Soviet nuclear blackmail. Temptations of a new Tauroggen or Rapallo would haunt a disarmed and isolated Germany broken out of the Western system of alliances and economic cooperation. The Western powers could thus consider the Rapacki Plan only in the context of general supervised disarmament, a European security system, and the solution of the German problem.

The similarity between the Stoica Plan and the Rapacki Plan is striking. The Rumanian proposal strives to keep the Balkan area free from atomic weapons. But, according to the Greek and Turkish governments, renunciation of atomic weapons would leave Greece and Turkey practically open to Soviet aggression. The Soviet Army, being supplied with the most modern arms, could, starting from the inner line, easily overrun the Greek and Turkish defense forces if they were not supported with rockets and atomic warheads. Greece has to put up with extremely difficult defense problems anyway, considering its long borders, the lack of depth of its territory (which would make a counteroffensive nearly impossible), and the exposure of its ports to aerial attacks. Tactical atomic weapons, be they in Greek hands or supplied by the American Sixth Fleet, alone establish a military equilibrium with the Soviet-bloc neighbors.

The diplomatic overture connected with the Rumanian initiative was cleverly handled by Bucharest. The fulfillment of the financial obligations established in the peace treaty, increase in trade with Greece, and the less aggressive tone of the propaganda paved the way for better relations with Athens. This diplomatic preparation contrasted strongly with the Bulgarian refusal to pay reparations to Greece. However, as in the case of the Rapacki Plan, the Rumanian initiative must be recognized as national in form, Soviet in content. It was supported by Bulgaria—which tended to discredit it in Greek eyes—but met with little enthusiasm in Yugoslavia. Seen from the Western side, these projects emerge as part of the general framework of Soviet-bloc policy.

The common elements in the Rapacki and Stoica Plans are obvious; so is the parallel between these two plans and the "five principles" of Bandung, which in Indian eyes should have become the basis for a permanent understanding with Communist China—before Mao Tse-tung's aggression against India. Guarantees of territorial integrity, nonaggression, nonintervention in internal affairs, equality, and collaboration for mutual benefit seem in the context of Communist policy an enlarged version of the regional initiatives of Rapacki and Stoica and born of the same general conception as Khrushchev's peaceful coexistence—unilaterally binding on the West. Nonaggression pacts, a preferred prewar instrument

of neutralizing non-Communist neighbors, have been discarded—
discredited as they were by Soviet aggressions against Finland, the
Baltic states, Poland, and Rumania—except for the proposal of a
nonaggression agreement between the Warsaw Pact and the North
Atlantic Pact. The aim to create a militarily and politically mushy
buffer zone, however, has not been abandoned.

Limited Western Aims

Confronted with the different projects of the Soviet bloc, the
West has shown little initiative aimed at the satellite countries.
It concentrates on the greater problems—disarmament, security
systems, and Germany—in which, however, scarcely any progress
resulted from the Western proposals. Russia's supremacy in Eastern and Southeastern Europe is not challenged by the West. In
order not to increase tensions and thus jeopardize chances for
eventual agreements leading to peace, the West goes out of its
way to avoid irritating the Soviet leaders. It prefers not to raise
the question of the Soviet territorial annexations, or that of the
undemocratic regimes violating the interallied agreements of the
war period and the peace treaties. It covers the Soviet interference in Finland's internal affairs with silence, and it has never
seriously considered non-Communist alternatives to any Communist regime—not even in the cases of Yugoslavia or Albania.
Pressure from outside could indeed increase the cohesion of the
Communist forces. But even if the West were totally inactive, as
it is for long periods, Communist demonology will always cast
Western states and statesmen in the devil's role—as imperialists,
neocolonialists, *revanchists*, or militarists—and no amount of ap-
peasement can liberate the West from this unilaterally assigned
role. The Western world can never appear as peaceful or peace-
loving in Communist terminology.

The West attempts to distinguish between the Soviet Union and
the other Communist states, and it gropes for signs of independent
responses. The possibilities of any other action are extremely
limited, given the basic proposition that in no instance should
force ever be used, or any internal movement of resistance supported militarily. The long-range goal remains, therefore, merely
to reach the population in sectors not completely isolated by Com-

munist police activity, and to establish contacts, if not with larger segments of the population, then with the pro-Western elites. This is done through cultural-exchange programs as well as informative broadcasts by the BBC, Voice of America, Radio Free Europe, and Radio Liberty. The diversity of the instruments of foreign policy, which include foreign aid (economic, technical, and military-assistance programs), intelligence, and propaganda, handled by different agencies, sometimes reduces clarity of purpose. The Communist countries, according to the Soviet plans, should behave as a bloc; the West attempts to distinguish and to play on the different national characteristics. The separate identities of the East European states, however, can claim only a tenuous existence under Soviet tolerance. There are no contacts with the West that cannot be immediately terminated should Soviet interests deem such action advisable.

In fact, the changes inside the Communist world affect the relations between the satellite countries and the West more than any initiative of the free world. Power struggles in the Kremlin, de-Stalinization, shifts of weights in the Soviet bloc due to economic developments, or changes in personal ties are hardly ever influenced by the West, but they determine the relationships between the Communist and the Western world. Increases in economic or military power in favor of the East or the West—be they real or only assumed—also influence the relationships between the two blocs. This is made clear by the effect on world politics of Russian rocketry successes and of the nuclear stalemate. The attraction of the West for the East cannot be fully secured by a West reluctant to use its power. The East knows hardly any restrictions.

The options available to the satellite countries are limited by the permanent threat of the use of Soviet power. Minimum options are available in different degrees to the various countries and their populations. A certain degree of cultural freedom may be granted by law or by practice to individuals, or it may be claimed by one or the other Communist states. Poland also grants a slight degree of political self-determination to individuals, allowing them to cancel some of the candidates named on the single list presented at elections. At the same time, Poland enjoys a greater degree of political autonomy than other members of the bloc. It follows a separate course in its agrarian policy, in its relations with the Catholic Church, and, most of all, in accepting American aid. Wherever a fissure opens, contacts with the West are established—but they remain on a low level.

Here again, Poland and Rumania play a special part. Especially in Warsaw a broad area of contacts has been established by Western institutions with members of the government and of the Communist and non-Communist elite. Teachers and students are exchanged, mainly with the United States. Poland also receives American aid in the form of credits and foodstuff, which at the end of 1962 amounted to more than $500 million. This aid reflects the Western interest in Poland and its population and is said to be recognized as such by the population. The Western contacts with Rumania are on a much smaller scale. All these exchanges are strictly peaceful. The West has not created a political slant by force, as the Soviet Union periodically does, by first applying pressure and then relaxing tensions to promote an atmosphere favorable to a conference in which the West, grateful for the relaxation, offers compromises.

Khrushchev's aspiration to American-Russian bilateralism in world politics does not meet with enthusiasm in the other Communist countries, which always fear agreements by the superpowers at their expense. Poland might wish to play its own role as an independent Communist state, but it will not achieve this goal as long as it is held in a vise between the Soviet Union and the unregenerate Stalinist regimes in Pankow and Prague. While this situation persists, Warsaw lacks the freedom of action to bargain for the recognition of the Oder-Neisse border by the non-Eastern world—a recognition Poles claim essential for national survival.

Yugoslavia—A Special Case

The only Communist country besides Poland that accepts Western aid is Yugoslavia; it began to do so after its expulsion by the Cominform in 1948. From 1949 to 1961, Marshal Tito's regime received $2.28 billion worth of American aid, one-third of this for military purposes between 1952 and 1957. Military aid, under which Yugoslavia received 553 airplanes, has stopped, but Tito is still allowed to buy U.S. surplus materiél (130 jets in 1961) on extremely favorable conditions. Apart from U.S. aid, Yugoslavia received substantial economic aid from West European nations.

Marshal Tito retained greater freedom of action than leaders of the other East European states after World War II because his partisans had contributed more to the liberation of their country, while Russian military support—given only since 1944—had only been complementary. Tito acquired the highest degree of freedom when, upon defying Stalin, he was expelled from the Cominform and the Soviet bloc cancelled its treaties of Friendship and Mutual Aid with Yugoslavia. The West saved him from total isolation by according him large-scale support. In 1953, Tito even concluded a treaty of friendship and collaboration with Greece and Turkey, which was expanded a year later into a formal alliance providing for cooperation and mutual assistance. This Balkan Pact made Yugoslavia *de facto* an associate member of NATO, to which it was linked by the alliance with Athens and Ankara.

Western support was granted to Tito, who had formerly shown himself as one of the most aggressive members of the Soviet bloc—shooting down American planes, claiming Trieste, aiding and abetting the Communist aggression by proxy in Greece—under the assumption that a nationalist deviation would weaken the Soviet bloc and that Yugoslavia would not export Communism. On the level of Party relations one may argue that indeed Yugoslavia has not exported Communism to the West. On the other hand, the Yugoslav state represented by Tito attempts to lead the neutralists onto a track that seems very little removed from Communism; his influence on Abdel Nasser in Egypt, Sékou Touré in Guinea, and Kwame Nkrumah in Ghana should not be underestimated.

The appeal of Titoism to the masses in the Soviet bloc has often been overrated. Titoism appears at best as "the poor man's freedom," the least of evils, which would gladly be accepted as long as there is no hope for anything better. As the events in Hungary clearly proved, the masses would not choose Titoism as an alternative to freedom from Communism; the pendulum moving away from Communism would not stop at Titoism—or perhaps not even at socialism.

Tito himself moves nearer or withdraws from Moscow—Yugoslavs claim, of course, that Moscow, not Belgrade, moves—according to forces of gravity generated by the Kremlin's foreign and internal policy. Tito shares the Soviet leaders' belief in the inevitable decline of the non-Communist West. His methods may differ from Russia's; he may believe that "different roads lead to socialism"; but as a dyed-in-the-wool Communist he will always concede higher value to the protection of "socialism" than to individual freedom. Djilas rightly states that "National Communism neither desires nor is able to transform itself into something other than Communism, and something always spontaneously draws it toward its source—toward the Soviet Union. It will be unable to separate its fate from that which links it with the remaining Communist countries and movements." Soviet concessions after the series of meetings with Khrushchev led Tito in 1957 to renounce American military aid and to recognize the Ulbricht regime, accepting a break of diplomatic relations with the German Federal Republic. He allowed the Balkan Pact to lapse into a deathlike catalepsy. In downgrading the Pact, Tito followed a line adopted by Greece after the anti-Greek excesses of September 6, 1955, in Turkey. A shadow secretariat moved first every year, then every two years, into another of the capitals of the member states, but in the fall of 1961, Tito sounded its death knell, proclaiming that he would not object to formal abolition of the agreement.

The Neutralist Conference of September, 1961, in Belgrade saw Tito adopting the Khrushchev line on Germany. He deemed himself strong enough to renounce the reassurance given him by the West, or thought he could find similar support from the neutralists. The political pendulum had brought Tito extremely near to the Soviet leader of the time; details about the fluctuations in Soviet-Yugoslav relations remain outside the scope of our observations. The new *rapprochement* between Tito and Khrushchev diminished Belgrade's influence in world affairs; the neutralists refused to accept Yugoslavia's proposed resolutions on the German question. But Yugoslavia still plays a role in Communist world politics similar to that of Pietro Nenni in Italian national politics: It provides a pervious field in which, through a process of osmosis, left-wing forces are drawn step by step into the Communist camp. Polycentric Communism may lose some of its radiation force acquired by the compactness of masses, but it may also appear more attractive to gullible left-wingers in the neutralist countries and in the West. Anticolonialism and neutralism, when taking the form of disengagement from the West, may be first steps into the magnetic field spread out by Communists.

The picture of Yugoslavia and of the other Communist countries changes, depending on whether the similarities between them are stressed or the dissimilarities put in focus. All Communists, dogmatists and revisionists alike, share the belief in the ultimate victory of their creed. The walls of barbed wire, mine fields, watch towers, and police controls do not provide the best way to improve relations between the Communist states and the Western world. They hamper Western contacts with the peoples of Eastern and Southeastern Europe, and they also give every Communist initiative the obvious character of a foray with ulterior motives. Even Communist countries are sealed off from Communist countries; behind the prison wall, the civil war of the Communist minority against the non-Communist majority, called class struggle, is relentlessly waged. Propaganda and reality remain locked in an unbridgeable dichotomy. However, the Berlin Wall set up on August 13, 1961, by Ulbricht is emblazoned with a slogan meant for the West: "The German Democratic Republic always radiates peace."

"Never Befriend the Oppressed . . ."

The inadequacy of Western reactions to the destruction of non-Communist forces in Eastern Europe through terror and rigged elections, to the overthrow of the Slovak regional government in November, 1947, and the *Putsch* in Prague of February, 1948; the lack of aid for the workers' uprising in East Germany in June, 1953, and the revolution in Hungary of October, 1956; the silence when Ulbricht's wall was erected on August 13, 1961, a flagrant provocation to the West—all these speak more eloquently in the Communist countries than all the propaganda aimed toward them by the West. The frivolous talk of a "rollback," which was not and could not be followed by adequate deeds, disillusioned the peoples of Eastern Europe. But as the West cannot forget their enslavement, the oppressed peoples cannot forget that freedom

exists in the world. The only means found so far by the West to alleviate their craving is the patent medicine of economic aid. The
West—especially the European governments—seem to follow the
humorous maxim of Ogden Nash: "Never befriend the oppressed
unless you are prepared to take on the oppressor."

Since Stalin's death, the Communist world has been in a state of
upheaval. As stated by Brzezinski, "Without a common power
center jealously to protect certain universal ideological imperatives, Marxism, even Marxism-Leninism, was shown to be inadequate in providing unity for international Communism. Diversity
of thought, emerging once the center's controls lapsed, immediately brought to the surface the divisive forces which survived
even in the heydey of Stalinist unity. National animosities, cultural affinities, territorial claims, specific ideological traditions, all
gradually came to the front." Thus changes may, in time, confer a
broader array of options to some Communist countries, affecting
their relations with the West. The West, however, is kept at bay
by Krushchev's threat to Berlin and the existence of Soviet super-
bombs; to the peoples under Communist domination it cautiously
offers the lollipops of cultural exchange and free wheat. Each
wave of de-Stalinization creates new unrest in the Communist
countries and unleashes centrifugal forces. An end to this development cannot be seen yet—polycentrism may only be a transitional
stage. Meanwhile the members of the Soviet bloc continue to live
under a system of enforced friendships with each other and compulsory enmity toward the non-Communist world.

NOTES

1. THE NEW SOCIETY
(pp. 3–25)

1. Ralf Dahrendorf, *Class and Class Conflict in Industrial Society* (Stanford, Calif.: Stanford University Press, 1959), pp. 31, 103.
2. Zbigniew K. Brzezinski, *The Soviet Bloc; Unity and Conflict* (rev. ed.; New York: Frederick A. Praeger, 1961), p. 75.
3. *Ibid.*
4. *Yugoslavia's Way,* trans. Stoyan Pribechevich, Program of the League of the Communists of Yugoslavia (New York: All Nations Press, 1958), pp. 19–20.
5. *Ibid.*
6. *Ibid.,* p. 25.
7. *Ibid.,* p. 26.
8. *Ibid.,* p. 27.
9. Josip Broz Tito, *Govori i Članci* (Zagreb, 1959), V, 233.
10. Fred Warner Neal, *Titoism in Action: Reforms in Yugoslavia, 1948–1954* (Berkeley, Calif.: University of California Press, 1958), p. 19; see also Boris Kidrić, "O reorganizaciji državne uprave," *Arhiv za Pravne i Društvene Nauke,* No. 2, 1950, pp. 8–9.
11. Radivoje Petković, *Local Self-Government in Yugoslavia* (Belgrade, 1955), pp. 65–115. Tito, *op. cit.,* V, 5, 234, 251; IX, 37; X, 236–37. There is little evidence in the new constitution regarding the withering away of the state. See *The Constitution of the Federal Socialist Republic of Yugoslavia: A Preliminary Draft* (Belgrade: Union of Jurists' Associations of Yugoslavia, 1962), p. 2, chap. ii, art. 9, pp. 14–16.
12. Tito, *op. cit.,* XI, 390.
13. *Ibid.,* VII, 331.
14. *Ibid.,* V, 242.
15. *Ibid.*
16. *Ibid.,* IX, 25; XI, 390.
17. *Ibid.,* V, 235.
18. *Yugoslavia's Way,* pp. 29–30.
19. *Ibid.*
20. J. V. Stalin, *On the Draft Constitution of the U.S.S.R.* (Moscow, 1936), pp. 19–20.
21. Alex Inkeles, "Social Stratification and Mobility in the Soviet Union: 1940–1950," *Transactions of the Second World Congress of Sociology,* II (1954), 479.

22. S. V. Utechin, "Social Stratification and Social Mobility in the U.S.-S.R.," *ibid.*, 55–62.

23. Milovan Djilas, *The New Class* (New York: Frederick A. Praeger, 1957), p. 27.

24. *Ibid.*, p. 61.

25. *Ibid.*

26. *Ibid.* Djilas' point seems to contradict somewhat Utechin's views concerning the restriction of vertical mobility in the Soviet Union. See Utechin, *op. cit.*, p. 8.

27. Robert V. Daniels, *The Nature of Communism* (New York: Random House, 1962), pp. 364–65.

28. *Ibid.*

29. Djilas, *op. cit.*, pp. 60–61.

30. *East Europe*, VI, October, 1957, 4.

31. Brzezinski, *op. cit.*, p. 402.

32. *New Europe*, X, September, 1961, 3–6.

33. Daniels, *op. cit.*, p. 44.

34. *Ibid.*, p. 367.

35. *Ibid.*

36. Nicholas DeWitt, *Education and Professional Employment in the U.S.S.R.* (Washington: National Science Foundation, 1961), p. 8; R. A. Feldmesser, "Equality and Inequality under Khrushchev," *Problems of Communism*, IX, No. 2 (March–April, 1960), 31–39.

37. DeWitt, *op. cit.*, p. 8.

38. Djilas, *op. cit.*, p. 62.

39. Dahrendorf, *op. cit.*, p. 108.

40. Djilas, *op. cit.*, p. 63.

41. *East Europe*, VII, July, 1958, 3.

42. Brzezinski, *op. cit.*, p. 9. The author gives figures on Polish intelligentsia lost during the war.

43. Jan Szczepański, "The Polish Intelligentsia," *World Politics*, XIV (1962), No. 3, 406–20, 414.

44. Tito, *op. cit.*, I, 298, 331, 334.

45. *Ibid.*, II, 84.

46. *Ibid.*, II, 386.

47. *Ibid.*, II, 415–16.

48. *Nowe Drogi*, July, 1957, p. 126; D. Zablocka, "Notes on the Intelligentsia," *Nowa Kultura*, September 7, 1958; Brzezinski, *op. cit.*, pp. 239–40.

49. Jan Szczepański, "Struktura inteligencji w Polsce," *Kultura i Spoleczenstwo*, IV (1960), 19–48.

50. Szczepański, "The Polish Intelligentsia," 417–18.

51. *Ibid.*

52. *Ibid.*, 419.

53. *Ibid.*

54. *Ibid.*

55. Jan Szczepański (ed.), *Z badán klasy robotnieczej i inteligencji* (Lódź, 1958); *Wyksztatcenie a pozycja spoleczna inteligencji*, 2 vols. (Lódź, 1959–60).

56. Szczepański, "The Polish Intelligentsia," 420.

57. *Ibid.*
58. Brzezinski, *op. cit.*, p. 204.
59. *Nepszava*, June 8, 1958; Brzezinski, *op. cit.*, p. 219.
60. François Fejto, *Behind the Rape of Hungary* (New York: David McKay Company, 1957); Tibor Meray, *Thirteen Days That Shook the Kremlin* (New York: Frederick A. Praeger, 1959); Brzezinski, *op. cit.*, pp. 219–22.
61. Brzezinski, *op. cit.*, p. 234.
62. *Ibid.*, p. 331.
63. *Pravda*, January 28, 1959.
64. *Rudé Právo*, January 9, 1961.
65. *East Europe*, X, February, 1961, 24. The Albanian population is estimated on the basis of figures given in Stavro Skendi (ed.), *Albania* (New York: Frederick A. Praeger, 1956). For figures on Yugoslavia's population, see Jozo Tomasevich, *Peasants, Politics and Economic Change in Yugoslavia* (Stanford, Calif.: Stanford University Press, 1954), p. 301; and *Jugoslavija. Savezni Zavod za Statistiku, Statistički bilten*, No. 223, January, 1962, pp. 50–51. Census for 1961.
66. Ryszard Turski, "Urbanization—Real and Latent," *Polish Perspectives*, V, No. 5 (1962), 10–16, 12–13.
67. Milorad M. Drachkovitch, "Tito's Yugoslavia in Khrushchev's Era," in Stephen D. Kertesz (ed.), *East Central Europe and the World* (Notre Dame, Ind.: University of Notre Dame Press, 1962), pp. 281–313.
68. On the shift of population from village to city and its implications in Czechoslovakia, see Jan P. Michal, *Central Planning in Czechoslovakia* (Stanford, Calif.: Stanford University Press, 1960), p. 85.
69. Dyzma Galaj, "Rural Sociology," *Polish Perspectives*, V, No. 7 (1962), 13–21, 14.
70. Turski, *op. cit.*, 12–13.
71. *Ibid.*
72. On these developments in agriculture, see Cvetko Kostić, *Seljaci industriski radnici* (Belgrade, 1955); and Vlastimir Mihajlović, "Kooperacija i polarizacija seljačkih gazdinstva," *Glasnik. Glavni Savez Zemljoradničkih Zadruga u Jogoslaviji*, No. 3, 1962, 10–15.
73. Slavko Komar, "Proizvodno-ekonomski problemi i zadaci u daljem razvoju poljoprivrede," *Komunist* (Organ of the Central Committee of the League of Communists of Yugoslavia, Belgrade), July, 1962, pp. 145–73.
74. Dyzma Galaj, "Sociology of New Industrial Regions," *Polish Perspectives*, V (1962), No. 3, 5, 5–11.
75. *Ibid.*, 6.
76. *Ibid.*, 8–9.
77. *Ibid.*
78. Jerzy Mikke, "After the Great Migration," *Polish Perspectives*, V, No. 3 (March, 1962), 19–25.
79. Irena Turnau, *Studia nad struktura ludnošciowa polskiego Wroclawia* (Poznan, 1960); review by Wiktor Sukiennicki, *Journal of Central European Affairs*, XXI, April, 1961, 113–15.
80. *Ibid.*
81. Dejan Djurković, "Razgovor o domaćem filmu," *Delo*, VIII, No. 3 (March, 1961), 340–60.

2. EDUCATION FOR COMMUNISM
(pp. 26–51)

1. While there is no single work on the subject, the evolution of education in the area to 1958 is fairly adequately covered in the existing scattered literature in English. For general background, see John S. Reshetar, "The Educational Weapon," *The Annals of the American Academy of Political and Social Science,* CCLXXI ("Moscow's European Satellites"), September, 1950, 135–44; and George Bereday, "Education and Youth," *ibid.,* CCCXVII ("The Satellites in Eastern Europe"), May, 1958, 63–70.

Developments in individual countries are presented in the chapters on education in the country handbooks published by Frederick A. Praeger (New York): Stavro Skendi (ed.), *Albania* (1956); L. A. D. Dellin (ed.), *Bulgaria* (1957), Vratislav Busek and Nicolas Spulber (eds.), *Czechoslovakia* (1957); Ernst Christian Helmreich (ed.), *Hungary* (1957); Oskar Halecki (ed.), *Poland* (1957); Stephen Fischer-Galati (ed.), *Romania* (1957); and Robert F. Byrnes (ed.), *Yugoslavia* (1957). Those in East Germany are reported in Paul S. Bodenman, *Education in the Soviet Zone of Germany* (U.S. Office of Education Bulletin, 1959, No. 26). Other studies worth noting are Herta Haase and Seymour M. Rosen, *Education in Rumania* (U.S. Office of Education, 1960); Elinor Murray, "Higher Education in Communist Hungary, 1948–56," *The American Slavic and East European Review,* XIX, No. 3 (October, 1960), 395–413; Irwin T. Sanders, "Communist-Dominated Education in Bulgaria: A Study in Social Relationships," *ibid.,* XV, No. 3 (October, 1956), 364–81; Joseph S. Roucek, "Sovietization and Russification of Bulgaria's Education," *Etudes slaves et est-européennes,* IV (1959), 68–78. See also U.S. Office of Education, *Selected Bibliography of Materials on Education in Poland* (1960); . . . *Czechoslovakia* (1960); . . . *Yugoslavia* (1961); . . . *Albania, Bulgaria, Czechoslovakia, Hungary, Poland, Rumania and Yugoslavia* (1958); Robert F. Byrnes, *Bibliography of American Publications on East Central Europe, 1945–57,* (Bloomington, Ind.: Indiana University Press, 1958); and the annual volumes of *The American Bibliography of Slavic and East European Studies for 1957–61* (Bloomington, Ind.: Indiana University Press, 1963).

For the general literature on the Marxist countries, see R. N. Carew Hunt, *Books on Communism* (London, 1959) and Marin Pundeff, *Recent Publications on Communism* (Los Angeles: University of Southern California Research Institute on Communist Strategy and Propaganda, 1962).

2. For the position of religion in education in these countries and Rumania to 1955, see Vladimir Gsovski (ed.), *Church and State Behind the Iron Curtain* (New York: Frederick A. Praeger, 1955).

3. Cf. Marin Pundeff, "History in Soviet Education Since 1958," *Harvard Educational Review,* XXXII, No. 1 (Winter, 1962), 66–80. The best single source on the Soviet reforms is Nicholas DeWitt, *Education and Professional Employment in the U.S.S.R.* (Washington, D.C.: National Science Foundation, 1961), which contains a bibliography. Important analyses of the Soviet changes, as well as educational developments in East Germany and Poland, are presented in Edmund J. King (ed.), *Communist Education* (London: Methuen, 1963). For materials published earlier, see U.S. Office of Education, *Bibliography of Published Materials on Russian and Soviet Education* (1960). Important analyses of the Soviet changes and of educational developments in

East Germany and Poland are presented in *Communist Education*, ed. Edmund J. King (London: Methuen & Co., 1963).

4. Oskar Anweiler, "Zwischenbilanz der sowjetischen Schulreform," *Osteuropa*, XI, Nos. 4–5 (April–May, 1961), 285–301, giving the tables of distribution of instructional time.

5. *Pedagogicheskii slovar'* (Moscow: Izdatel'stvo Akademii Pedagogicheskikh Nauk, 1960), I, 143–46.

6. *Osnovy kommunisticheskogo vospitaniia* (Moscow: Gosudarstvennoe izdatel'stvo politicheskoi literatury, 1960), pp. 14, 17, 159–60.

7. *East Europe*, August, 1959, p. 47, quoting *Scinteia*, June 11, 1959. See also the excellent article by Randolph L. Braham, "The Rumanian Schools of General Education," *Journal of Central European Affairs*, XXI, No. 3 (October, 1961), 319–49, and Constantin Sporea, "Kommunistische Erziehung in Rumänien," *Der Europäische Osten*, No. 83, September, 1961, pp. 517–23.

8. *East Europe*, December, 1962, p. 27, quoting *Rabotnichesko Delo*, September 30, 1962.

9. *Ibid.*, January, 1959, p. 49, quoting a monitored broadcast of Radio Sofia. See also A. Mandikoff, "Remodeling Education," *Survey*, No. 39, December, 1961, pp. 113–19.

10. *East Europe*, November, 1962, pp. 31–33, quoting speeches by the Minister of Education and Culture Nacho Papazov and Party Secretary Todor Zhivkov.

11. Text in *Gesetzblatt der Deutschen Demokratischen Republik*, No. 67, December 7, 1959. The previous education reform law it supersedes is the "democratization" law issued in May–June, 1946, in the five *Länder* of the Soviet zone.

12. *Sovetskaia Pedagogika*, No. 6, 1961, pp. 127–32.

13. *New York Times*, June 10, 1962.

14. For the time allocated to polytechnical training in the various grades, see *Sovetskaia Pedagogika*, No. 1, 1961, pp. 100–15.

15. *Magyar Közlöny*, No. 74, October 17, 1961.

16. Russian texts in *Sovetskaia Pedagogika*, No. 4, 1961, pp. 98–137. The decisions of the Central Committee were implemented by a law enacted on July 15, 1961 (*Dziennik Ustaw*, No. 32, July 21, 1961).

17. Vladislav Ozga and Roman Pol'ny, "Obsuzhdenie voprosov reformy shkoly v Narodnoi Pol'she," *Sovekskaia Pedagogika*, No. 1, 1959, pp. 96–109. See also Jacob Ornstein, "Ferment in the Polish Classroom," *Journal of Central European Affairs*, XX, No. 1 (April, 1960), 69–83; Nellie Apanasewicz and William K. Medlin, *Educational Systems in Poland* (U.S. Office of Education, 1959); Richard Hiscocks, "Education in Poland," *International Journal*, XIV, No. 4 (Autumn, 1959), 259–71; and Siegfried Baske, "Die Entwicklung des polnischen Schulwesens seit 1944," *Osteuropa*, XII, No. 3 (March, 1962), 181–89.

18. *Yugoslavia's Way*, trans. Stoyan Pribechevich (New York: All Nations Press, 1958), pp. 222–29. The best analysis of the "Yugoslav way" is George W. Hoffman and Fred Warner Neal, *Yugoslavia and the New Communism* (New York: Twentieth Century Fund, 1962); for developments in education, see pp. 234–36 and 373–77.

19. Translation in Vera Tomich, "The Legal Basis, Organization, Administration, and Program of the Secondary Schools in Yugoslavia," Ed.D. dissertation, University of California, Los Angeles, 1960.

20. *East Europe,* October, 1962, pp. 27–28, quoting *Zeri i Popullit,* July 21, 1962.

21. Oskar Anweiler, "Bildung und Produktion: Grundfragen der Schulreformen in Osteuropa," *Oesterreichische Ost-Hefte,* I, No. 1 (1959), 3–8.

22. For the papers and comments given at the seminar, see *Sovetskaia Pedagogika,* No. 3, 1961, pp. 11–111.

3. Agriculture and the Peasant

(pp. 55–81)

1. Among the regional approaches, one should mention Irwin T. Sanders (ed.), *Collectivization of Agriculture in Eastern Europe* (Lexington, Ky.: University of Kentucky Press, 1958). The main body of comparable area statistics made available includes 1959 as the last year, but developments until the spring of 1963 are, of course, considered.

2. Cf. the pioneering work by David Mitrany, *Marx Against the Peasant: A Study in Social Dogmatism* (Chapel Hill, N.C.: University of North Carolina Press, 1951), reprinted with a new foreword by Crowell-Collier Publishing Company (New York, 1961). The "workers-peasants alliance" and the toleration of private property are concessions due to expediency.

3. A useful source for this period is *European Agriculture: A Statement of Problems* (Geneva: United Nations, 1954), chap. iv.

4. *Economic Survey of Europe, 1960* (Geneva: United Nations, 1961), chap. iv, analyzes the developments of the late 1950's. See also *Economic Survey of Europe, 1961* (Geneva: United Nations, 1962), especially Part 1, chap. ii; and U.S. Department of Agriculture, *The Agricultural Situation in 1961–62 in the Soviet Union and Other Eastern European Countries* (Washington, D.C., September, 1962).

5. Details on the institutional structure are contained in A. M. Petrushev, *Sel'skoe Khozyaystvo Evropeyskikh Stran Narodnoy Demokratii na Sotsialisticheskom Puti* (*Agriculture in the European People's Democratic Countries on a Socialist Path*) (Moscow, 1959).

4. Industry and Labor

(pp. 82–117)

1. Cf. pertinent sections in Nicolas Spulber, *The Economics of Communist Eastern Europe* (New York: John Wiley & Sons, 1957); Jan Wszelaki, *Communist Economic Strategy: The Role of East Central Europe* (Washington, D.C.: 1959); Naum Jasny, *Soviet Industrialization, 1928–1952* (Chicago: Chicago University Press, 1961); V. Winston, "The Satellites—Economic Liability?," *Problems of Communism,* January, 1958; S. J. Zyzniewski, "Economic Perspectives in Eastern Europe," *Political Science Quarterly,* LXXV, No. 2 (June, 1960).

2. Details of early postwar developments may be gleaned from *Patterns of Economic Growth, 1938–1958* (New York: United Nations, 1960); *Economic Survey of Europe, 1960* (Geneva: United Nations, 1961); *World Economic Survey, 1959* (New York: United Nations, 1960); Spulber, *op. cit.;* T. P. Alton, *The Polish Postwar Economy* (New York: Columbia University Press, 1955); Jan M. Michal, *Central Planning in Czechoslovakia* (Stanford, Calif.:

Stanford University Press, 1960); Wolfgang Stolper, *The Structure of the East German Economy* (Cambridge, Mass.: Harvard University Press, 1960); R. L. Wolff, *The Balkans in Our Time* (Cambridge, Mass.: Harvard University Press, 1956).

3. Cf. *World Economic Survey, 1959*, pp. 114, 122, 124.

4. Cf. Appendix, pp. 118–19, for iron and steel production. Relevant details to 1956 are in United Nations: *Economic Bulletin for Europe*, III, No. 1 (1951); *Economic Survey of Europe Since the War* (Geneva, 1953), pp. 59 ff; *Economic Survey of Europe, 1955*, pp. 208–46; *1956*, pp. A-35–A-45; *1957*, chap. vii; *World Economic Survey, 1955*, pp. 96–110; *1956*, pp. 235–44; *1957*, p. 133; and Spulber, *op. cit.*, pp. 253 ff.; Norman Pounds and Nicholas Spulber (eds.), *Resources and Planning in Eastern Europe* (Bloomington, Ind.: Indiana University Press, 1957); *The Annals of the American Academy of Political and Social Science*, CCCXVII, May, 1958, 22–44.

5. Further references to this phenomenon are in S. J. Zyzniewski, "Economic Perspectives in Eastern Europe," *loc. cit.*, 213; the possible ramifications on foreign economic relations have been discussed in S. J. Zyzniewski, "The Soviet Bloc and Underdeveloped Countries," *World Politics*, XI, No. 3 (April, 1959). The strain upon Soviet resources seems to have led to some reluctance to increase exports to Eastern Europe, and the leveling of shipments that developed in 1953 contributed to the growing crises of 1954–56. Cf. *International Affairs* (London), XXX, No. 1 (1954), 40–49; *Economic Survey of Europe, 1957*, chap. vi, pp. 8 ff.

6. Cf. *Economic Survey of Europe, 1956*, chaps. i and ii.

7. Cf. *Economic Survey of Europe, 1957*, chap. ii; *1958*, chap. i; *1959*, chap. ii; *1960*, chap. ii; *World Economic Survey, 1958*, pp. 267 ff.; *1959*, pp. 114, 122, 124; *1960*, pp. 217 ff.

8. Among the recent studies devoted to the complex problems of the bloc's planning and operational dilemmas are Gregory Grossman (ed.), *Value and Plan: Economic Calculation and Organization in Eastern Europe* (Berkeley, Calif.: University of California, 1960); Alfred Zaubermann, "The Polish and Soviet Quest for a Criterion of Investment Efficiency," *Economica*, XXIX, No. 115 (August, 1962).

9. Cf. *Rude Pravo*, June 26, 1958; *Zahranici Obchod*, No. 7, July, 1958; *Neues Deutschland*, August 7, 1958; *Hospodarske Noviny*, August 17, 1958; *Trud*, August 20, 1958; *Pravda*, December 17, 1958; *Mirovaia Ekonomika i Mezhdunarodnie Otnosheniia*, No. 1, January, 1959; *Voprosy Ekonomiki*, January–February, 1959.

10. Cf. *Voprosy Ekonomiki*, No. 3, March, 1959, 34 ff.; No. 1, January, 1960, 17 ff; *Vneshniaia Torgovlia*, No. 4, April, 1959, 6 ff.; *Mirovaia Ekonomika i Mezhdunarodnie Otnosheniia*, No. 1, 1959, 4 ff.; *Voprosy Ekonomiki*, No. 3, 1961, as translated in *Problems of Economics*, IV, No. 2 (June, 1961), 43 ff.; *Kommunist*, No. 1, 1961, as translated in *Problems of Economics*, V, No. 2 (1962), 59; *Pravda*, June 17, 1962.

11. Reportedly, a decrease in the types of metalworking machines being produced was effected in 1959, from 3,347 products to 2,340. Other details on specialization are in *Economic Survey of Europe, 1956*, chap. ii; *Mirovaia Ekonomika i Mezhdunarodnie Otnosheniia*, No. 4, April, 1959, 27 ff.; *Economic Bulletin for Europe*, XI, No. 1, 57–76; *ibid.*, No. 3, 45 ff.; *East Europe*, VIII, No. 7 (July, 1959), 40 ff.; *Voprosy Ekonomiki*, No. 9, 1959, pp. 95 ff.;

ibid., No. 1, 1960, 12 ff.; *ibid.,* No. 11, 1961, 91 ff.; *Vneshniaia Torgovlia,* No. 7, 1961; *Economic Survey of Europe, 1960,* chap. ii; *ibid., 1961,* chap. ii.

12. "It cannot be denied that in the present period of rapid industrial expansion, the securing of necessary raw-material supplies for member nations constitutes one of the cardinal points of CMEA planning," I. Vajda, "Hungary and the CMEA [COMECON]," *The New Hungarian Quarterly* (Budapest), II, No. 3 (1961), 129.

13. Cf. S. Skrzypek, "Soviet-Satellite Economic Developments: New Trends Toward Supranational Planning," *The Polish Review,* VI, No. 4 (Autumn, 1961).

14. G. Karkhin, "The Socialist Community: Possibilities and Prospects," *International Affairs* (Moscow), No. 8, August, 1962.

15. Indicators of output in major industries since 1959 are in *Economic Survey of Europe, 1961,* chap. ii, p. 7.

16. See Appendix II, pp. 118–19, for statistical details of employment, per-capita output, and real wages. Also, cf. United Nations, *Report on the World Social Situation* (New York, 1961), *European Housing Trends and Policies in 1960* (Geneva, 1961), *Economic Survey of Europe, 1961,* for additional commentary on living standards and housing.

17. Some twenty-five barter agreements among bloc members have already been signed for the 1961–62 period. (*International Affairs,* No. 11, November, 1962, p. 67.) The problems of prices, capital mobility, and conflicts of interest have been recently summarized in M. Gamarnikow, "The Future of COMECON," *East Europe,* XI, No. 6 (June, 1962), 3 ff.

18. Analyses of COMECON's role in recent years have varied among Westerners. While most have stressed that integration will reinforce Soviet ascendancy, the opposite implication appears in R. S. Jaster, "CEMA's Influence on Soviet Policies in Eastern Europe," *World Politics,* XIV, No. 3.

19. Additional details on both the industrialization process and Titoist reforms to 1956 can be gleaned from pertinent sections of R. L. Wolff, *op. cit.,* and C. P. McVicker, *Titoism* (New York: St Martin's Press, 1957). The more recent developments are discussed in "Economic Planning and Management in Yugoslavia," *Economic Bulletin for Europe,* X, No. 3.

20. *Economic Bulletin for Europe,* XIII, No. 2; *Economic Survey of Europe, 1961,* chap. i, pp. 43 ff.

21. Additional details on recent innovations (planned or implemented) are in *Economic Survey of Europe, 1960,* chap i, and P. Landy, "Reforms in Yugoslavia," *Problems of Communism,* X, No. 6 (1961).

22. Industrial output in 1962, at midpoint, was running at an increase of only 4 per cent, and the acerbity of Tito's remarks in May of that year portended a period of austerity for the Yugoslav people. (*East Europe,* XI, No. 6 [June, 1962], 32 ff.)

6. THE INTERNAL POLITICAL ORDER
(pp. 159–94)

1. Russell Brain, *The Nature of Experience* (New York: Oxford University Press, 1959), p. 3.

2. See particularly Zbigniew K. Brzezinski, *The Soviet Bloc: Unity and Conflict* (rev. ed.; New York: Frederick A. Praeger, 1961); Ferenc A. Vali,

Notes

Rift and Revolt in Hungary (Cambridge, Mass.: Harvard University Press, 1961); and Hugh Seton-Watson, "Five Years After October," *Problems of Communism*, September–October, 1961, pp. 15–21.

3. See Edward Táborský, *Communism in Czechoslovakia, 1948–1960* (Princeton, N.J.: Princeton University Press, 1961), p. 105.

4. This account is based on Andreas Theimer's excellent article: "Der Prager Germinal, die tschechische Literatur zwischen Tau und Frost," *Wort und Wahrheit*, XV, February, 1960, 93–100.

5. *Ibid.*, 94.

6. See his "Warsaw Notebook," *Soviet Survey*, No. 35, January–March, 1961, pp. 26–30.

7. See her *The Rich Nations and the Poor Nations* (New York: W. W. Norton, 1962). A possible application of this concept is found in the excellent review article by György Hollo, "Das Regime Kádár," *Wort und Wahrheit*, XVI, May (1961), 395–97. In the author's opinion, the three decisive factors that have helped to keep the essentially weak Kádár group in power in post-revolutionary Hungary were a power vacuum, a moral vacuum, and the excessive preoccupation with materialism.

THE CONTRIBUTORS

L. A. D. DELLIN is Associate Professor of Economics and Chairman of the Program of Russian and East European Studies at the University of Vermont. His articles on Eastern Europe and Communism have appeared in American and foreign scholarly journals, and he is the editor of *Bulgaria,* published in 1957.

WILLIAM E. GRIFFITH is a Research Associate at the Center for International Studies, Massachusetts Institute of Technology. He is the author of *Albania and the Sino-Soviet Rift, The East European Thaw,* and of numerous articles on Soviet affairs.

ANDREW GYORGY is Professor of Government at Boston University. He is the author of *Geopolitics, The New German Science* and *Governments of Danubian Europe* and the editor of *Problems in International Relations.*

MARIN V. PUNDEFF is Associate Professor of History, San Fernando Valley State College, and Consultant to the Slavic Division, Library of Congress. He is a frequent contributor to professional journals, the author of *Tensions in the Soviet Captive Countries: Bulgaria,* and contributing author to *Government, Law, and Courts in the Soviet Union and Eastern Europe.*

HANS E. TÜTSCH is foreign editor of the *Neue Zürcher Zeitung.* He has traveled extensively in Europe, Asia, North Africa, and the United States and has written a number of books on the Arab countries, North Africa, and Italy. His latest book, *From Ankara to Marrakesh,* will appear in the near future.

WAYNE S. VUCINICH is Professor of History at Stanford University. He is the author of *Serbia Between East and West* and a frequent contributor of articles and special studies to scholarly journals.

JAN H. WSZELAKI, a member of the Polish diplomatic service until his resignation in 1945, teaches at the School of International Service, American University, Washington, D.C. He is the author of a number of studies on East European economics.

STANLEY J. ZYZNIEWSKI is Associate Professor of History at the University of Kentucky. His articles on Russian history and Soviet-bloc economic relations have appeared in professional journals here and abroad.

This volume was prepared with the assistance of JOSEPH BABICKI and JOSEPH S. ROUCEK.

THE EDITOR: Stephen Fischer-Galati is Associate Professor of History at Wayne State University and Associate of the Russian Research Center, Harvard University. He is the author of *Ottoman Imperialism and German Protestantism*, *Rumania: A Bibliographical Guide*, and of articles and studies on the history of Eastern Europe.